It Shouldn't Be This Hard to Serve Your Country

It Shouldn't Be This Hard to Serve Your Country

Our Broken Government
and the Plight *of* Veterans

David Shulkin

PUBLICAFFAIRS

NEW YORK

PublicAffairs
Hachette Book Group
1290 Avenue of the Americas, New York, NY 10104
www.publicaffairsbooks.com
@Public_Affairs

Printed in the United States of America

First Edition: October 2019

Published by PublicAffairs, an imprint of Perseus Books, LLC, a subsidiary of Hachette Book Group, Inc. The PublicAffairs name and logo is a trademark of the Hachette Book Group.

The Hachette Speakers Bureau provides a wide range of authors for speaking events. To find out more, go to www.hachettespeakersbureau.com or call (866) 376-6591.

The publisher is not responsible for websites (or their content) that are not owned by the publisher.

Print book interior design by Amnet Systems.

Library of Congress Control Number: 2019947214

ISBNs: 978-1-5417-6265-7 (hardcover), 978-1-5417-6264-0 (ebook)

LSC-C

10 9 8 7 6 5 4 3 2 1

This book is dedicated to United States veterans and their families. Veterans, you are why I came to Washington, why I fought so hard to strengthen and reform the VA, and why this entire story exists. My one wish in sharing my story is to help readers understand why the VA is such a vital and irreplaceable American institution. Without the VA's existence, and the dedicated men and women who work there, it would not be possible to honor our promise to care for the brave men and women who have sacrificed so much for our freedom.

Contents

It Shouldn't Be This Hard to Serve Your Country

Prologue

Jumping in Headfirst

As both a physician and former volunteer fireman, part of my attraction to rushing into crisis situations is not knowing what I'll find when I get there. The same was true when I entered government. I had little preparation for my transition from the private to the public sector. Because government presents an entirely new set of rules and a culture completely different from anything I'd ever experienced, I had to reset expectations and quickly develop an approach that I thought would work.

This book is the story of my service, first as under secretary, then as secretary of the US Department of Veterans Affairs (VA). When I was first summoned to Washington, there were chilling reports of excessive wait times for VA medical care in many parts of the country. There was also an unacceptable breakdown in delivery of mental health and addiction care, which left veterans of Iraq and Afghanistan to fend for themselves during epidemics of traumatic brain injuries and posttraumatic stress—neglect that led to myriad suicides and overdoses. The VA health care system was all but publicly declared to be on life support.

So when the call came, I knew I could not say no. It was my time to serve.

Many of my colleagues questioned my decision to enter government service, insisting that coming to the VA would expose me to reputational risk, while others pointed out that it would be a financial blow. But my sense of civic responsibility easily overshadowed those voices. I went in knowing that running the VA would be the greatest test of my managerial skills and that it would require putting to use everything I had learned during my past thirty years in health care management.

There are more than twenty million American veterans, more than 40 percent of them living in rural areas, and many of them rely on VA benefits just to get by. More than nine million of our veterans rely on VA health care, a system that is spread across the entire country, with approximately one thousand facilities and more than 350,000 employees. It's the largest health care system in the country and one of the most complicated organizations in the government. Dealing with the size and scope, budget realities, capital deficits, and political pressure surrounding the VA is nearly impossible under the best of circumstances.

Working for two different administrations under two very different presidents also presented special challenges and insights. President Obama was analytical, pensive, and at times appropriately cautious. This approach ensured that improvement initiatives were carefully planned, but it also led to a slower adoption of change. President Trump and his team shot first and aimed later, but this tumultuous and frenzied environment actually allowed me to take more risks, move faster, and in many cases make more meaningful change.

Using the experience I gained in the Obama administration and the freedom I was given in the Trump administration, I took advantage of the opportunity to change the VA. We broke new ground by publishing our wait times and quality data, expanding benefits for mental health services, and adding benefits for those with Other-Than-Honorable discharges. We dramatically increased our technological sophistication through greater reliance on telehealth and by moving toward a new electronic health record system that would connect seamlessly with the Department of Defense. We made real advances in timely access to care, and we implemented important changes that resulted in veterans having more choice in where they received their care. In large part, we found a formula for moving away from the status quo and getting the system back on track.

Part of that formula involved working more closely with the private sector and making the VA more competitive with industry practices. This was essentially a middle ground between a fully government-run organization and privatization. With Americans polarized over almost every issue, I hoped that caring for veterans wouldn't get entangled in the usual DC gamesmanship. The longer I was in the capital, the more I was sorely disappointed.

Much of my narrative deals with the factions pushing me to simply close the VA or at least large parts of it that weren't working well. But I didn't see how shutting down a system specifically designed to care for veterans could be in the veterans' best interests. My strong belief is that my job was to find solutions—no matter how many problems plagued the VA—in order to make the existing system work better.

We made real progress during my time at the VA. The morale of the workforce was growing. We were passing new legislation. We were working more closely with our community partners, and we were making the structural changes to ensure sustainable improvements. I had found a way to get things done despite the turmoil within the Trump administration, and things seemed to be running smoothly.

Until they weren't.

To be clear, I did not set out to tell the story of how much the VA accomplished in three years and how I was fired by a Trump tweet on the eve of passing the most important bill in the history of veterans' medical care because I wanted anyone to feel sorry for me. I am telling my story because, in my opinion, the VA is still in grave danger. Its doctors, its administrators, and most importantly our veterans are at risk as never before.

In large part, Washington works not just when you have the right plan but also when you have the right alignment of interests. Much of what I did as secretary was to work with the veterans' groups, Congress, VA employees, and the administration to find the right path forward. Ultimately the political chaos that became evident within the Trump administration overtook the ability to get the job done. My struggle with the internal political appointees and their outside allies became the biggest challenge of my tenure in government.

The VA was once thought to be the only part of the federal government that was above politics. But under President Trump, the VA's mission and resolve were undermined by the people we used to refer to—jokingly for a while, until it was no longer funny—as "the politicals." Some of them are associated with the Koch brothers' empire, which many people believe has the shortsighted goal of dismantling the VA, based on the mistaken belief that private industry can necessarily care for veterans more effectively.

As someone who has spent his life in the private industry of medicine, not of political manipulation, I can assure you that "the politicals" are wrong. But they infiltrated the VA and at least one of the veterans' groups, and they managed to accumulate influence and greatly impact the politics of veterans' care. If we don't figure out a way to stop them, they are fully capable of destroying the VA. They are also capable of undermining the VA's long history of public service in our country.

What the politicals ignore is that the private sector, already struggling to provide adequate access to care in many communities, is ill prepared to handle the number and complexity of patients that would come from closing or downsizing VA hospitals and clinics, particularly when so much of what the VA does involves the mental health needs of people scarred by the horrors of war. Working with community providers to adequately ensure that veterans' needs are met is a good practice and something I strongly encouraged. But privatization leading to the dismantling of the department's extensive health care system is a terrible idea.

The VA's understanding of service-related health problems and its special ability to work with veterans cannot be replicated in the private sector.

Maintaining a strong VA is also an essential piece of the puzzle that is the United States national security system: we cannot expect our sons and daughters to risk their lives and fight for our freedom unless we keep our promise to care for them if and when they return home broken, injured, or traumatized. There is no excuse for not holding up our end of the bargain. The mission set forth by President Abraham Lincoln to care for those who have "borne the battle" is a sacred duty.

One year after I became the secretary of veterans affairs, the environment in Washington had grown so toxic, chaotic, and subversive that it became impossible for me to accomplish the important work that our veterans need and deserve. When I left, I promised to continue to speak out against those seeking to harm the VA by putting their personal agendas ahead of the care of our veterans. This book is one way I hope to honor that commitment.

I am also worried about the future of public service generally, which appears increasingly bleak as important positions remain unfilled and while cabinet secretaries are hired, fired, and publicly humiliated as if our national government were a reality television show. After I was fired by a tweet, I told my wife—and then repeated the thought in an op-ed I wrote for the *New York Times*—"It should not be this hard to serve your country."

The time I spent in government changed me and my family forever, but it also gave me a renewed sense of purpose, as well as a belief that systems in government *can* be improved. It's not hopeless, but it is a long road without any quick or easy solutions. It also reaffirmed my belief that as long as we have the need for a military to defend our country, the VA must continue as a strong and effective system willing and able to serve those injured during their service. It is important that Americans understand what the VA system is, how it works, and why it exists. If we are willing to commit to our veterans as they have to us, we can all work together to build a safer, healthier, and prouder country.

David J. Shulkin, MD
Ninth Secretary, US Department of Veterans Affairs

1

Wild Goose Chase

I WAS TYING UP THE LOOSE ENDS OF MY TENURE AS UNDER SECRETARY for health of the Department of Veterans Affairs and racing to a meeting with Texas congressman Beto O'Rourke when I received a call from Michael Cohen.

I had met Cohen in New York City when I was running a hospital system there and he was trying to join the board. I didn't want to keep the congressman waiting, and I thought about letting the call go to voicemail, but given that Cohen's most notable client had recently been elected president of the United States, I decided to answer.

"I need you to speak to someone right away," he blurted out, which was typical of Michael. Always insistent, rarely forthcoming.

"I'm going into a meeting," I told him. "I've literally got one foot in the door."

"Just hold on."

I stepped back into the corridor and heard a strange electronic gurgle, and then Cohen introduced me to someone named Ike.

"Mr. Trump asked for my advice," this gentleman explained in a thick Israeli accent. "He wants me to help with the VA."

With Donald Trump's inauguration only a couple of weeks away, we Obama appointees were being shown the door, and I doubted that my schedule would be heavily booked once the new team took over. If only to be polite, I told "Ike" that I looked forward to meeting him at some point in the future.

"Good. So dinner tonight."

At first I thought he was joking. But he wasn't, and I sensed that he was not going to take no for an answer. I paused. "I'll look at my schedule," I said. "Let me try. Where would you like to meet?"

"At my club in West Palm."

There was no "obviously" attached to this absurd proposition, but it was implied. Who was this guy? How could a man I never met expect me to fly from Washington, DC, to Palm Beach, Florida, for dinner on a few hours' notice? I guess this was the kind of entitlement that came from being in Trump's inner circle—or maybe this was the kind of entitlement it took to be in Trump's inner circle.

Members of my staff had already gone ahead into Beto's office, and now heads began poking out, accompanied by hand motions to let me know that the congressman was waiting and I needed to hurry up and get off the phone.

"I need to go," I told Ike. "I'll call you back after my meeting."

But Ike didn't take the hint. Every few seconds a different head appeared, and each time the hand motions were more animated, but Ike kept talking as if we had all the time in the world. I would've cut him off, but if he really was a conduit to Trump, I thought that he might be my one chance to stay in my current job and continue the work I cared about: helping veterans. Maybe I was grasping at straws, but at the very least, this guy in Florida could be a way of getting my concerns registered with the incoming administration.

At this point, the congressman himself peered out into the hall, giving me a look that asked how much longer I would be.

Ike pressed me for an answer on a West Palm meeting. He told me he would have his assistant set up the details. I hung up and stepped into Beto's office.

What I had no way of knowing was just how much this moment marked the transition between two very different worlds. The men

I had just spoken with on the phone, Michael Cohen and Marvel Comics chairman Ike Perlmutter, represented a dealmaking culture that often made it difficult to ascertain genuine motivations. The congressman I was about to meet with represented something much more straightforward.

Beto O'Rourke has since become a political celebrity, but I first knew him simply as one of the more involved members of the House Veterans Affairs Committee. With the Obama administration packing up to leave at the end of their term, I was most likely going to be looking for a new job. For his part, Beto was giving up his House seat in order to run for the Senate against Ted Cruz.

When I first came to Washington, Beto let me know that he had no patience for VA failures and VA excuses. At our initial meeting, he told me he had developed his own proposal for the El Paso VA; Beto had a plan to focus on behavioral and primary care and to collaborate with the University Medical Center (a private hospital) for most other services. Beto and I had developed a strong relationship built on trust, and we both wanted to make sure that a proper transition plan was in place for veterans' health services in his district. We did not want to lose momentum during the time it took for a new under secretary to be nominated and confirmed.

When I stepped into the room with Beto, I apologized for the interruption occasioned by Cohen and Perlmutter before sitting down to delve into the VA situation in his district once again. Beto wanted me to update him on how we were going to position his plan for implementation under a new under secretary in the next administration.

I tried to focus on the issue at hand, but I had gotten out about ten words when my phone rang again.

It was Ike. I had to take it.

"There's one more flight today from DC to Palm Beach," he said. "You need to be on it."

I hung up, gave Beto a pained look, and said, "I'm sorry. I have to go."

I ran to my car, where my VA-assigned driver waited for me in front of the Capitol. "Let's get to the airport, Dennis. I have a plane to catch." Dennis smiled and stepped on the gas.

The VA is a massive bureaucracy that employs 377,805 people. (Microsoft, by comparison, employs 134,000; General Motors, about 180,000.) Established in 1930 and made a cabinet-level department in 1989, the VA provides near-comprehensive health care services for nine million eligible veterans at VA medical centers and outpatient clinics located throughout the country. Beyond health care, the agency provides disability compensation, vocational rehabilitation, education assistance, home loans, and life insurance. It also provides burial and memorial benefits to eligible veterans and family members at 135 national cemeteries. But 85 percent of what the VA does is to provide medical services for veterans, which is the 85 percent I managed as under secretary for health under President Obama.

In 2015, when I was first approached about coming to the VA, many of my colleagues expressed concern that the job was a no-win situation for me. They felt it was a surefire way to ruin my career leading large hospital systems—a career that had been marked by distinction. They warned that the VA was simply too big and complex to change. Others pointed out that it did not make sense to accept a dramatic pay cut in return for such enormous headaches. But I took the job because I felt a sense of responsibility to our nation's veterans. The VA had been in crisis mode for years before I arrived, but after seventeen months as under secretary and a great deal of progress on many fronts, I felt optimistic, energized, and even more responsible than ever, which is why I dashed out of a congressman's office to meet with a stranger in Florida.

En route to the airport, I called my wife. "I need you to see if I can get on the next flight to Palm Beach," I said. "I don't have time to explain. Just drop what you're doing and call me back. Please!"

As always, Merle came through, and I made the plane.

Just before takeoff, Ike's assistant, Marisol, called to tell me that since the flight wasn't arriving in Florida until early evening, she had moved the meeting from dinner to breakfast. She informed me that she secured a room for me at Mar-a-Lago, the old Merriweather Post estate built in the 1920s and acquired by Donald Trump in 1985. With 126 rooms and private quarters measuring 62,500 square feet, it would soon become known as the Southern White House. I thanked Marisol for her thoughtfulness but refused the offer and booked myself a room at an inexpensive hotel nearby. Then I buckled up for what I expected would be a bumpy ride.

2

The Power of Adaptation

I HAVE ALWAYS BEEN A PROBLEM SOLVER. FOR YEARS, MY WIFE HAS called me Mary Poppins, saying that I pop into situations where there is trouble, fix the problem, and then pop out to do the same thing somewhere else. The day I turned sixteen, I joined the local volunteer fire department. Later, after I left academic medicine to launch a start-up that measured hospital quality, I became a volunteer fireman once again. I keep a small emergency kit in my car and frequently pull over to offer help when I see an accident with injuries. Especially as a health care administrator, I am drawn to turnarounds, which is exactly the kind of transformation the VA needed.

I came of age just after the Vietnam War, during a time of relative peace and an all-volunteer army, and as a result, I never served in uniform. But I was born on a military base in Highland Park, where my dad was an army psychiatrist. One of my most vivid childhood memories is seeing how my dad contained his emotions as he watched his patients struggle to overcome psychological wounds. Sometimes he brought these men home and paid them to work around the house. I often found strangers trimming our bushes or painting a part of the house even though we had done these chores ourselves just a few weeks before. When I asked him about this, he simply smiled and explained that we were helping them help themselves.

I spent my twenties focused on my medical education, and by the time I finished my training, I had worked in three VA hospitals. VA hospitals were fantastic places to learn because, at that time, there was little supervision by attending physicians, which meant that we interns and residents got to do much of the care ourselves. I specialized in internal medicine, but when I saw the huge problems our country faced in health care delivery, I took management training and rose through the ranks of hospital administration.

Through it all, though, I maintained my clinical work. I enjoy seeing patients. I also believe that the only way for hospital administrators to truly see whether their efforts are creating the desired effect is for them to stay in close touch with the patients themselves. During my time at the VA, I did more than just see individual patients, though. Especially during my first months as the VA's under secretary for health, I traveled extensively to tour VA facilities, get to know veterans and staff, and observe firsthand the type of overall care veterans were receiving.

My first chance to really get to know some of the people I was working for—and some of the obstacles they were working to overcome—came when I attended a winter sports clinic in Aspen, Colorado, one of the eight adaptive-sports events the VA runs each year.

Getting off the forty-seat flight that took us from Denver up into the mountains, I counted eight service dogs and eleven wheelchairs. My seatmate on the short flight was a Vietnam veteran who had lost his left leg. Alex, his eighty-five-pound golden retriever service dog, slept peacefully on top of my feet the whole trip.

At the hotel, check-in was slow because several veterans were asking for bathrooms that were wheelchair accessible, rooms close to the elevator, and recommendations for where to buy dog food. In the lobby, we saw many veterans with one or two prosthetic limbs, others who were paralyzed, and some who appeared anatomically normal but suffered from invisible wounds of warfare and were accompanied by their emotional support dogs.

In clinical practice, I had always focused on the patient's physiology. In Aspen, I began to understand the power and the necessity of a more holistic definition of health and well-being that framed the VA's more comprehensive approach. It was also a humbling demonstration of the sacrifices these veterans had made for our country and of what we now owed them in return.

In the year or so before I came to Washington, the VA had made the wrong kind of headlines, when the length of time it took to get an appointment reached crisis proportions. There were allegations that forty veterans may have died while waiting for care in the Phoenix system alone. Other reports alleged that many thousands more nationwide were kept waiting too long or never received services. Pushing poor management into alleged malfeasance, staff were said to have manipulated wait times to make the data seem more acceptable. This rolling fiasco led to the resignations of both the VA secretary and the under secretary. By the time I arrived, the agency's harshest critics were advocating that we simply turn off the lights, close up shop, and turn the job over to the private sector.

But here on the Colorado ski slopes, I saw the VA functioning with a passion and a compassion that can't be accounted for in an efficiency report or a profit-and-loss statement. Instructors had come from VA hospitals all over the country, many of them paying their own way just to be part of this experience. To give me some small idea of what the veterans were experiencing in adaptive skiing, two of these instructors loaded me into a metal chair that pressed my knees together firmly and had two skis in the front and one in the back, took me up the chairlift, and then guided me down the slope. I'm not sure I've ever been more terrified. I cannot imagine how difficult the loss of mobility may be for anyone, let alone for veterans who previously prided themselves on their physical abilities but lost those abilities in service to their country. And for this same reason, I could understand why on this mountain so many found the experience to be freeing, exhilarating, and, for some, life changing.

The size and complexity of bringing four hundred disabled veterans to a ski resort was like a military operation in itself. Along with volunteers to help individuals, the VA brought trailers of equipment for adaptive skiing and technicians to customize the equipment for individual needs. VA staff set up a field hospital next to the hotel in a large canvas tent, complete with beds and procedure rooms. Everyone hoped this facility would not get much use, but the past several years had suggested that now and again, medical intervention would be necessary.

As the week progressed, and as I skied down the trail with some of the veterans, I could see the fear and anxiety of the first-timers give way to excitement and joy. Many who returned year after year told me that the ability to compete and to master a sport had renewed their hope and confidence. Some told me they had been depressed and even suicidal until they discovered adaptive sports. Others confided that they had been able to reduce or even stop medications after getting involved in these events.

After dinner one night, each of the veterans was invited to a reception for his or her particular military branch. The first one that my wife, Merle, and I attended was for marines. Of all the services, the marines may be the most tight-knit, and as though sensing that I might feel a little out of place, three of the veterans came to the front of the room and asked for everyone's attention. Each of them was missing a limb or had a service dog. Asking me to join them up front, they presented me with a marine pin and began a small ceremony proclaiming me as an honorary marine. During my years as a physician, I've seen many heartrending dramas in emergency rooms and cancer wards, and I'm not someone easily moved to tears, but it was hard to maintain my composure while being recognized by these men who had given so much.

3

An Interview Unlike Any Other

Arriving at Mar-a-Lago to meet with Ike Perlmutter was like stepping into a James Bond film. My car rolled through majestic gates and up the long driveway to let me out at the canopied entrance. Entering the main building, I was greeted by a very pleasant young woman seated behind a bronze desk.

"Good morning, Dr. Shulkin," she said. "Mr. Perlmutter is expecting you."

She led me through a high-ceilinged hallway into a vast space with marble floors, gold walls, and glass chandeliers. This room opened onto a veranda with about thirty tables set for breakfast. Only one was occupied.

The two men sitting there looked to be in their early seventies. The first to speak was Ike, short but solidly built, who introduced himself and then with a gesture to his companion said, "This is Dr. Moskowitz."

I still had no clear idea why I had been summoned to Florida, but I sat down, ordered coffee, and listened as Ike began telling me how he had emigrated from Israel after serving in the Six-Day War of 1967. He also told me how much he cared about what was happening to our veterans and that he was not happy with the current situation at the VA. He also reiterated that the president-elect had asked him to help fix these problems.

"So, Bruce," he said, turning to Dr. Moskowitz, "tell him—"

"I practice in West Palm," Moskowitz began. "Everybody from migrant workers to some very wealthy people. I also treat a lot of veterans who can't get good care from your VA." I blinked.

He then went on to tell me how he had trained with Dr. Toby Cosgrove, the CEO of Cleveland Clinic. He also knew the CEOs of Johns Hopkins, Mayo Clinic, and Partners Healthcare—the group that manages the Harvard teaching hospitals. I was aware that the president-elect had met with some of these leaders to discuss running the VA. I also heard some talk of Dr. Cosgrove's becoming Trump's nominee for secretary of VA.

Ike and Bruce took turns asking me about my experience at the VA—what I thought was working and what was not. They asked me about VA staff, use of technology, and interactions with the private sector. The conversation flowed easily, but the purpose of the meeting still eluded me.

We talked for about ninety minutes before it was time to say goodbye. In preparing to leave, I made sure to express my wish, however unlikely, to remain as under secretary under President Trump in order to finish the job I had begun eighteen months earlier. A simple nod from each was their only acknowledgment of my request.

Before heading back to DC, I spent the morning touring the West Palm Beach VA. I had recently had my first success in recruiting a senior executive from the private sector to the VA, and she had just assumed the role of medical center director there. I promised her that I would visit and spend time with her management team, and this was my opportunity to do so before I left my job as under secretary. Afterward, I got a ride back to the airport and traveled home.

Back in the capital, I spent the rest of the afternoon in my office, then, as per usual, hopped on an Amtrak train to head home to Philadelphia, where my wife maintained her medical practice. Merle and I met in medical school and have been married for thirty-one years. She is a dermatologist in private practice and one of the few doctors I know who still loves to practice medicine as much as when she first graduated. We have two children. Danny, our oldest, graduated from NYU and earned his MPA there before starting to work for Horizon Blue Cross. Jennie was a nationally ranked tennis and squash player who completed her undergraduate studies at the University of Pennsylvania and then law school at Harvard. Following graduation, she became a law clerk to a federal district judge in the Eastern District of New York.

When my train arrived at Philadelphia's Thirtieth Street Station in the midst of a snowstorm, Merle picked me up, and we drove to White Dog Café in Haverford, about twenty-five minutes outside Philadelphia. Given that the snow was really heavy, I pulled the car up close to the entrance to let her get out. Then, as I ventured across the parking lot to try to find a space, my cell phone rang.

Ike's number flashed on my caller ID. I picked up. "Where are you?" he barked.

"Philadelphia."

"No. You need to be in New York. Reince will call you with details."

It didn't seem wise to take a call from the soon-to-be White House chief of staff, Reince Priebus, in a noisy restaurant, so I decided we had to leave. I frantically motioned to Merle, who was already seated. Startled and a little upset, she got up from the table, and we left the restaurant without eating.

We went home and waited for a call, which was not exactly the way we had hoped to begin our weekend. Especially since the call never came.

Merle and I tried to get some rest, and the next morning, Saturday, January 7, I called Ike to see if he knew what was going on. "Donald is expecting to see you at Trump Tower today at 2:00 p.m.," he said.

I hung up in a panic. It was a little after 11:00 a.m., and our home outside Philadelphia is a two-hour drive from Manhattan under the best conditions. Today's conditions were approaching whiteout, but this was not a meeting to miss.

Without really thinking, I threw on the first suit in my closet, grabbed my car keys, and yelled to Merle to get her coat. She was barefoot, and I told her to just grab her shoes and put them on in the car. Moments later we swerved out of the driveway and made our way along the snow-covered roads toward the interstate. I drove faster than I should have, but few other drivers were crazy enough to be on the road in a blizzard like we were. After about an hour of sustained panic, my cell phone rang. It was Reince Priebus.

"Sorry not to have called sooner, but we're all set. You'll be meeting with the president-elect on Monday at 2:00 p.m." *Monday*, not today.

We found the nearest exit, turned around, and headed back home.

Later that afternoon, Priebus called again, this time with some questions for me—mainly, it seemed, to help him figure out how I had gotten on his call list. He wanted to know how I knew Trump. I told him I didn't. He seemed perplexed that I had no connection to the Trump campaign. He also wanted to know how I became under secretary for Obama. I explained that there is a statutory commission that selects the nominee for a presidential appointment. I also told him that I was a doctor and that I had served as a chief executive of health care organizations for more than a decade. Without commenting on any of this, Priebus asked me to meet with him for lunch on Monday prior to my meeting with the president-elect.

On Sunday, still mystified but intrigued, I took a train to New York, this time with a carefully packed overnight bag. I stayed in our Manhattan apartment with our son, Danny, and slept on the couch in the living room. Late in the evening, Ike called to see if I was all set for the meeting. Clarifying some final details, he asked me if I wanted to enter Trump Tower through the main lobby or use a private entrance to avoid being seen. A year and a half into my service in Washington, I still didn't quite understand optics and the strategy behind these kinds of decisions. I saw no reason to hide a meeting with the president-elect. "I'll go through the front door," I said.

The next day, I headed over to Trump Tower, around which the NYPD had set up a security corridor extending two blocks in all directions. I wasn't quite sure what to expect, but even if this meeting was nothing more than an exit interview, I wanted the chance to tell the president-elect where progress was being made at the VA and what direction his new administration should take. At worst, this was my chance to give input to the people to whom I would be passing the baton. At best, I might convince the president-elect to let me stay in my position as under secretary and continue the work we were doing.

The police weren't letting anyone through without ID, and those who passed the first check had to wait in long lines to be searched and scanned. Fortunately, from my days working in New York City, I had become an honorary NYPD police surgeon, so I flashed my badge and moved through without a word.

Just inside the building, I was met by several Republican National Committee staffers, who escorted me to the lobby restaurant. As Priebus and I shook hands, he told me that he no longer had time for lunch. I said I understood, but knowing that he was from Green Bay, I added, "By the way, congratulations on the Packers' win this weekend."

He smiled and said, "You know, maybe I do have time for a quick bite."

Making our way through the small restaurant, we were stopped by swarms of diners who all seemed to want their picture taken with Reince, so I became the amateur photographer as table after table stood up to pose with him. We took a back table, ordered chicken Caesar salad, and spent most of our time casually discussing our families and nonpolitical interests. I gleaned nothing of substance and no explanation for why I was summoned to New York. After lunch, he escorted me upstairs.

As we approached the inner sanctum, Steve Bannon came out to greet us and escort me into Trump's office, familiar to millions as the set of *The Apprentice*. Against a wall of glass, the president-elect sat at a huge desk covered with copies of *Time* magazine with his picture on the cover as Person of the Year. A part of me wondered where the secret cameras were hidden.

As we shook hands, Trump announced to his staff in the room, "He's a good-looking guy." He then quickly repeated, "He's a good-looking guy, isn't he?

Taken aback, I could think of nothing better to say than, "Nice to meet you, Mr. President-Elect."

As various staff members came and went, he picked up one of the magazines and said to me, "See this, have you seen this?"

"Yes, I have, sir. Congratulations."

Glancing around the room, I noticed that the one nonglass interior wall was filled with awards and plaques from events honoring Trump. I sat down in the only chair facing him, across the desk.

"Get me Ike Perlmutter on the phone!" Trump shouted.

He had an intercom but evidently chose not to use it. Whoever was taking orders on the other side of the wall never responded verbally, but in less than a minute, Ike was on speakerphone.

"Ike! I have Dr. Shulkin here."

"Yes, Mr. President. I think you'll be very impressed. I met with him last week, and I think he understands what's going on at the VA."

"Okay, Ike, I'm going to talk to him and see what I think." Without saying goodbye, Trump pressed a button to hang up the phone.

It seemed by now that most of Trump's inner circle were milling about in the room behind me—Jared Kushner, Kellyanne Conway, Steve Bannon, and Reince Priebus.

"Ike is an amazing guy," Trump said. "He started with nothing, you know. Nothing but the clothes on his back, and now he runs Marvel Entertainment. You know he made four of the top ten movies? So how do you know him?"

"I just met him, Mr. President-Elect. Michael Cohen introduced me."

I saw a flash of recognition across Trump's face. "You know Michael?"

I nodded.

Suddenly, there was another yell. "Get Michael Cohen in here right now!" Within seconds, Michael Cohen appeared. "Michael, you know this guy?"

"Yeah. He used to run Morristown Hospital. Your family was treated there."

Trump smiled at this memory. "Oh, yes. They treated us very well. Very well."

Jared and Kellyanne were having a side conversation, which they took outside. Then Trump turned to me and asked, "So what's the best hospital in the city?"

"Well, Mr. Trump, I think it depends on—"

"You know, I used to think well of this one place, but I know a guy who went in there feeling okay, and they just chopped his *thing* right off! They chopped *it* off! I wouldn't go there for *anything* now."

Once again, I wasn't quite sure what to say. "Yes. Well . . . no hospital is good at treating every condition," I managed.

"So if you were sick, where would you go?"

Before I could answer, he looked over at Michael Cohen. "So, Michael, what do you think of this guy?"

"Donald, he's the best in his field."

"You really think so, huh?" Looking back at me, Trump asked, "So what do you think of this guy McDonald?" Bob McDonald, the current VA secretary and my boss, had been appointed by President Obama to replace General Eric Shinseki, the VA secretary forced to resign in the midst of the wait-time crisis.

"I think he's one of the best leaders in the country," I answered truthfully. "He's been making really good progress, and I think he should stay."

"Yeah, I've heard good things, but there is no way we can keep him, just not possible. What do you think we need to do?"

Then, answering his own question, Trump said, "I'll tell you what we need to do: we need to make sure our veterans aren't waiting for care."

"Mr. Trump, you're absolutely right."

"We have to fix this thing. It's a mess. Do you think we can fix it?"

"We've been making big improvements on the wait times. We've developed same-day access, and we're getting more veterans—"

He cut me off again. "I want our veterans to get the best." Then he repeated, "They really created a mess here. Can we fix it?"

Once again, I assured him that I was committed to doing just that.

Trump ruffled through a few papers on his desk and then looked up. "The VA's an important place, but there are some good ones and some bad ones. But I'll tell you what's messed up. They come back with PTSD. You know what's really bad? They come back and their wives or girlfriends didn't wait for them."

I swallowed.

Trump paused for a moment and then looked up as if actually seeing me for the first time. "You know, you don't really fit the bill. The generals . . . now they fit the bill. But can they fix health care?"

Not waiting for my response, he continued. "Who do you think would make a good secretary?"

"Well, Mr. Trump, Bob McDonald is doing a great—"

Trump cut me off to ask about a certain African American candidate from the navy. He asked if I thought he could fix health care.

I said I did not know anything about the gentleman.

"What about this CEO of Exxon Mobil?"

Before I could answer, he moved on to, "What are you . . . like, the number-two or number-three guy at VA?"

"I'm number three, sir."

Jared and Kellyanne came back in, still engrossed in their own private conversation, passing a piece of paper back and forth. Soon Reince Priebus and Steve Bannon were drawn in, and the volume of their sidebar escalated.

After a moment, Reince interrupted. "Mr. Trump, we need your approval on this press release. It's about Jared's role in the administration."

Trump glanced at the paper for a split second and then, without reading it, handed it back. "Just tell me what it says!"

"I don't think we should release it just now," Kellyanne said.

"Well, I do," Jared countered.

Having seen all of these people parodied relentlessly over the past several weeks on *Saturday Night Live,* I couldn't help thinking that I'd stepped into a skit with Alec Baldwin and Kate McKinnon.

As the tension increased, Reince leaned over to me and whispered, "Dr. Shulkin, we need to resolve this. Would you mind stepping out for ten minutes?"

I rose from my chair, but Trump swatted me back down. "David can hear this. Stay."

I sat back down.

The debate continued, with Trump sitting quietly, until the group seemed to reach some kind of resolution. Then Trump turned back to me. "So why is it so broken? The VA."

"Well, there are many reasons, starting with—"

"I think we need to let the veterans go wherever they want."

"Well, there needs to be a coordinated effort—"

"I'll tell you what: we're going to fix this thing. If you were in charge, what would you do first?"

"I would make sure that we had—"

"Do you think we can fix this thing?"

"Yes, Mr. President-Elect, I do."

We went on like this for another thirty minutes or so while the others wandered in and out. Finally, Trump turned to Priebus, Bannon, and Cohen and asked, "So what do you guys think?"

Heads nodded in approval.

"Get Ike on the phone!" Trump yelled.

Within seconds, Ike was once again on speakerphone.

"Ike, impressive guy. You've got a good guy here. I like him."

From West Palm, Ike said, "Donald, he's your guy. Toby and all the others that you've met, they all endorse him. I wouldn't steer you wrong."

Then the president-elect turned to Michael Cohen and said, "Next time you see him, you can call him Mr. Secretary."

Confused, I stood, shook Trump's hand, and left the office.

I took the long elevator ride down to the Trump Tower lobby, where I was met by a barrage of camera flashes and bright lights from TV crews. Reporters shouted, "Dr. Shulkin! Did you meet with Donald Trump? Dr. Shulkin, who'll run the VA?"

I had no idea, mostly because I had no idea what had just happened.

I smiled and waved shyly but said nothing. Then I made my way quickly into the crowds on Fifth Avenue, where I was once again unrecognizable.

4

The Call to Serve

Before the strange phone call from Ike Perlmutter that eventually landed me at Trump Tower, I was coming to terms with having to end my work on behalf of veterans. It took me a while to realize it, but what I was being offered through these confusing interactions with the Trump team was a new beginning. What took me even longer to realize was the awkward and unusual nature of the position I was going to be in as an outsider coming into Trump's inner circle.

I have never been particularly political. I certainly was not a "Trump guy." And even though I was appointed as the VA under secretary by President Obama, I was not an "Obama guy" either. My primary loyalty was to the men and women in uniform who served our country and to the VA mission providing their health care.

Oddly enough, my first contact with the Obama administration shared a number of similarities with my first contact with the Trump team, beginning with a series of similarly mysterious and awkwardly timed phone calls. Certainly the most dramatic of these came from Air Force One.

It was December 19, 2014, and I had just arrived home after my two-hour commute from northern New Jersey to Philadelphia. Our family was leaving the next morning for a ten-day trip to South America, and I had not packed yet. When the phone rang, Merle instructed, "Don't get that. It's six o'clock on a Friday afternoon, and we're on vacation."

I glanced at the caller ID, though, and all that registered was "0000000000," which piqued my curiosity.

When I picked up, the caller asked, "Is this Dr. Shulkin?"

"Yes. Who's this?"

"This is the Air Force One operator. Please hold."

After a moment, a woman came on and said, "Dr. Shulkin, this is Anita Breckenridge, White House deputy chief of staff. The president is on his way to Hawaii and wanted to know if you'd consider being our nominee for under secretary of the VA."

Strange as it was to be getting a call from the president's plane, it was not a total surprise.

In the summer of 2014, I attended a board meeting in Washington, where I was invited to lunch at the Metropolitan Club by Eric Larsen, an affable man in his forties who appeared to know everyone. For whatever reason, he had done his homework on me, and it turned out that we had a number of friends in common.

Toward the end of our meal, he asked me a deep question. "David, you've had a truly great career, but do you have any regrets?"

I started to say no, just reflexively, but then I paused and said, "You know, maybe just one. Not spending any part of my career in public service. I've been reading about the wait times mess at the VA, especially down in Phoenix, and I wonder if I could've made a difference."

After lunch, I took a train back to Philadelphia, and as usual in the Northeast Corridor on a Friday afternoon, the train was packed. We barely reached the outskirts of Washington when my cell phone rang.

"Hello, Dr. Shulkin. This is Jonathan McBride at the White House. I wanted to know if we could talk to you about running the VA health care system."

Thinking this might be a prank, I asked, "How did you get my number?"

"We have our ways," he said mysteriously. "Could you meet with us this Monday in DC?"

I continued on my way home to Philadelphia and then headed back to Washington a little more than forty-eight hours later.

In the capital, I met with a special commission appointed by the secretary of VA and headed by deputy secretary Sloan Gibson. The first question before this twelve-member panel was from Bob Wallace, the executive director of the Veterans of Foreign Wars. "If you were under secretary," he asked me, "who would you be working for?"

I hesitated for a moment, taking into account that the under secretary obviously works for the president and for the secretary of VA, and technically for the American people. But then I answered, "I would be working for the veterans."

Bob smiled, sat back in his chair, and said, "We've asked that to each of the other seven candidates. You're the first one to give the right answer."

This interview led to yet another trip to Washington a few weeks later, so I could meet with then-VA secretary Bob McDonald.

This time my destination was the block-long VA headquarters on Vermont Avenue. When I arrived at the tenth floor, the secretary greeted me in the doorway to his office, his West Point ring conspicuous on his outstretched right hand. Every VA secretary before me had come from a military background.

We stepped into his office, where the large windows looked out onto Lafayette Park and directly through the park to the White House.

"This is what you'd call an artilleryman's dream shot," McDonald joked.

I looked out the window and could see the snipers positioned on the roof of the White House, their binoculars aimed out toward us.

Bob showed me his office, including the magnificent view of the Washington Monument from his window. To our left was Dolly Madison's House, and below, Lafayette Park, with its statues of

Generals Lafayette, Rochambeau, Kosciuszko, and von Steuben, all heroes of the American Revolution.

We talked about my belief that health care must be patient centered, metric driven, and totally transparent about outcomes. I told him I would bring my private-sector experience to the VA and that this could create some friction with those who wanted to maintain the status quo. Bob smiled and said, "That's exactly what we're looking for."

We talked about the lengthy process of vetting and confirmation, and as we stood to say goodbye, Bob reached across his desk and extended his hand to offer me his "challenge coin," an ancient military tradition now extended to all senior levels of government. "I want you to have this," he said, "to thank you for agreeing to serve."

With these preliminaries out of the way, it looked like my path to the nomination as under secretary was pretty clear, but it still took many months and many cartons of paperwork. Each time I completed one set of forms, another arrived, and after a while, I realized that the reason for sending these out in this "death by a thousand cuts" fashion was that anyone seeing the mountain of paper all at once would flee in terror. With this incremental approach, though, your sunk costs increased with each form you completed, and you persisted if only to recoup the investment.

A few weeks later, Merle was in our local supermarket when a woman living about ten houses down stopped her in the dairy aisle. "You know it was the strangest thing. The other day, a man from the FBI came to my house and said he wanted to ask me some questions about your husband. Is everything okay?"

Even after the FBI completed its investigation, I still had to face a series of interviews with White House staff. I was impressed by the Obama administration's compulsivity. They wanted zero surprises and refused to nominate someone who might embarrass the president.

5

Transitioning to Public Service

THE ANNOUNCEMENT OF MY NOMINATION FOR UNDER SECRETARY was scheduled for 3:30 p.m., March 18, 2015. Merle and I had been asked not to tell anyone prior to this day, so the news took many of my family, friends, and colleagues by surprise. I realized I had accepted the nomination without even knowing what the salary would be and knowing that it came with zero vacation days and no personal days. None of it mattered to me.

Since this was a Senate-confirmed position, I began to set up face-to-face meetings with key members of the relevant committee. Created in 1970, the Senate Committee on Veterans Affairs has fifteen members, and at this time, the breakdown was eight Republicans and seven Democrats, with Republican senator Johnny Isakson from Georgia as chair.

As far as I could tell, Senator Isakson was a well-liked, straightforward, and thoughtful politician who genuinely cared about veterans. My meeting with him went well, with him promising that the upcoming hearing would contain no surprises and no partisan games.

Over the next two weeks, I met with almost every member of the committee. I was always accompanied by a staffer from the VA Congressional Affairs team, who supplied me with a standard bio on each senator. This was helpful, but the staffers also gave me instructions that I found troubling, because the path they advised went against everything I believed in. Throughout my career, I have always tried to be up-front and completely candid, but these staffers urged me not to answer any question in a way that committed me to a specific position, which could then be used against me in the confirmation hearing. Their preferred response was to say, "Senator, if confirmed, I will give that issue my full consideration." I had always valued transparency, so this felt very unnatural to me.

Despite staff advice, when a senator asked my opinion, I gave it, truthfully and completely, which I thought worked perfectly well. After all, these were savvy, knowledgeable people who wouldn't be satisfied with platitudes and evasions. For instance, Louisiana senator Bill Cassidy, a physician who specialized in liver disease, entered politics specifically because he was frustrated with our public health system. Cassidy and I talked about problems with access, best practices in managing hepatitis, and strategies to implement best practices across a geographically diverse system.

Each senator seemed deeply committed to veterans, had genuine concerns, and helped me to develop a stronger understanding of the issues.

My confirmation hearing for under secretary was scheduled for May 5, 2015, in the Dirksen Building on Capitol Hill. Merle and my daughter, Jennie, joined me in the large wood-paneled room with high ceilings and large portraits of past committee chairmen.

I sat alone at a small table in front of a semicircle of senators on a raised platform. After Chairman Isakson called the meeting to order, I gave an opening statement about my family history and my desire to give back. I detailed my experience as a physician and hospital CEO and spoke of my intent to use both my medical knowledge and my managerial skills to fix the problems that the VA had experienced so very publicly over the past several years. This was followed by a round of questions from each senator—a ritual familiar to anyone who watched the hearings for then Judge Brett Kavanaugh's confirmation to the Supreme Court—rotating between Republican and Democratic. The senators used most of their allotted five minutes to espouse their positions, mostly for the benefit of voters back home, with maybe one question thrown in at the end and leaving very little time for a substantive response. Overall, though, I got the sense that the hearing went well.

Based on initial feedback, the White House called and told me to prepare for a quick confirmation vote. The White House suggested I tell my current employer that I would probably need to resign in a few days to go to Washington.

I called the head of Atlantic Health System, Brian Gragnolati, and informed him of my impending confirmation. He responded quickly, and that same day, we announced my temporary replacement at the hospital.

Then, with equal dispatch, the White House called me back and said, "It looks like we might've been too optimistic. It seems we have some holds."

I had just quit my job. Great.

The concept of a hold was new to me, but as I soon learned, any senator can unilaterally declare a hold on a nomination, and the process stops. A senator may use it to extract a concession—whatever he or she feels is needed. I had four of them, all from Democrats. Senator Sherrod Brown of Ohio organized a hold with two other senators over the unwillingness of the VA to recognize the claims of national guard airmen who flew in C138s.

When I came back to Washington to meet with Senator Brown, he knew his facts cold, but I had also done my homework. After our discussion, which included Secretary McDonald and representatives from the White House, it was agreed that the VA would expand coverage, and the three holds were lifted.

The last hold was placed by Senator Kirsten Gillibrand, whose concern also dated back to Vietnam and Agent Orange. She wanted coverage for "Blue Water" navy veterans, those who served on ships well off the coast of Vietnam but who still might have been exposed to the chemical, used as a defoliant, and later shown to cause cancer and other serious diseases. The VA had already recognized the claims of the "Brown Water" sailors, those who served on rivers or in harbors and even those on vessels docked in Vietnam for just a few hours. There was no definitive science to back up the claims of the Blue Water veterans, but Senator Gillibrand, for one, was leading the fight to offer presumptive coverage.

When I met with her, she expressed her frustration that her experts on Agent Orange had not been given a fair hearing and that their data was not being taken seriously. I promised the senator I would give all of the data full and fair consideration. She thanked me and told me that she now felt heard. Senator Gillibrand lifted her hold.

I was gaining perspective on the new world I was entering. I would be, in effect, reporting to a board of the 435 members of Congress. This was on top of the direct stakeholders in the VA—the veterans we served—who were even more vocal through advocacy organizations.

Even though the wheels of this democratic process turned very slowly, at least we were now back on the path toward confirmation. On June 24, 2015, I was in DC, looking at a number of apartments for my new weekday home, when the White House called. "This could be the day. The vote may come this afternoon. We'll call you."

Shortly thereafter, I boarded yet another Amtrak train back to New Jersey with my cell phone close at hand. At four o'clock the phone rang. It was the White House.

"Bad news. Looks like you have a new hold from Senator Sullivan. Unlikely you'll get confirmed before the July recess as we'd hoped. Sorry."

I couldn't help thinking how this "advise and consent" aspect of representative democracy sounds great in theory, but for the individuals involved, trying to manage mundane considerations like knowing whether I'll have employment next month and wondering if or when I should rent an apartment can be a pain in the neck.

Only a few minutes later, a member of the VA congressional affairs team called and said, "Sir, Senator Sullivan from Alaska is asking to speak with you right away. Okay if we arrange that?"

"Sure," I said.

"Sir, you're breaking up. Before you talk to the senator, I think you better get off the train and find a quiet place."

Just then the conductor announced, "Next stop Aberdeen, Maryland." I grabbed my suitcase and jumped off.

Finding a quiet corner of the small station, I waited for the call. The staffer told me the Senate would only be in session another half hour before they recessed. Nothing like coming down to the wire!

My phone rang. "Dr. Shulkin, this is Senator Sullivan. I'm standing on the floor of the Senate as we speak, and I am going to make this real simple. Alaska isn't like the other states. Our veterans' problems are different. I need you to commit to me that if confirmed, you'll come out and visit Alaska within your first ninety days. What do you say?"

Knowing that my job was being held hostage, but also knowing that this trip was an opportunity to help veterans, I replied, "Senator, we're going to Alaska."

A few minutes later, I was confirmed by unanimous consent.

6

Stand Down

M Y SWEARING IN WAS SCHEDULED FOR 7:30 A.M. ON JULY 5, 2015. Bob McDonald was traveling in Hawaii, so in his place, Sloan Gibson, the deputy secretary, administered the oath. With the uncertainty about my employment resolved, my family and I visited the under secretary's suite for the first time. My new office was positioned two floors directly below Bob McDonald's, and it shared the same expansive view of Lafayette Park, the White House, and the Washington Monument. The north-facing window peered directly over the Church of the Presidents, where Abraham Lincoln used to pray. There was nothing on the walls, and with the aesthetically refined eye of a dermatologist and a woman with good taste, Merle began planning where to place my diplomas and family mementos.

The front-office staff at the Veterans Health Administration (VHA) arranged a welcoming reception for me. They escorted Merle, Danny, and me to the under secretary's large conference room, graced by a worn wooden podium with the VA emblem. The room was filled with what looked to me like at least a hundred staff members. A gentleman I never met opened the proceedings with formal comments that included a recitation of my credentials. Then Carolyn Clancy, who served as acting under secretary before my confirmation, offered a few words of introduction and turned the microphone over to me.

I knew this was an agency beleaguered by crisis, scandal, and the accompanying bad press, and that morale was likely low. I offered a few encouraging words, but I kept my comments short and focused mostly on the privilege I felt to be joining in such an honorable mission.

We posed for some pictures and then stood in place for a receiving line. The staff quickly queued up to greet Merle, Danny, and me with a handshake and a personal welcome. Their precision signaled to me that they had been through this meet-and-greet with a new boss many times (in fact, roughly once every two years). I couldn't help imagining many of them glancing at their watches, wondering how long I was going to last.

Soon after, I got right to work. I met with my new staff and shared the issues on my mind. Even though I was not prepared to articulate it fully at the time, I was already developing a long to-do list for transforming the delivery of health care to our nation's veterans. I rattled off the top five items on my list: we had to fix wait times, better coordinate care in the community, improve employee morale, work more seamlessly as a system to implement best practices, and regain veteran trust.

That alone was a heavy agenda for any agency and for any administrator. How much time we would have and how far we would get remained to be seen. Judging from the muted reaction to my list of priorities, I really wondered whether my team was up to the task—or, for that matter, if I was.

Another task at the top of the to-do list was to find the right chief of staff. I knew I needed to find someone from inside the VA who could help me understand the system. I heard repeatedly that there was really only one person who fit the bill, and her name was Vivieca Wright Simpson. Vivieca (like Cher, everyone knew her by her first name) had worked at the VA for more than thirty years and knew all the ins and outs of the agency. But the culture at the VA did not encourage active recruitment of people from their current positions. I needed to wait and see if she applied, and fortunately she did. I hired her immediately.

Vivieca was an imposing figure in the VHA, not just because people respected her and knew her as a no-nonsense administrator, but because she knew the strengths and weaknesses of everyone else, as well as who was trustworthy and who was not.

Even with Vivieca on my team, I still felt the need for a little more firepower in my inner circle in order to launch a major reform. In my previous position, I had worked with a very effective agent of change, Dr. Poonam Alaigh, who had been the commissioner of health in New Jersey under Governor Christie before starting her own consulting firm. As a consultant, she had helped me establish a new accountable-care organization for Atlantic Health. Like me, she kept her hand in clinical medicine. After a full week of work, she often spent Saturdays and Sundays seeing patients at the Lyons VA Medical Center in New Jersey. I used to say to her, "Aren't you exhausted by the time the weekend comes around?"

She always told me, "I don't know. I just love the veterans. I can spend hours with them, listening to their stories, and I can tell that I make a difference when I'm working there."

I knew that if I called her and told her I needed her and that the veterans needed her, she would agree. This is how she came on board as a senior adviser to me.

I began to communicate our new priorities, and the organization responded positively. Of these priorities, nothing was more important than access to care—the issue that had led to the departure of the previous secretary and under secretary.

"How many veterans are waiting right now for care?" I asked.

"We have about 350,000 veterans waiting more than thirty days for appointments right now," my team responded.

My follow-up question was whether they thought that was a reasonable number. The team looked perplexed. I think they thought it was either one of the dumbest questions ever asked or a trick. But I was sincere. I didn't know the answer.

"How do we know whether these 350,000 veterans are suffering harm while waiting for care?" I asked.

"Well, we really don't know," the team responded.

"The job of any health system," I said, "is to match the clinical need of a patient to the time when his or her care is delivered, and the VA must have the same objective." I began to feel more like a lecturing professor than a newly minted government employee.

Then I pressed further. "Do we have a way of determining the clinical urgency of a veteran?"

My team responded, "Not really. VA has thirty-one different ways of ordering a consult. There's a spectrum from very urgent to routine, with twenty-nine other variations in between."

Now I was baffled. I had never heard of anything like this. Creating thirty-one different categories meant that we ended up knowing almost nothing about the real clinical urgency of our patients' condition. I tried to understand how we got to thirty-one. All I could imagine was that anytime someone wanted to add a category to the list, it was approved. Yet probably no one felt they had the authority to remove any categories. So over the years, the list of choices just grew and grew.

"Starting next week," I said, "I only want two categories: *urgent* or *routine*."

My team studied my face, trying to ascertain that I was serious (as I almost always am). They then went to work. By the following week, there were simply two choices for ordering consults, and clinicians were asked to reorder all previously ordered consults using this new directive. By the end of that week, we had the answer to my original question: there were fifty-seven thousand urgent consults waiting more than thirty days.

Coming from the private sector, my standard for responding to an urgent consult was forty-eight hours or less. In fact, as a physician, if I felt my patient had an urgent need, I almost always personally called and arranged for him or her to be seen. I couldn't imagine letting my patient wait for thirty days or more. I had suspected that the VA had a problem. Now we not only confirmed it, but we actually quantified it.

I reassembled my new team. "How does the military respond to a critical task?"

One of my staff yelled out, "I think it's called a stand-down, sir." As I learned, a stand-down is a military term for soldiers who have to focus on a mission.

I responded, "Well, we need a stand-down, and we need it now, because we have an emergency on our hands!"

I issued an order for every VA medical center in the country to remain open that upcoming Saturday for the VA's first "Access Stand-Down." My objective was to contact every veteran on the list of fifty-seven thousand and confirm that they had been seen and cared for, and if not, to get them seen right away.

The inevitable pushback surfaced. Excuses included: "We don't have any veterans who are waiting for urgent care," "This weekend isn't good for us since our chief of staff already planned vacation," and "We can't get any of our staff to come in over the weekend."

My response was firm: *No exceptions*. I wanted everyone to understand that when it comes to our new priorities, we would all act together, as a system, as the VA.

With the mission identified, everyone went to work, and the planning for that Saturday was unlike any operation I had ever run or been a part of. The team at VA headquarters broke the fifty-seven thousand patients into location-specific lists. The assistant under secretaries, led by Dr. Thomas Lynch, got on conference calls with field leaders across the country and began to detail the expectations and the approach we planned. We reached out to our academic partners, and many of them joined and opened special clinics on that Saturday just to see veterans. Our veterans service organizations (VSOs) sent volunteers to help with the phone banks. Staff around the country volunteered for their local stand-downs. You could feel the energy rising as people prepared, and many commented that it felt good to finally be doing something rather than just hearing about the problems at the VA.

I participated that Saturday in the Access Stand-Down at the Philadelphia VA. When I arrived at the medical center, the entire cadre of clinical leadership was gathered in the conference room in the director's suite, and each had a list of veterans' names. In preparation for the stand-down, some had already reviewed their lists and knew which veterans had issues that had already been addressed and which ones needed care now. I was impressed by the seriousness and thoroughness of these professionals and the pains they took to ensure that no veteran was overlooked. By the end of that day, I felt confident that at least in Philadelphia, while there might still be veterans waiting for care, there were no veterans waiting for care that was clinically *urgent*.

By the end of the weekend, after literally hundreds of similar stand-downs around the country, the list of fifty-seven thousand veterans waiting for urgent care was down to less than one thousand! The response from leaders across the country was reassuring, to say the least. Many felt good about what we had accomplished, and maybe more importantly, people were proud to be a part of something bigger than themselves. The VA worked together as a system that day. My goal was to make that "systemness" become an everyday reality.

7

The Way Forward

WHILE IT FELT GOOD TO MAKE PROGRESS, I KNEW WE HAD JUST begun our work to improve access for veterans. One weekend activity wasn't enough. We needed a sustained effort.

I stared out of my office window at the Washington Monument, and while the view seemed to change each time I looked, it was always inspiring and uplifting. And then it hit me: the VA needed its own Declaration of Independence—a Declaration of *Access*. I typed out the first draft, complete with ten principles that every leader should aspire to in order to ensure that veterans' needs were adequately addressed. The most important tenet of the declaration was same-day access. Same-day access was the only way I knew to ensure that no veteran with an urgent clinical need would ever again wait for care. I gave my draft declaration to Dr. Poonam Alaigh and asked her to share it with the field before coming back to me with a final document.

Poonam enlisted the help of Dr. Steven Lieberman, a VA physician who had been detailed to Washington from the field, and together they created a process for rolling out the Declaration of Access called a "sprint." They brought in leaders from the field and people from the VA Central Office to work on my draft of the declaration and turn it into a document that all could embrace. A week later, they were in my office, ready to present it to me. Their final document was strong, and more importantly, it had support both from the field and from the central office. The plan was to list the elements of the declaration and enlarge it into four-foot-by-three-foot posters with room for the signatures of the leadership team in each of our medical centers. The declaration would then be publicly displayed for all to see.

As I traveled around the country visiting VA Medical Centers, I saw that each one proudly posted the declaration in their administrative offices or their lobby. Each was signed by the leadership team and sometimes clinicians and staff as well. For many, it was a visible commitment to fix access issues. Even more fundamentally, it allowed them to regain a sense of purpose.

The next part of the plan was to get each leader to understand his or her respective numbers. This meant knowing how many urgent consults they had and also knowing their wait times in each of their clinical areas. This was easier said than done.

The VA measured wait times in numerous ways, in a system so convoluted that only a federal agency could come up with it. When people from the VA spoke about wait times, they were often using different definitions. In effect, they might as well have been speaking different languages.

I suggested that we go to a single metric that, in my opinion, reflected the veteran experience: measure the time from when the veteran requested an appointment until the time he or she was seen.

I believed that another essential element in improving performance was transparency. We needed to make our wait times public. The VA data department, under the direction of Dr. Joe Francis, did a great job in developing a new system. Joe had been a resident in internal medicine with me at the University of Pittsburgh, and I remembered him as a very smart guy. What he lacked in political skills, he made up for with his data and analytic talents. One day, Joe came into my office and proudly showed me his new reporting tool. I said, "This is exactly what I've been looking for, Joe. You're a genius."

But not everyone felt the same way. Deputy Secretary Sloan Gibson undoubtedly recognized the power of this tool, but he was concerned about the reaction when Congress, or possibly reporters, found out that their local VA was not performing. However, playing it safe in the past hadn't gotten the VA where it needed to be and most likely wouldn't in the future.

Shortly after I was confirmed as secretary, we publicly posted all of our wait times, which meant that all VA leaders knew their data and where they needed to focus their improvement efforts. The VA became the first and only health system in the country to take this step. With the exception of posting emergency room wait times, I believe this is still true today.

By the end of 2016, we had established same-day access for primary care and mental health issues in all VA locations. This in itself was a major accomplishment, but in conjunction with options provided in the community, this helped ensure that veterans with urgent needs would be cared for in a timely manner. Toward the end of my time at the VA, we conducted a study comparing wait times in the VA to those in the private sector, and we published our findings in the *Journal of the American Medical Association* in late 2018. What we found was not only that the VA improved access over the past several years while the private sector had not but also that VA wait times were now overall better than those in the community. Even with this tremendous progress, there remained much work to be done to ensure that veterans received care when they needed it.

My private-sector experience had taught me that health care needs to be patient focused, outcomes driven, and transparent about results. I realized that bringing this viewpoint into a huge bureaucracy might create friction with those more comfortable with the status quo. In addition to this natural inertia, government service presented an entirely different culture from anything I had ever experienced before. The VA was closely aligned with the military—rules based and very disciplined. Getting the hang of the regulations, the protocols, and the endless acronyms of government took a while.

Where I really lacked understanding was of the political knife fighting beneath the surface of so many of Washington's closed-door meetings, evening receptions, and photo-ops. The VA's harshest critics—the ones who wanted to privatize VA health care—were well funded, persistent, and utterly ruthless. Their determination to sandbag my efforts to fix the VA was only a peripheral concern during the Obama years. It was after the Trump team took over that they became a subversive force within the VA itself, a Fifth Column to be reckoned with each and every day.

Given the turmoil the VA had been experiencing for years—the wait-time crisis, independent inquiries finding "significant and chronic system failures" and a "corrosive culture," an alleged breakdown in delivery of mental health and other critical services, a hepatitis epidemic, a surge in veteran homelessness, and an alarming rise in veteran suicide rates—it was not entirely surprising that there was pressure from far-right groups to shut down the VA and turn to the private sector to care for veterans instead. But these advocates didn't play fair. For all the VA's myriad sins that had led to the wait-time crisis, there was evidence that slamming understaffed facilities like Phoenix for not being able to see every patient within fourteen days was a politically motivated setup to further privatization. The fact is, most private systems don't meet a fourteen-day target either. People often refer to Washington as a swamp, but a minefield might be a better metaphor.

During my eighteen months as under secretary for health, I was doing everything I could to address these issues (along with many others), but eighteen months is a very short time frame for solving such complex problems. They say it takes a long time to turn an aircraft carrier around, and at least during the Obama administration, my experience was very similar. It was only when Mr. Trump arrived in Washington that the game started changing again—this time quite dramatically.

8

On the Road

STILL FINDING MY WAY AND LEARNING TO MANAGE SUCH A HUGE institution, I had to balance being in Washington—engaging with staff and policymakers in the capital—with being out in the field to see firsthand what was happening in different VA centers throughout the country.

Whenever I toured a facility, I asked the medical center director to take me to an area they were really proud of and also to an area of the hospital that they least wanted me to see. After some prodding to convince him or her that I truly meant what I said, the director usually obliged.

One of my early visits as under secretary was to the Tampa VA, where the director took me to an inpatient unit. There were four veterans in the hospital room with an adjoining Jack and Jill bathroom that connected to another hospital room with four more veterans. This meant that eight men or women shared a bathroom, and the shower was down the hall—shared by all veterans on the floor!

On the other hand, Tampa's Polytrauma Center was state of the art. It was large—perhaps one hundred thousand square feet—as well as bright and airy, and people there displayed smiles on their faces and walked around with evident pride. There was an internet café next to a rock-climbing wall, a physical therapy facility, and a swimming pool equipped with lifts so that paralyzed veterans could participate in aquatic exercise.

I wanted a VA where all of the foundational services—those necessary for veterans in particular, such as care for traumatic brain injury, posttraumatic stress, rehabilitation, prosthetics, and orthotics—were built and run like the Tampa Polytrauma unit but where there were no outdated facilities like Tampa's inpatient facility.

When I got back to DC, I asked for a survey of all VA hospitals that had patient rooms holding four or more patients. Within two weeks, we tallied 1,257 rooms like this throughout the country. The standard now in private hospitals is to move toward singles, which has been proven to reduce infection and to facilitate a more relaxed environment for healing. I asked for each VA to develop a plan to eliminate all four-to-a-room situations within three years. Some leaders thought it was an impossible task and simply ignored me. Where would they get the funding? How would they staff these new rooms? But many others were willing to try, and in a short period of time, we were gaining ground.

One of the benefits of site visits was to see firsthand how the problems of VA facilities varied from region to region. As part of a western tour, I spent time with Senator Tester at the Fort Harrison VA, where I was glad to see that Montana veterans seemed generally pleased with their VA. The problem for us in Montana was finding enough clinicians willing to work in America's wide-open spaces, far from the major urban centers.

But not all remote VA facilities are out west. A few months before my trip to Fort Harrison, I flew in an eight-seater to Chelsea, Maine, near Augusta, to visit the Togus VA, the nation's first veterans' hospital. Built to serve Union veterans of the Civil War, it looked every bit its age, but the staff was committed and caring, and the veterans I spoke to seemed very fond of their facility.

I then went on a five-hour drive to Caribou, in the far northern part of the state. Later, I found out that I could have taken an easy flight, but the local officials didn't tell me this because they wanted to impress upon me just how large Maine was, especially given that veterans often had to drive these kinds of distances to the Togus VA whenever they needed care that was more complex.

Senator Susan Collins and Congressman Bruce Poliquin met me in Caribou, where the VA clinic was embedded in the Caribou Medical Center. The VA staff took care of the primary care and some specialty needs of their patients, but the local hospital provided the lab, radiology, and inpatient services as needed. It worked for the VA, and it worked for the community. It was successes like this that inspired the Choice Program to give veterans more options for care—a program that became one of the major areas of controversy during my tenure at the VA, which I'll discuss in far greater detail later in the book.

I spoke to a full room in Caribou, which made me uneasy, because usually a room full of veterans meant that there was some problem or controversy. But not here. These veterans simply wanted to make sure I understood just how satisfied they were with their care and make sure that I didn't come in and mess it up with undesired changes. I agreed to keep my hands off, at least for the time being.

At the end of my stay, the local veterans presented me with a hand-carved wooden bowl made in Caribou. It was a lovely gift, but it was the first item I had been given as a government official, and I wasn't sure if I could keep it. I sent it to be evaluated by our ethics officials. Finally, after some Solomonic inquiries into the value of wooden bowls compared to the federal price limits on gifts, they determined that I could accept it. Later, after the political winds in Washington shifted, such questions of propriety became increasingly probing. In fact, they became weaponized.

Another of my early trips was to Chicago, where I visited the Jesse Brown Medical Center at 10:00 p.m., without advance notice. When I ran hospitals in the private sector, I learned that a health care facility in daytime can be a very different place from that same institution in the middle of the night, when there are fewer staff and far fewer supervisors. For these reasons, at least in part, there are higher mortality rates and more errors at night. As president and CEO of Beth Israel in New York City, I often came to the hospital after midnight and wandered the floors. I shared my findings in a *New England Journal of Medicine* article and was surprised by the number of clinicians I heard from afterward who had similar concerns about the performance of hospitals during off-hours.

At the entrance of the Chicago facility, I flashed my VA ID to the security guard, hoping not to attract special attention. The last thing I wanted was to make people aware that the under secretary was on site. Leaders can learn a lot about their organizations just by being inconspicuous observers. Fortunately, all VA IDs look the same, and he simply waved me through.

I sat in the emergency room for an hour, talking with patients and family as they waited. I also walked the patient floors and then other areas like radiology and the laboratory.

I was impressed with the attentiveness of the staff and the way they interacted with patients. The floors were quiet as expected, but staffers were busy, perhaps wondering who this stranger was wandering around, looking into rooms and asking questions.

While in the Windy City, I also visited the North Chicago VA facility, a joint venture between the VA and the Department of Defense. Given that this was an active navy base, sneaking in at night unannounced was not an option. Instead, I was greeted with a formal ceremony, complete with naval officers ringing a bell four times, the equivalent of being "piped aboard." As was my custom, I asked my host to take me somewhere especially problematic. In this case, the medical center director rose to the challenge. "Let's go to the Simulation Center," he said.

My host and I entered a cavernous space with the high-tech design you might expect in Silicon Valley or at MIT. The Simulation Center was one of 130 such facilities in the VA system where staff could practice with surgical devices and procedures before using them on patients. The VA's use of virtual-reality technology put the VA far ahead of most medical training facilities in the country. The only problem was that the Simulation Center stood only partially completed and very empty. The medical center director explained that this project had begun nearly four years earlier with a budget of $10 million—the cap for VA construction projects without congressional approval. As the project got closer to completion, it became apparent that there was no way to complete it for under $10 million, so construction simply halted. The building had sat empty for more than a year, with no plans to move ahead.

When I returned to Washington, I mentioned the Simulation Center to the central office management team, who were unaware of the problem. We went to work to find a solution, which wasn't easy. It literally took an act of Congress to raise the budget for the Sim Center to $20 million so that construction could proceed.

During another swing through the Midwest, I visited the Madison, Wisconsin, VA where my paternal grandfather had worked as a pharmacist many years before. The pharmacy staff there presented me with my grandfather's mortar and pestle that he had used to mix medications so many years before. I was immensely proud and know my grandfather would have been as well.

Honoring my preconfirmation commitment to visit Alaska, I flew north, where my first stop was the Anchorage Medical Center for ambulatory care. The center was adjacent to an air force hospital, and the way the two facilities worked together was another impressive example of commonsense symbiosis. Simply put, not all that many young air force personnel stationed in Alaska require hospitalization. In fact, without the veterans, the beds would have remained vacant. Moreover, air force medical staff needed to keep up their skills in order to be ready, should they be faced with an emergency, and caring for veterans made that possible.

Senator Sullivan and I flew to the Kenai Peninsula, where we met with a community center full of veterans. There was standing room only, and this time I was uneasy for a different reason. I had been warned that Alaskans generally were skeptical of people from Washington, but this group was downright hostile. The negative energy was so intense that Senator Sullivan felt it necessary to stand up and remind the audience that I was his guest and that they should show me respect. A few months later, I met with the senator again, and he told me he was glad I got out of that room alive.

My trip to Alaska allowed me to see not only how VA policies affected veterans but also how policies affected that other huge population I was responsible for: the federal employees who cared for the veterans.

Linda Boyle had been the nurse executive in Anchorage, but when her boss left, she stepped in as acting medical center director. Linda was clinically sharp, knew her operational metrics, and was eager for feedback and mentorship. She was also personable and knew all her staff by name. Most importantly, she fit in really well with the Alaska community.

Linda applied to become the permanent medical center director, which I was glad to see. All too often, the second or third in command at a VA facility decides that moving up to the top job simply is not worth the modest pay increase if it means a massive increase in headaches and risks.

Unfortunately, Linda was not selected for this position, and it would've been inappropriate for me to intervene. Many months later, however, Linda was offered the position of medical center director in the Central Alabama Health System, and she took it. From what I saw, Linda's experience was a very typical VA career progression. Employees often relocated three, four, even five times, starting at a lower-complexity VA or in a less desirable region, working up to a more complex institution or preferred location. The degree of commitment I observed in many of these people was truly admirable.

In Los Angeles, I met Skye McDougall, acting director of the VA's Desert Pacific Healthcare Network. In 2015, she testified before Congress about the Phoenix wait-time crisis. She was accused of knowingly misrepresenting the facts after answering a question about comparable wait times in Los Angeles. Later, an inspector general's report found that she had not intentionally given false testimony but had been responding to a different question. Nevertheless, the damage to her reputation had been done. She became a target of VA critics and a punch line for talk-show hosts on late-night TV.

When we met, Skye confided that the VA central office had not allowed her to respond to the allegations, which left her with no way to defend herself. She wanted a fresh start within the organization and wanted to leave Los Angeles. She asked for my support to move to an open network position in Arizona. This district included Phoenix, which was most certainly the toughest VA in the country to run. Not only had it been the center of the wait-time crisis, but it had been without steady leadership for many months. The position was even less attractive because it was temporary. I was reducing the number of networks, and this one was scheduled to be combined with another one in Southern California. Still, Skye was eager to make the move. She went through the thorough selection process, was the top-ranked candidate, and was offered the job. Then Arizona senator John McCain called me.

The senator made it clear that he didn't want Skye coming to Arizona. He felt that the Phoenix VA was still recovering from the scandal and that the last thing it needed was someone accused of lying to Congress leading it. I knew that Skye was capable and had been treated unfairly, but I also knew that Senator McCain was a strong advocate for veterans and that his support was essential for gaining the legislative traction we needed to get things done for the VA. I was in a tough position.

I told the senator that my priority was to find the best leader for his region and that Skye was that person. On the other hand, I told him, I would consider his request if he would help me recruit a strong candidate from the private sector in her place. He agreed.

Senator McCain made a number of calls to health care leaders in and around Phoenix, and over time, with his help, we identified a few promising candidates. Not knowing then that all these candidates eventually would turn us down, I called Skye and told her

I couldn't recommend her for Arizona. Instead, I helped her move to a network position elsewhere.

Skye then applied to lead the region covering Mississippi, Alabama, and Louisiana. With my support, she attained the appointment, but the announcement of her transfer immediately prompted calls from congressional leaders in the Deep South. Their position was essentially this: "If John McCain didn't want her, we don't want her either."

I tried to explain that Skye was the right person for that job. It was also true that, for this location, we had no reasonable hope of recruiting someone from the private sector. At this point, I began to regret my concession to Senator McCain.

Skye got the job, and she moved to Jackson, Mississippi, with her eyes wide open. She worked hard and developed strong relationships with the local community, including the veterans service organizations and the state veterans affairs officers. She tackled many tough issues in the medical centers in her region, and I am happy to say that she slowly but surely gained the trust of most members of her congressional delegation.

Despite the multitude of VA problems revealed to me on my travels, I also saw firsthand the tremendous commitment of so many VA staffers and a spirit of service that was truly inspiring. This is one aspect the media doesn't cover.

On a trip to Missouri, I toured the St. Louis VA Medical Center with Senator Claire McCaskill, where we met a young African American phlebotomist. We found out that a few weeks earlier, when this woman was leaving for the day, she saw an older veteran sitting alone in the waiting area. He seemed upset, so she approached him and asked him what was wrong. Apparently, his test had been delayed, and he had missed the van to take him home. Now he had to stay overnight, probably on the street, until the van came the next day. She said she had a car and could drive him home.

"But I live four hours away," the veteran informed her.

"That's okay," she said with a shrug. "I'm not doing anything special tonight anyway. Let's get going."

Senator McCaskill hugged the employee and then hugged me, too. There seems to be an easy bond among people committed to helping veterans.

9

Moving and Shaking

Back in Washington, I needed to build an entirely new management team, but VA positions often do not offer competitive salaries, and the agency's overall low morale didn't help recruitment. The hiring process itself was too long and complicated, which often weeded out the best candidates. Perversely, I wasn't allowed to see résumés, which were instead filtered by the human resource professionals and then sent to a committee of three Senior Executive Service (SES) employees. This panel would then review the already-filtered group of candidates and apply specific criteria to make a final determination. Included in these criteria were prior government experience, veteran status, and a number of other factors that were never quite clear to me. Someone with exactly the qualifications I was looking for could very easily slip through these many cracks.

The first candidate sent over to me was someone who worked for the Federal Aviation Authority (FAA) and had spent a long time in government but had absolutely no health care experience. When I asked to see the résumés of the other candidates, I was told *no*. So I rejected the candidate from the FAA, and the process of reposting for the position began again. Time and time again, I referred experienced health care executives who had worked with me in previous positions to apply for open VA hospital jobs, but they never made it through the screening.

Before coming to the VA, I called a number of former government leaders and asked their advice on how to approach the VA job. The common refrain was the need to focus on key priorities. Government was so complex, bureaucratic, and sluggish that attempting to take on too much could lead to getting nothing done.

The textbook approach for an outsider taking charge of an organization is to act as an observer and learn about the culture, maybe for as much as six months, before setting new priorities. But I didn't need to absorb the culture to know what the problems were. President Obama had brought in an outsider—me—precisely because the agency was in crisis. Fifteen months after the wait-time fiasco, there was still no plan for dealing with that persistent problem. I could see very quickly that the agency also adhered to a formal chain of command. People waited for their leaders to give instructions, while many of their leaders were like deer in headlights. So I stepped up.

"Here are our priorities," I told the team. The first was to fix access to care. The second was to improve employee engagement. The third was to support the dissemination of best practices throughout the system.

If these were not the perfect three priorities, they were close enough, and at least we would begin to move. Later I added two more priorities: better coordination of care in the community and gaining veteran trust.

There seemed to be a sense of relief that we had a direction—*any direction.*

The VA hadn't always been sluggish and timid. Its last great era of radical reform was in the 1990s, led by under secretary for health Dr. Ken Kizer. He accelerated the movement from inpatient care to ambulatory care and dramatically increased the number of VA outpatient clinics now found throughout the country. He created regional networks, called VISNs, which oversaw the coordination of services in more than twenty different parts of the country. His third landmark innovation was to usher in the era of electronic records, making the VA the first major system to be paperless. The Kizer era for the VA signaled high levels of employee engagement and promoted a culture of innovation. The VA became known as a leader in technology, safety, and quality outcomes, but in many ways, the VA rested on those laurels for a long time.

When I brought leaders together from across the country, I often asked, "If VA were a publicly traded company, what year would the stock have been the highest?" Invariably, old-timers said it was in the early 1990s under Ken Kizer. But not even Kizer was immune to political sniping. After implementing so many changes, he was apparently unpopular with some of the veterans service organizations, and their political clout was said to have led to his departure.

While I was a great admirer of Kizer's vision and leadership, I believed that his relentless focus on competitive innovation had led to unintended consequences. In the private sector, health care professionals had stopped viewing quality improvement as a competitive tool and, quite the opposite, had made a concerted effort to share best practices. The VA hadn't followed suit, which had led to a highly decentralized system that evaluated all VA medical centers on a one-to-five-star scale, with a forced distribution so that there could only be 10 to 15 percent of medical centers in the top rating, which generated a kind of zero-sum mind-set among VA medical center directors. When I arrived at the VA, leaders told me that because of this rating system, when they found a way to solve a problem, they wouldn't readily share the solution with their VA colleagues in other parts of the country.

Looking for a way out of this morass, I found VA Pulse, a recently instituted and underutilized digital platform that I referred to as the VA's Facebook. Pulse was the great equalizer, because any staff member could sign on and engage in conversation with any other VA colleagues or leaders. I saw this as a great way to solicit ideas on best practices from front-line staff and clinicians, and with my encouragement, best practices began to pour in from around the country.

We focused on those that aligned with the five priorities I had articulated: access, employee engagement, care coordination, building veteran trust, and best-practice dissemination. The ideas ranged from how to redesign a Code Cart tray to make resuscitations more reliable, to group visits for veterans to promote efficiency, to direct scheduling of appointments for audiology and optometry. After a vigorous screening progress, we winnowed down our 250 submissions to the thirteen best, which we designated as our "gold status" ideas.

Then, taking a cue from the popular television show, we launched a series of "Shark Tank" events, each of which would produce a winner. Instead of billionaires bidding their own money, our sharks were VA medical center directors bidding on their commitment to implementing these best practices.

At the Madison, Wisconsin, VA, for instance, a pharmacy intern named Ellina Seckel developed a system of pharmacist-run medication clinics to help reduce the workload of primary-care physicians. She found using pharmacists to manage patients' medications reduced wait times for veterans wishing to see primary-care physicians, which resulted in enhanced quality of care and improved patient satisfaction. Within a short time, 25 percent of all primary-care appointments were being managed by pharmacists. After the Shark Tank event, this best practice spread to El Paso and then Kansas City and then around the country. Now, more than 1.9 million VA prescriptions are being written by pharmacists.

We then formalized a VA diffusion council to oversee the spread of these best practices, creating a best-practice dashboard—the VA diffusion hub—so people across the country could find these solutions whenever they identified problems at their sites. We created a Best Practice Fellowship so those who led best practices at their sites would have time to teach others and even travel to other VA facilities to promote their innovations.

Our Shark Tanks channeled competitive juices while showing people that problems within the VA could be worked on collectively and systemwide. Using this approach, the size, scope, and diversity of VAs could be seen as an advantage rather than as an excuse for a glacial pace of change.

One of the reasons the best-practice initiative was so successful was the individual I assigned to lead it: a White House Fellow named Dr. Shereef Elnahal, who found a way to launch the best-practices program without any dedicated resources or any budget.

Shereef was one example of an innovation strategy I used in the VA generally, which was to give young people a chance to make an impact early in their career. I worked with several White House Fellows, and each time I gave them projects, they were expected not just to learn but to actually drive results.

After identifying best practices from VAs around the country, we wanted to share them with health care professionals around the country. The result—a book entitled *Best Care Everywhere,* published by the Government Publishing Office in 2017—is filled with examples of work being done by various VAs around the country. To me, it represents the incredible ability of the VA to collaborate and progress when all players involved make it a priority.

Any health care effort to attain greater collaboration must necessarily take into account nurses, a major constituency that could be a vital force for reform or a major roadblock to success. The VHA employs more than sixty thousand of these important health care providers and is the largest educator of nurses in the country. The VA Nursing Handbook, maintained by the Office of Nursing Services in Washington, was long overdue for an update, so even before my confirmation, I was questioned on whether or not the VA would grant authority to advanced-practice nurses, including nurse anesthetists, to practice outside the supervision of a physician.

I heard from hundreds of nurse anesthetists who felt that their current status prevented them from caring for as many veterans as they could have otherwise. The anesthesiologists felt exactly the opposite. These physicians argued that over the years, they had worked hard to establish a team-based approach in which they supervised the team and worked well with the nurses. They felt that any change in the model would jeopardize the quality of care.

There seemed to be no common ground. Then, in addition to hearing from the nurses and the doctors—both urban and rural ones—the professional associations began to weigh in, as did nearly half of the members of Congress. In total we received more than three hundred thousand comments. The sentiment was about 50 percent for and 50 percent against.

I met for a briefing from our chief nursing officer, Donna Gage, then met with the American Association of the College of Nursing, and next with the American Society of Anesthesiologists to get their perspectives. Using an established, team-based approach within the VA system, I got commitments from the anesthesiologists to continue to work with nurse anesthetists and further explore expansion of their scope of duties in a thoughtful way. The data showed that, unlike many other clinical areas in the VA—especially primary care and behavioral health—there was no access problem in anesthesia. So when I met again with our Office of Nursing Services, I told them that I had decided to move forward with full-practice authority for advanced-practice nurses, but not for nurse anesthetists, for whom the supervision requirement would remain. I also communicated my decision to Secretary McDonald, who I knew had also been lobbied on this issue. The Office of Nursing Services was then supposed to take my decision, finalize the appropriate language in the nursing handbook, and transmit the draft handbook to Office of Management and Budget for their review and comment prior to publication of the regulations in the Federal Register.

Between formulating my opinion and publicly announcing my decision, I met with the Congressional Nursing Caucus and the Doctors Caucus. I explained my rationale for supporting full-practice authority for advanced-practice nursing in medical and psychiatric areas, where there was a need for additional access, but not in anesthesia, where no such problem existed.

Then, just as I thought I had put this chapter behind me, I started receiving frantic calls from members of Congress. They accused me of not telling the truth and of doing the opposite of what I had promised. I also started receiving calls from the Office of Management and Budget, asking for further clarification on my decision to grant nurse anesthetists full-practice authority.

I was astounded. I had clearly communicated that I did *not* support full-practice authority for nurse anesthetists. But apparently, the Office of Nursing Services had written the regulations to support this practice anyway.

Now I had a much bigger mess to clean up. I began with a very candid conversation with the VA Office of Nursing Services, and I requested that they immediately revise the regulations to reflect my original intent. I quickly contacted members of Congress and the press to make sure they understood that I had not changed my mind and that we were correcting the language that had been submitted to the Office of Management and Budget. The department's public affairs team didn't want me to speak to the press about this, but I was adamant about clarifying my position. Over their objections, I went ahead and scheduled media interviews. The correct version of the regulations was finally published in the *Federal Register* on December 14, 2016. I truly don't know if this policy fiasco was a misunderstanding or not, but a mistake this large had shaken my confidence in the internal processes and taught me that I needed to make organizational changes to ensure that something like this didn't recur.

When I became secretary under President Trump, this kind of flouting of my directives became all too frequent. I learned very quickly that, in these cases, it wasn't just a matter of miscommunication but a purposeful strategy aimed at getting rid of me and any other obstacles to privatizing the VA.

Another power constituency I needed to engage was external: the veterans service organizations (VSOs). The first congressionally chartered VSO was the Navy Mutual Aid Association, established in 1879. Today, there are more than thirty of these organizations, plus perhaps forty thousand other US-based nonprofit organizations dedicated to helping veterans and military families. I spent most of my time with the "big six," which included the American Legion, AmVets, Disabled American Veterans, Paralyzed Veterans of America, Veterans of Foreign Wars, and Vietnam Veterans of America. Each had an executive director to represent its point of view, although most also elected commanders.

Some in Washington were fond of saying that the VSOs' influence was fading and that they represented only the older veterans, but this was far from the truth. I found the VSOs relatively open and supportive of change, as long as it made sense for their members. I think they recognized that the status quo was a losing strategy but that a complete privatization or dismantling of the VA was out of the question.

Rick Weidman, executive director of the Vietnam Veterans, was the most candid and outspoken of these leaders. When he didn't like something or someone, he didn't keep it to himself. The first time I met him—at a reception shortly after my nomination as under secretary—he made a beeline for me and then wasted no time letting me know that if I were to be confirmed, I would have a lot of work to do. He told me I'd have to start by cleaning house of the VA bureaucrats he felt were blocking progress. "You'll make more progress at VA through subtraction rather than addition," he told me. Then he rattled off a bunch of names of people he thought were terrible.

During the Obama administration, Concerned Veterans of America was viewed not as a legitimate VSO but as a lobbying group financed by the ultra-right-wing Koch brothers. During the Trump administration, this would change, and the Koch-sponsored group would be welcomed to the table and become a major player, especially in the push for privatization.

As under secretary, I typically hosted a breakfast meeting with the big six once a month but consulted with them more frequently as issues arose. I also had extensive contact with the

Military Officers Association, the Wounded Warrior Project, the Military Order of the Purple Heart, the Blinded Veterans Association, and the Iraq and Afghanistan Veterans of America. For me, this was not playing a political game but rather consulting with an organized group of concerned customers. Veterans kept the VSO leaders on their toes, and when the VA was not performing well enough, those leaders let me know. In addition, many of the VSOs had a historical and political perspective on issues that I lacked, as well as a network in the DC rumor mill that was much deeper and stronger than mine. If there was a problem brewing on Capitol Hill or with the press, the VSOs usually knew about it before I did, which made them crucial allies.

These groups also were helpful when it came to getting the word out to veterans, getting feedback on policy initiatives, and celebrating and honoring veterans' events and veterans themselves. Many of the executive directors became my confidants and provided me with objective advice and counsel rather than with a specific agenda in mind. Most of all, they were instrumental in keeping me in touch with the people I was appointed to serve.

10

No Man Left Behind

IN THE FALL OF 2015, I MET WITH PRESIDENT OBAMA AND SECRETARY McDonald to present the VA's improvement plan for the coming year.

As I arrived at the West Wing waiting area, an aide to the president appeared and told me that the meeting would be in the Oval Office. I was excited, because I had never been in the Oval before. The aide walked me down the hall until President Obama stepped out of the Oval and greeted me.

"David, how are you?" President Obama asked. "I'm looking forward to our meeting." Then he added, "I smelled some gas in the Oval Office, so I don't think we should go in there. Let's meet in the Cabinet Room."

I found it a little strange that if the president of the United States smelled gas in his office, there wasn't more commotion, an evacuation, or a visit from the local fire department. But he seemed calm, and I followed him to the Cabinet Room.

I had never been in the Cabinet Room before either, and before long, Secretary McDonald and Rob Nabors, McDonald's chief of staff, arrived, along with Vice President Biden and about a dozen members of the president's staff.

The president began with a pep talk, exhorting us to push hard during this last year of his term. He then proceeded to ask if there were any political barriers in our way that he could help remove. Secretary McDonald then gave an overview of our strategic direction, focusing on the VA's efforts to become a truly veteran-centered culture that was more service oriented and customer responsive. Secretary McDonald next asked me to share our plans for the following year at the VHA.

I focused my initial comments on access to care. The president listened intently and then asked questions about where we were making progress and where we were still struggling. He also asked about our ability to hire the necessary health care professionals. He wanted to know about the support we were receiving from Congress and if there was resistance to change from staff. My face brightened when the president said, "David, you tell people that you are doing these things on my behalf, and if you need me to come with you to any meetings to make that clear, you just ask."

The first chance I had to catch my breath was the week between Christmas and New Year's Day. Congress was out of session; many people were away on vacation, and Washington traffic was eerily light. I looked forward to catching up on reports I needed to review and presentations I needed to prepare. An even greater luxury was having a moment to eat lunch at my desk and read the newspaper.

On December 29, 2015, I picked up the *New York Times* and found a front-page story about a cluster of suicides. Corporal Tyler Schlagel, a marine veteran, had killed himself a few weeks before, the fourteenth marine in his unit to take his own life.

So much for my peaceful lunch. I felt sick to my stomach, and my mind began to race. I called Rear Admiral David Lane, who was serving as the medical officer and director of health services of the marine corps. Admiral Lane was very familiar with this marine unit and shared my determination to find ways to improve the situation. The marine corps had been proactive on suicide prevention, and the admiral welcomed the VA's collaboration. This began a strong working relationship between our two organizations in which we met regularly and developed a joint action plan.

I called my suicide-prevention team together and asked for ideas. Headed by Dr. Caitlin Thompson, this team also included Dr. Harold Kudler, the VA's head of psychiatric services. Our discussions focused initially on just getting a better understanding of the data, but I also wanted action, so I asked them to organize a suicide summit with the best minds in medicine. I also said I wanted it within thirty days.

To my dismay, the team told me the earliest they could get a summit of this type together was late spring, with the fall being much more likely. To me, this was clearly an emergency, so I repeated that I wanted it done in thirty days. When they still pushed back, I took out a calculator and rapidly punched in the numbers. If twenty-two veterans killed themselves each day, then each passing month meant another 660 lives lost. I held up my calculator screen for them to see my estimate. Then I punched in more numbers and held up my screen again. If we delayed the summit by six months, we'd lose four thousand lives. The team left my office red-faced, but they agreed to my deadline.

I was still learning the ways of government and discovering what the infamous Washington red tape meant in practice. In order to get a room large enough to hold the suicide prevention summit, we needed to rent a banquet room in a hotel. But for the VA, renting a banquet room meant conducting a formal contract process and getting competitive bids from potential vendors. Two days before the deadline, we found a hotel in DC that met our needs, just in time to let the summit's attendees know where to show up on February 4.

Another idea that my staff resisted was inviting members of Congress, but I knew that if we wanted to actually implement the summit's solutions, we needed Congress to be an active participant.

Everyone we invited attended, and they all wanted to speak. This included Chairman Isakson, Chairman Miller, and Ranking

Member Brown, who brought with her Martin Luther King III, Beto O'Rourke, and a number of others. We asked Lee Woodruff, writer, activist, and wife of Bob Woodruff, the ABC News anchor injured by a bomb in Iraq, to moderate, and she was terrific at keeping people focused. President Obama taped an introductory message for us, and Secretary McDonald made a special effort to be present, even though he had another commitment.

The meeting attracted two hundred mental health professionals, caregivers, military officers, family members, and veterans. One of the more powerful moments was when air force veteran John Heitzman and army veteran Brent Rice told their stories of being suicidal, recovering from their despair, and then dedicating themselves to helping other veterans suffering in similar ways.

We left with a list of actions that included elevating the Suicide Prevention Office to directly report to the under secretary, adding additional resources for suicide-prevention coordinators throughout the country, creating three new tele-mental health hubs to expand tele-mental health offerings, expanding the use of peer counselors, and ensuring same-day access to mental health care.

VA researchers developed a research program, ReachVet, that used big data and predictive analytics to identify veterans who had up to eighty times the risk of suicide over the next year. Despite much hesitation from people around me, I told the researchers that it was time to move this project from the research lab to the clinical setting. Using ReachVet data, suicide-prevention coordinators at each VA medical center started to contact these veterans and connect them with appropriate resources. Veterans were generally pleased that people from the VA were calling to check on them and offer help. Staff at the medical centers reported that these calls likely made many lifesaving connections.

Another way we were addressing veteran suicide was by expanding the use of emotional support dogs. The VA had been reluctant to expand the use of service dogs beyond veterans with physical disabilities and consequently began conducting a research study to determine if there was evidence that service dogs benefitted veterans with emotional challenges. I was unwilling to wait for the results of another multiyear, multimillion-dollar VA study that denied benefits in the meantime. During my short time at the VA, I had already witnessed so many veterans' lives dramatically improve as a result of adopting a service dog. So while the study's results were still pending—and until the unlikely event that the finalized results proved that emotional support dogs *weren't* worthwhile—I ordered VA to open access to emotional support dogs through the VA's new Center for Compassionate Innovation.

Developing strategic partnerships was another one of the strategies I supported to better address suicide prevention. Almost 70 percent of veterans who commit suicide do not use VA health care services. In order to help these veterans, we needed to work more closely with community organizations, veterans service organizations, and companies that knew how to reach a target population. In this respect, we partnered with Johnson & Johnson, whose CEO, Alex Gorsky, was a former Army Ranger and deeply committed to the veteran community. Alex and I assembled a team of individuals from the VA and Johnson & Johnson to meet on a regular basis and develop a multifaceted plan that included research for better diagnosis and treatment as well as a campaign for better public outreach. We even recruited Tom Hanks as the national spokesperson for this effort, which we called "Be There for Veterans."

In January, President Obama launched the VA into another initiative with his Cancer Moonshot, an effort to focus various agencies on cancer issues under the leadership of Vice President Joe Biden. The strategy was to pool the resources of the federal government, multinational pharmaceuticals, biotechnology companies, academic centers, and oncologists in order to find ways to alleviate suffering from cancer and expand access to new drugs and therapies. This was personal for the vice president, who had just lost his son Beau to brain cancer.

During a White House meeting, the heads of each agency presented a five-minute summary to the president and vice president of opportunities they saw for breakthroughs. I had not yet presented my report when the Secret Service approached the president and whispered in his ear. The president interrupted and said he had to leave to attend to urgent business and then added, "But first I want to hear what David has to say."

I walked though my analysis of our Million Veteran Program, which allowed us to collect the largest database in the world linking veteran clinical data with genomic data. This enabled us to do research using genomics at an unprecedented scale that would allow for breakthroughs in discovery and treatment. The president listened intently, processed the information, and then began firing questions and throwing out ideas on how to maximize the opportunity. I was impressed that, despite whatever urgent business he had to attend to, President Obama was still totally engaged and gave my presentation his full attention.

After this launch, the Moonshot team met almost every week, with the vice president in charge. He brought on a very capable lead administrator, Greg Simon, who had battled with cancer himself. From my perspective, what was holding the VA back was gaining access to supercomputers to run our data in the Million Veterans Program. The Department of Energy (DOE), on the other hand, holds some of the most powerful supercomputers in the world.

Greg did some matchmaking, and before we knew it, we had an interagency agreement between the VA and the DOE to utilize their supercomputing capabilities. Without the intervention of the White House, interagency agreements of this complexity can take years. But Greg took the initiative as seriously as the vice president did. One day, Greg came to the meeting wearing blue pants and a black tuxedo jacket from the evening before. When I quietly pointed this out to him, he looked down at his mismatched outfit and just laughed. How could he spend time worrying about whether his clothes matched when he was trying to find a cure for cancer? I couldn't argue with that logic.

The White House also helped us reach out to industry, including IBM, the developers of a powerful analytic tool called Watson.

Through the White House, we were able to arrange a donation from IBM so that Watson's analytics could begin helping ten thousand veterans suffering from cancer. Watson would help interpret the genetic testing involved to match treatments with tumor types. The commitment we had to the Moonshot seemed to remove layers in decision-making. What would have taken months to arrange using the usual government procurement processes took only a few weeks.

We were also committed to ameliorating hepatitis C, an epidemic that disproportionately affected veterans. Yet the search for a solution to hepatitis C opened up still another crisis for the VA. In 2013, a drug had been released on the market that could actually cure hepatitis C, and I wanted the VA to be the first health system in the country to eradicate the disease from our patient population.

Early work on the drug—later acquired by Gilead and marketed under the brand names of Harvoni and Sovaldi—was carried out by Dr. Raymond Schinazi, a researcher at Emory University who had also worked for the Atlanta VA since 1983. As a result of the commercialization, Dr. Schinazi personally made over $400 million.

The CBS Evening News picked up the story in December 2015, alleging that research for the drug actually had been conducted at the VA but that when Schinazi formed a company to sell the development, the VA got nothing. Adding to the whiff of scandal (or at least alleged VA incompetence), a single treatment with the drug was reported to cost up to $84,000. The Department of Veterans Affairs got a significant discount, but even so, the VA could hardly afford the new medicine, despite the claim by some that the VA was instrumental in its development. The VA spends about $2 billion a year on research, and when that research is successful, it's supposed to benefit veterans, not federal employees' wallets.

The chairman of the House Committee on Veterans Affairs, Jeff Miller, decided to hold hearings, but suspecting that the inquiry was going to be more political than factual, Dr. Schinazi chose to retire before he would have to appear and be demonized. He had, in fact, never been a full-time VA employee, and none of his work on the hepatitis drug had been done at the VA or on VA time.

While reassuring to me, I knew this distinction would not satisfy members of the House committee. As an indication of Dr. Schinazi's dedication to veterans, even after he made $400 million from the sale of his drug to Gilead, he remained committed to veterans and continued to work for us, doing important research on viral replication. It was only the harsh, inquisitorial spotlight of Washington that caused him to quit.

Nothing was out of line in this particular case, but my investigation of it revealed that the process at the VA for protecting intellectual property was, to say the least, very lax. We never consistently required our researchers to disclose patentable discoveries, and we had not executed agreements with our academic partners in research, relying instead on these partners to self-report payments. In 2014, and despite our enormous investment in research, the VA collected less than $500,000 in patents and royalties.

At the hearing, I set the record straight about Dr. Schinazi, but I was also very candid in saying that our process in technology transfer and IP was inadequate and needed a major upgrade. Not long after, I announced a search for a new head of this area and the appointment of an advisory board to make recommendations on how best to bring this part of the VA up to the standards in the industry. That day, my strategy of transparency over defensiveness worked well.

It was entirely fitting that Congress should be concerned about the VA's access to the latest drugs for hepatitis C. Veterans have higher rates of hepatitis C infection than the general population, with the number of cases among veterans estimated to be as high as 160,000. New antiviral medications like the one developed by Dr. Schinazi, which work as nucleoside analogues and interfere with the ability of hepatitis C viruses to replicate, became available only in 2014, but they yielded cure rates of approximately 95 percent.

As previously mentioned, these drugs were incredibly expensive, and because the VA's budget was approved two years ahead of time, there had not been enough money budgeted to buy the new drugs. Nonetheless, in 2015, the VA allocated $696 million for hepatitis C drugs, which represented 17 percent of the entire VA pharmacy budget. The upside of this huge expenditure was that, in all but a few cases, the new drugs actually *cured* the disease, meaning that there would be no need for subsequent, perhaps even more expensive treatments like liver transplants.

Dr. David Ross, the director of our hepatitis program, wanted to treat as many patients as possible, regardless of cost. As the under secretary, though, I had to actually implement the program, ascertain that it was well executed, and ensure that it did not bankrupt the VA. So we worked with Congress to identify the costs associated with a plan that was incredibly expensive but could eliminate hepatitis C from the entire veteran population. Not surprisingly, Gilead (the manufacturer of the breakthrough drug) used their considerable political clout to ensure funding.

In March, we announced that Congress had allocated $1.5 billion for these new medications. But even with funding secured, there were not enough hepatologists in the VA—or perhaps in the country—to run a program of this size through our specialty clinics. We began to work with our primary care doctors and our pharmacists to train them on using the new drugs. Using our electronic records, we identified veterans with hepatitis C and contacted them to come into the medical centers for treatment.

By the summer of 2016, the number of new weekly starts on medication reached almost twenty-three hundred. Since that time, the VA has treated well over one hundred thousand veterans and was on track to eliminate hepatitis C from the entire population within two years.

Unfortunately, rather than allowing the VA latitude, our authorization required 100 percent of the $1.5 billion to be used toward buying the drug. This meant we couldn't use it toward the pharmacists, nurses, and doctors we needed to administer the drugs. The sad irony was that shortly after we received the $1.5 billion authorization, Merck came out with a similar drug, and the price of Gilead's medicine dropped by almost half. So we found ourselves with more money than we needed for the drug but no authorization to spend the surplus where it could do the most good.

I was frustrated, seeing this as a classic example of lobbying and congressional logrolling that was making it difficult to do the right thing for veterans. We worked with Congress to allow some of the funding appropriated for the drugs to be transferred to other related purposes, and in time, Congress gave us this flexibility.

11

"I AM"

ANOTHER KEY DEMOGRAPHIC OF CONCERN FOR US WAS THE DISABLED veterans, and here adaptive sports were an integral part of the VA's approach, as I had seen in Aspen earlier in the year. In May 2016, Merle, Danny, and I attended the Invictus Games at Disney's ESPN Wide World of Sports in Orlando, Florida. The Department of Defense was the official host, but the VA helped by providing medical support and services.

Invictus is an international event created by Great Britain's Prince Harry, inspired by the Wounded Warrior Games in the United States. The motto of the games is "I am the captain of my fate. I am the master of my soul," which is a line from the poem "Invictus," written by William Ernest Henley. This motto, or often just "I am," was on display everywhere at the games. The previous year, at a reception for the prince at the British embassy in Washington, we had gotten to know the CEO of the games, Vicky Gosling, a Royal Air Force veteran who retired after twenty-one years with the rank of group captain. When we met the prince, he was personable and down-to-earth and very passionate about the cause. After Prince Harry stepped away, Merle and Vicky continued to chat and discovered that they had much in common: a commitment to helping veterans and a love of travel and tennis.

Prior to the opening ceremonies, Vicky, Merle, Danny, and I were invited to the stadium to greet the first lady. I had never met Michelle, and when she arrived, I reached out to shake her hand. She bypassed my gesture to wrap her arms around me and then gave Merle and Danny each a big hug, too. With a warm smile, she said, "I'm a hugger." Then she continued, "Barack and I are so grateful for what you're doing for our veterans, and we can't thank you enough. I am so glad you're here and making such a difference."

President George W. Bush, who had started an institute to improve the lives of veterans, also attended the event. In conjunction with the games, the Bush Institute hosted a special symposium at the Shades of Green, a facility run by the Department of Defense to give soldiers and their families time to decompress from the stress of military life. The former president joined a panel that included Prince Harry and several severely wounded veterans to discuss the power of positive thinking and sports in the healing process.

After the symposium, we had a chance to speak with President Bush. He told us that each year, he hosts a hundred-kilometer mountain bike ride with twenty to twenty-five wounded warriors. He emphasized how much these participants inspired him. After leaving public office, President Bush took up painting. One evening, he proudly introduced me to a number of veterans who were the subjects of portraits he created. It was clear he had gotten to know each of these veterans and their stories personally.

The Invictus Games themselves were terrific. You could sense the bond developed between competitors, and while each athlete aimed to win, there was also great camaraderie and mutual support. We spent time with athletes and their families and listened to their stories of injury and recovery.

At the Britain vs. USA volleyball game, we got a chance to speak again with Prince Harry. His security team wanted to keep him off to the side, but he insisted on walking through the stands to meet the athletes and their families. We also spent more time with Vicky Gosling, whose friendship and generosity, oddly enough, would play an unexpected role in my departure from the VA many months later.

Many of those assisting in the games were employees of the Orlando VA, and as the games were winding down, they asked us to tour their recently opened state-of-the-art sixty-five-acre facility in Lake Nona, a growing biotech district near the airport. If anyone wanted an example of VA transformation, this was the place.

Sadly, not long after we left, another event in that city captured national attention—a senseless shooting at the Pulse Nightclub targeting the LGBTQ community, leaving forty-nine people dead, fifty-three wounded, and many more traumatized. I was back in Washington when the news broke, but I immediately called my deputy under secretary for operations, Steve Young, and told him that I wanted to mobilize our mobile medical units and get them on site as soon as possible. I asked him to call back with a progress report within an hour.

But a second call with a much larger group of VA leaders raised concerns about deploying our mobile medical units to help these victims. This made no sense to me. Who else had the number of psychologists, grief counselors, social workers, doctors, and emergency staff that we did? Emergency preparedness was one of our core missions. But according to these staffers, VA lawyers said that our legislative mandate was to serve veterans, not to respond to civilian emergencies. I didn't care what the lawyers said, and I instructed our people to proceed with dispatching the mobile units.

I took responsibility for this decision because I felt it was the right thing to do. I remember thinking that if this were my last decision as under secretary, I could live with it. I had taken the job to make a difference in people's lives, and this was a prime opportunity to do just that. I also knew that under Title 38 Code of Federal Regulations, the VA is permitted to share medical resources during natural and man-made disasters and terrorist attacks.

On my command, the VA deployed its mobile medical units from a number of our medical centers, including Orlando; Jacksonville; Macon, Georgia; Columbia, South Carolina; and Pasco County, Florida. In all, four mobile units and twenty-seven crisis responders went on site, and in the course of the next twelve days, VA staff took care of more than five thousand people. Some were veterans; many were not.

VA staff was involved in grief counseling, death notifications, coping skills, late-night phone calls, support groups, and distribution of food and supplies. I was told that the staff on site felt good about what they had done. Still, some people in the central office were grumbling that I had overstepped.

I decided to use this as a teaching moment. I wasn't going to hide from my decision but rather use it to help reset VA culture. At a session of our leadership teams from around the country, I talked about the controversial nature of my choice and why I made it and said that I wanted them to act as leaders in the same ways. I told them they needed to make principle-based decisions and then explain their actions to others within their organizations. I received a lot of feedback that day from VA leaders around the country, most of whom expressed pride at being part of an organization that was mission oriented and principle based.

About a month later, at the White House summer lawn party, President Obama took me aside and said, "David, thank you for what you did down in Orlando. That really made a difference, and I was very proud of the VA."

That summer, I celebrated my first anniversary as under secretary. My new "family"—the VA staff—held a party with balloons, cake, and a slideshow of the many things we'd already accomplished. Merle contributed many of the pictures. The slideshow showed twelve months as under secretary, which included forty-three congressional hearings and presentations, 345 subject-matter-expert interviews, 242 written media responses, and forty-one trips outside of Washington. I hoped we were just getting started.

12

Turbulence

M Y SECOND YEAR AT THE VA BEGAN VERY MUCH LIKE MY FIRST, with a heavy travel schedule and persistent problems. The ongoing presidential contest between Donald Trump and Hillary Clinton had become nasty and divisive, with conflicting narratives about email servers, hacked emails, and Russian interference.

With President Obama's term coming to an end, I assumed that my time in government was limited. So I was excited that, after speaking at the Disabled American Veterans conference in Atlanta, Secretary McDonald and I were invited to fly back to Washington on Air Force One. If there was one experience that I wanted to have in Washington before I left government, this was it.

We were driven to the tarmac in the secretary's Suburban by his security detail and boarded the plane. All passengers other than the presidential party were expected to board well ahead of the president's arrival so that the plane could immediately take off as soon as he arrived.

As the plane waited on the tarmac, we heard an announcement every few minutes updating us on the president's arrival time: "POTUS twenty minutes out," then "POTUS fifteen minutes out," and so on. As soon as the president was on board, the door was sealed, and the plane started to move.

About an hour into the flight, President Obama came and sat directly across from me, with a small table between us. He removed his jacket and loosened his tie before telling Secretary McDonald and me that he just got off the phone with Mr. Khizr Kahn. Mr. Kahn was the father of a fallen American soldier and a recent speaker at the Democratic National Convention, where he expressed criticism of Trump's immigration proposals. His family had since been targeted for his comments. The president told Mr. Kahn how much he appreciated his son's service and that his sacrifice on behalf of American freedom would not be forgotten.

After that the president switched gears, and the conversation lightened. So I took his cue and told him proudly, "Mr. President, my daughter just got into Harvard Law School."

The president said, "That's fantastic, David. I think it's a great place. You know, Michelle and I spent some time there, and Malia is going there, too." Of course I knew, but I liked how he didn't assume that everyone did. The president said, "You know, here's what I would tell her: relax, have a good time, and it'll all work out." Jennie still keeps an eight-by-ten photograph in her room of the president speaking to me on Air Force One that day, with a text bubble from me to her reading "Jennie—the president spoke to me for ten minutes with advice he wanted me to give you about Harvard Law School."

Around this same time, I accompanied Vice President Biden on a tour of Memorial Sloan Kettering in connection with the Cancer Moonshot. Vice President Biden follows his own internal clock, and he is such a people person that whenever someone wants to say hello or take a selfie, he almost always acquiesces. This means, of course, that he often falls behind his tightly packed schedule.

We had four events that day in New York, and during those that involved fundraising, I stayed outside and waited for the vice president to finish. While waiting, I saw one of his aides gathering a collection of Biden's challenge coins, and I offered to trade him one of mine for one of the vice president's. He rejected my offer and told me why: At an event some years before, the aide had seen a young boy in a wheelchair waiting patiently behind some barriers to catch a glimpse of the vice president. Feeling bad that Biden was running an hour behind and the boy would have to wait so long in the hot sun, the aide gave him one of the vice president's coins. The boy was thrilled. Moments later, when the vice president finally came out to greet the crowd and shake hands, he reached into his pocket for one of his coins to give to the same little boy. When he offered it, the boy promptly said, "No thank you, I already have one." Later that day, the vice president made it clear to his staff that he would be the only one handing out his coins in the future. When I became secretary, I adopted the same policy.

On the first of September, I flew to Seoul, South Korea, for the second international workshop on veterans' affairs. It was a great conference overall, and President Harry Truman's grandson was one of the speakers. I met with Korean and Vietnam veterans, along with young military students and other health care professionals. Also present were veterans affairs officials from Australia, Canada, New Zealand, and the United Kingdom. I presented our approach to rehabilitating returning soldiers with traumatic brain injury and PTSD. There was a good interchange of information among countries, and it was useful to see the similarities among our allies' veterans' needs.

Shortly after my return from this new view of the grand horizon, one of the VA's most persistent domestic trouble spots boiled over again: the Phoenix VA. A new medical center director, Rima Nelson, had been named, but she too carried baggage. Years earlier, while she had been an acting director in St. Louis, fifteen hundred patients were exposed to contaminated dental equipment that increased their risk of infection. Rima had done the right thing by shutting down the service until she could ensure that the environment was safe. Nevertheless, the press was very critical of an alleged safety lapse. Given this history, Senator McCain and other members of Congress were speaking out against Rima as the new director. I was convinced that she was the best person for Phoenix (our most high-profile and politicized facility), where there had been six acting directors since 2014.

Most leaders in the VA system didn't want to go anywhere near Phoenix. I had spent almost a year seeing if I could attract a candidate from the private sector, but at government salary and the real risk of reputational damage, there were no contenders. Rima was not only willing to go; she said she looked forward to the challenge. I spent all afternoon on calls to plan a strategy for how I could support her and fight the political headwinds. I decided that the best way to support Rima in Phoenix was to be there with her on her first day of work, so I booked a flight.

I knew emotions were running high in Arizona. Veterans were angry, the staff was on edge, and the local media was hostile. There was even a billboard in front of the Phoenix Medical Center that read, "Veterans are Dying. VA is Lying." With this new controversy over the new director, I knew things had the potential to get nasty. So for the first time since entering government service, I requested a security detail.

The day was not easy, but along with all the anger came a lot of support, and I was glad I was there personally to stand behind Rima.

Returning to problems in Phoenix, I had come full circle, which was compelling proof—as if any more were needed—that "fixing" an organization is never a matter of "one and done" but rather a matter of endless maintenance, fine-tuning, and recalibration.

Spending so much time responding to problems in Phoenix made me realize that a leader's job is to make sure situations like this don't happen again. It was clear as daylight to me that the VA was spending too much time responding to crises instead of preventing them. Each day, another situation popped up, and our attention had to quickly turn toward damage control somewhere else. I wanted a system that could identify problems before they became crises. Toward that end, we launched the Healthcare Improvement Center (HIC), an electronic monitoring system that used the VA's extensive data to predict where the next urgent situation might arise. Using key performance measures, operational metrics, and clinical indicators, we developed an early-warning system for low-performing medical centers and those at the highest risk for crisis. For example, the HIC was able to identify when the nurse vacancy rate became too high in Little Rock, Arkansas, which allowed the VA to quickly pivot to same-day job offers to avoid shutting down beds. Additionally, when the HIC identified a poorly functioning ultrasound probe at the Popular Bluff VA (eventually leading to a national recall), the VA was able to remove it.

With the 2016 presidential election around the corner, I began to wonder how much time I had left in Washington. During my tenure at the VA, I became acquainted with Scott Gould, who was the VA's deputy secretary before I arrived. Scott and his wife, Michèle Flournoy, were both politically savvy in the best possible way. Michèle had been the Department of Defense's under secretary of defense for policy, and as the 2016 election approached its climax, she was rumored to be the likely nominee to head the Department of Defense under Hillary Clinton. In the spirit of optimism and new beginnings, Scott and Michèle invited us to an election-night party at their house. Aside from the pleasure of good company, I thought it wouldn't be a bad idea to nurture my relationships with the new team that just about everyone expected to soon be running things in Washington.

Shortly after 8:00 p.m., the election results started rolling in, and everyone was in good spirits as they clustered around the television set. People were tracking the numbers closely with spreadsheets and vote-tracking software on their tablets that I did not even know existed. By 9:30 p.m., though, people started to look worried. By 10:15 p.m., it felt like we were gathered for a funeral. Then people started to leave, not sure what to say to console the hosts or each other.

Heading home, Merle and I stopped at a bar across the street from our apartment to watch the election results for another hour or so, but when we went to sleep that night, we still didn't know the final outcome. In the morning, like most Americans, we woke up surprised to find that Donald Trump was our new president. If I had any hope of staying on at the VA to finish the work I'd started, I was going to have to get to know a different crowd. The prospects for success seemed minuscule, and it would be several long weeks before I heard from Ike Perlmutter.

Especially that year, I found it comforting that Veterans Day comes right on the heels of Election Day—signaling that despite our political affiliations and the nationwide divide a presidential election can cause, we can all come together as Americans to honor our heroes.

The period leading up to Veterans Day 2016 was a busy time for me. On November 10, I took the train to the Iraq and Afghanistan Veterans of America Gala in Manhattan and then hurried back to Washington to attend the White House Veterans Day breakfast at 7:00 a.m. the next day. Assuming that this was likely to be our last significant event in Washington, my family joined me.

At the breakfast, we had a chance to speak with President Obama. Merle told the president, "We are really going to miss you."

He smiled at her, leaned down to Merle's ear, and whispered, "David should stay at VA." We were a little bit baffled. How did he expect me to do that?

After a lovely buffet, we then headed out to Arlington National Cemetery for the laying of the wreath at the Tomb of the Unknown Solider. Danny and Jennie were allowed to march out in the procession with us, and we stood directly behind Bob and Diane McDonald.

The president was greeted by a twenty-one-gun salute, and then a bugler played taps while he laid the wreath. We were taken to the amphitheater at Arlington to hear the president's speech, which contained a very optimistic message, especially considering that it was only three days after the election. President Obama advised us to look to our veterans as examples for how to behave, and he was right.

The following week, Secretary McDonald and I were scheduled to go to New Orleans for a ribbon-cutting ceremony. We had been waiting for days for the arrival of the Trump transition team, but we hadn't heard from them and were still unsure of when they were going to show up. Rather than wait, we decided to simply carry on as before, which meant going to the opening, although we stayed close to our phones in case someone was trying to reach us. The event was to celebrate a new VA medical center, replacing the facility destroyed by Hurricane Katrina. It had taken eleven years to locate the new property, obtain the funding, and build the new facility, so this was a proud moment.

Under Secretary McDonald's leadership, the VA had made a great deal of progress. We hadn't attempted a top-to-bottom, systemic restructuring of the way the VA did business; instead, we focused on fixing immediate problems and making incremental but meaningful improvements. Even with everything we were able to achieve, I wondered whether we might have relied too much on consensus and not been sufficiently bold in our actions. The important thing, though, was that we would be leaving the VA in better shape than it was when we arrived.

13

The World Turned Upside Down

Several more weeks passed before the Trump "landing" team arrived, but then the political maneuvering began almost immediately. Individuals who had been involved in the campaign were sent into each agency to develop postinauguration plans. It was rumored that these teams had been hastily pulled together, which may explain why it took so long for them to show up.

Accompanying me to the first few meetings with the Trump team was Dr. Richard Stone, then serving as my principal deputy under secretary. In meetings up until this time, Dr. Stone had deferred to my opinions. Even though I encouraged all my team members to speak their minds, Dr. Stone was a retired army general, and I think it was out of respect for my higher rank that he had demurred.

But now I saw a new Dr. Stone. He took a far more active role in working with the VA staff in preparing their presentations, and he told them that there would be no landing-team meetings without him. He also took the lead in discussions, where he had no problem disagreeing with me in front of the Trump people.

Soon I was asked to attend fewer and fewer meetings, with my scheduling staff being informed that "Dr. Stone's attendance would suffice." Within three weeks, a memo was sent out to VA staff saying that there was no need for any "political appointees" from the Obama administration to attend any further meetings.

Naturally, I thought the landing team would benefit from my perspective and understanding of the VHA, and I felt particularly bad for Bob McDonald, who, despite his extensive expertise, was excluded from what we had both hoped would be a transfer of knowledge. I knew that he too wanted to make sure that this new team understood our plans and how they might build on the substantial progress we had made.

I spoke about my concerns to retired general Michael Meese, who was leading the landing team as it related to the VA, and I let him know that I wanted to be helpful. I also told him of my interest in remaining as under secretary. I even told him that I thought that Bob McDonald was doing a great job and should be considered to remain as secretary. General Meese was a gentleman, listened politely, and said that he would share my messages with the decision-makers. Nothing changed. It appeared that both Bob McDonald and I had been written off as players for the wrong team.

Interestingly, while I was effectively barred from official meetings, nothing stopped individual landing team members from reaching out to me. Some contacted me privately and asked to meet off site, either early in the day or after work. I got the impression that there was significant internal competition and more than a little confusion.

Many commentators have speculated that Trump entered the Republican primaries as a marketing ploy, with no expectation of actually winning the nomination, much less the general election. Certainly there was nothing about his transition team that suggested a great deal of advance planning.

One notable member of the landing team was Darin Selnick, who previously had served on the Commission on Care—a group created by the 2014 Choice Act to provide recommendations for reforming the VA health care system. Darin told me that he supported the idea of my staying on as under secretary, but I couldn't decide whether he was sincere or playing me. There was something about him that I didn't trust.

Meanwhile, Dr. Stone did everything he could to give the impression that he was taking over my role at the VA. Several staff members expressed discomfort with Dr. Stone's new aggressive style, saying that they felt torn between having to decide if they were on "Team Stone" or "Team Shulkin."

I knew this wasn't good for the organization, and I arranged to speak with Dr. Stone. But when I expressed my concerns, he denied that he was trying to replace me, and he gave me his assurance that he too was on "Team Shulkin."

"We all need you to stay," he said, but here again I couldn't gauge his sincerity.

As inauguration day drew closer, the landing team began telling people they had completed their plan for the VA but were unable to share it publicly. Most assumed that Dr. Stone would become acting under secretary for health on January 20. I thought they were probably right.

It was during this interregnum period that I received the strange phone call from Michael Cohen that led to my even stranger meeting with Ike Perlmutter and Bruce Moskowitz at Mar-a-Lago, and then the strangest meeting of all with the president-elect at Trump Tower. Even after those encounters, I remained unsure about my future but assumed I was leaving like the other Obama political appointees. I prepared my letter of resignation, which was very emotional for me, but I hesitated to turn it in. Meanwhile, I made use of every last second to continue the work I was doing at the VA. Staff started buzzing, "Why isn't he cleaning out his desk? It's over. Doesn't he get it?" I did get it; I just didn't *want* to.

Each day, new names floated in the media as likely candidates to be nominated as secretary. Most of those suggested were former military officers, although politicians and media personalities were included as well. Then, on January 11, Fox News reported that Mr. Trump was finally about to announce his pick for the secretary of the VA.

Obviously, I was keenly interested in the press conference, scheduled for 11:00 a.m., but at that moment, I was at a myVA meeting at George Washington University. The myVA Initiative, launched under Secretary McDonald, had twelve breakthrough strategies associated with it, each of which was designed around a problem veterans experienced. VA teams were assigned to each problem and given metrics, goals, and timelines. Bob had also established a veterans' experience office focused on better defining and improving the customer experience.

Like me, Bob was trying to make the most of his last moments at the VA to do everything he could for the veterans. This is why, when the president-elect was about to take the podium and begin his press conference, Bob and I were on our own platform, fielding questions about the future direction of the agency. Like a school kid passing discreet notes in class, one of the other panelists, Scott Blackburn, signaled to me to look over at his phone. His screen displayed a betting app that allowed people to wager on who the next VA secretary would be. There were eighteen names on his screen. Number one was Jeff Miller, the Florida congressman who chaired the House Committee on Veterans Affairs, favored thirty-one to one. Next was Pete Hegseth, the Fox News personality and former head of Concerned Veterans of America at twenty to one. Number nine was Bob McDonald.

I turned back to the questions from the audience, but a few moments later, my colleague tapped me again. A new name had popped up at number nineteen with only 2 percent of the vote—*me!* Now, this I really found funny. But then I started thinking back to Trump's cryptic remark: "Next time you see this guy, you're going to be calling him Mr. Secretary." People often called me Mr. Secretary, though, even while I was under secretary. Besides, the whole interview had been spent asking me who I thought should be secretary. Nothing about it seemed like a job interview for me becoming the *secretary!*

I reminded myself that the VA secretary, by tradition, was always a veteran, often with a distinguished military background. Moreover, I had not heard a word from Trump or any of his staff after that meeting in Trump Tower. A year and a half earlier, as they prepared for my official nomination as under secretary, President Obama's team had been compulsive in their planning. They had asked me to be present in Washington when the announcement was made, had me review and approve the press release, requested a list of industry validators that would be available to speak to the press on short notice, provided me with a call list of key senators and congressmen to approach shortly before the public announcement, and prepped me for interactions with the media. I assumed that if I were being considered for any position in this new administration, similar discussions and planning would have occurred. But there was nothing—*utter silence.* So I really hadn't entertained any notion of becoming the president's nominee for secretary. The most I hoped for was to be allowed to continue in my current role as under secretary.

On the other hand, if there was any chance that Trump had actually meant that he was going to choose me as secretary, I didn't want to be sitting in front of five hundred people in an auditorium when he announced it.

I abruptly got up from the panelist table, walked out of the conference, and returned to VA headquarters. When I arrived, I found several members of my staff meeting in the conference room attached to my office. I took out my phone and asked the assembled group if they wanted to see something funny. I opened the betting app and said, "Look, they've got me at number nineteen."

Vivieca, my chief of staff, glanced at the phone, looked at me, and corrected, "No. You're now number three." I stared at my phone in disbelief.

I rushed to my office, closed the doors, and turned on the television, sitting alone as the president-elect began his remarks.

He covered a number of issues, mostly relating to his preparation for assuming office. About fifteen minutes into his remarks, he said something to the effect of, "And I have the nominee for my new VA secretary here." Then Trump reached into his inside suit pocket and pulled out an envelope, as if he were announcing the winner of an Oscar. Time stood still for me as he fumbled with opening the envelope. When he finally extracted the paper with the name of his VA nominee on it, he said, "I am pleased to announce the new head secretary of the VA will be . . . David Shulkin."

I was incredulous. There was no one with me to ask if he had, in fact, said my name. But as he went on with his remarks referring to "David" and promising that "David is fantastic," it began to sink in that I was indeed his nominee.

Immediately my phone rang. It was Rick Scott, the governor of Florida. "I just wanted to congratulate you," he said. I thanked him and hung up, wondering how he had gotten my cell phone number. My phone kept ringing, and I could see the caller IDs of friends and colleagues. I was too stunned to talk to anyone, though, so I let them all go to voicemail. Then my office door flung open. Vivieca and Poonam stood in my doorway, shouting, "Oh my God! What just happened?"

Word soon spread throughout the building, and a small crowd of staff started to gather outside my office. My executive assistant told me that the press was calling and wanted a statement, and by the end of the afternoon, there were seventeen media requests for interviews. I still hadn't had any contact with the Trump team and was not sure how they wanted me to handle this, which is why a little communication and planning would have been useful.

Later, someone at the George Washington Conference informed me that after the announcement had been made, many people in the audience started to look at their phones, which is how Bob McDonald heard the news. He then made an announcement about my nomination and concluded the conference.

I was worried about how Bob might react to this news and knew I had to see him right away. I went to his office as soon as he returned from the conference. It was obvious that he was not happy, but Bob was always professional and a gentleman, and he told me that he was pleased. I tried to explain that the nomination was unexpected, but he didn't seem to believe me. I can understand why. After all, the story made very little sense.

I told Bob how sorry I was that things had happened this way and mentioned that I had told Trump that Bob was doing great work and should stay. Bob said he appreciated that but that I should've told him before I met with Trump. I explained that under normal circumstances, I would have, but I was given strict instructions not to tell anyone except Merle. I don't think anything I said mitigated Bob's sense of betrayal.

One of the very first people to come to my office to congratulate me was Rich Stone, proclaiming what wonderful news this was and how happy he was for me. Maybe he was being genuine. After all, it was the under secretary position he was after, and now that position was free. I think he was mightily surprised when I told him to think about whether he would be a good fit in my team going forward. The next day, Stone told me that he was returning to the private sector. It was unfortunate to lose a capable executive, but I supported his choice, and we parted ways on good terms. It was no surprise, however, that upon my departure as secretary, one of the first moves of Trump's political appointees was to bring back Dr. Stone as acting under secretary.

14

Confirmed: Our Lives Are Forever Changed

I HAD ALREADY BEEN THROUGH THE BARRAGE OF FEDERAL PAPERWORK to become under secretary, so this second time around, the vetting process, though just as cumbersome, seemed much easier. Senator Isakson told me he planned to hold a confirmation hearing as soon as possible.

During the interim, I remained in my role as under secretary, with Bob Snyder, McDonald's former chief of staff, as acting secretary. In deference to my nomination to become secretary, though, Snyder consulted with me on most major decisions.

I knew all of the members of the Senate Committee on Veterans Affairs and much of the Senate leadership, but even so, I requested a series of meetings with many of them in order to address any issues or concerns they might have. In the back of my mind was my earlier experience of senators placing holds on my confirmation until an issue had been cleared up or a promise made.

Given my new public profile, and knowing that if confirmed I would be in presidential succession, VA security was now escorting me everywhere. On one particular weekend, a security team drove me home from Washington to Philadelphia to check the routes and alternate routes and to size up security risks our house might present. They also met with the Philadelphia Police, Philadelphia VA Police, and our local township police. This was the first time in a very long while that Merle hadn't had to drive to Thirtieth Street Station to pick me up from my train.

I spent the weekend at the kitchen table completing my vetting forms. (The kitchen table, located in the center of the house, is my preferred working spot, and it drives Merle crazy that I monopolize this room and cover it in stacks of paper, my computer, and coffee mugs.) Once again, I had to list every foreign trip I ever took, every talk I ever gave, and every honorarium I ever received. While the paperwork was tedious and mind-numbing, it certainly beat spending the weekend moving my stuff out of my office and my Washington apartment and starting to look for a new job.

Taking on this higher post had nothing to do with personal ambition. As for "personal gain," I could make significantly more money going back into the private sector. Oddly enough, owing to an anomaly in the federal job rankings, the promotion to secretary actually meant a pay *cut* from what I was making as under secretary. I wanted this job only because I wanted to continue working with veterans and see through the changes I had already implemented and planned to implement in the future. I hoped that Trump's behavior would improve once he assumed the responsibility of the presidency and that he would bring the country together after what had been an extremely contentious election. If unification was his plan, I wanted to be part of that team. If unification was *not* his plan—as we soon saw that it wasn't—I wanted to be a high-level official representing bipartisanship and working toward lifting our fellow Americans up instead of bringing them down.

Even so, I was apprehensive about joining this administration. I knew there were reputational risks, and in hindsight, I should have been much more concerned than I was. Without a background in politics, I was naïve in thinking that if I was careful about my choices and remained a good person, I wouldn't find myself immersed in scandal. *That only happens to bad people,* I thought. I'm sure many people still think this way. Unfortunately, my family and I now know better.

On Monday morning, my first telephone call was from Marisol, Ike's assistant. The second was from Dr. Bruce Moskowitz, who was speaking with Toby Cosgrove and the rest of the group that I was told would be helping to advise the VA. After consulting with VA legal counsel, I told Ike and Bruce that in government, any advisory group needs to be officially sanctioned and meet the requirements of the Federal Advisory Committee Act. If they didn't want to go that route, any recommendations provided needed to come from them as individuals. I made clear that while they could offer advice to me as private citizens, they could not have an official role at the VA. They both confirmed that they understood and agreed to give advice and feedback only informally and as individuals. Time would tell how well this strange relationship was going to work.

The first time all the nominees for cabinet positions in the Trump administration met was in a secluded building on Eighteenth Street. The group included three doctors (Ben Carson, Tom Price, and myself). There were also four congressmen, three former governors, two four-star generals, one senator, a navy SEAL, and a number of businesspeople who had prior relationships with President Trump.

In the week prior to the inauguration, I received a list of activities from Cabinet Affairs. There was going to be an orientation for cabinet members, four black-tie events, two lunches, two additional ceremonial events, and four inauguration balls as well as an after-party at the soon-to-become-controversial Trump International Hotel.

Given that we had so many events in a row, Jennie's childhood bedroom in our Philadelphia home became Merle's wardrobe room for spreading out all of the gowns, cocktail dresses, and business suits she needed for the range of functions we had to attend.

Over the next few days, we were inundated with even more invitations—especially for events sponsored by veterans' organizations. On the day we attended the Veterans of Foreign Wars Medal of Honor event at the Hyatt on Third Street, Merle and I tried to work the room quickly because we only had half an hour before we had to move on to an event for big donors at the Library of Congress. At the Library of Congress was a very different group— one with huge diamonds, plastic surgery, and genuine minks very much on display.

We then moved on to a party sponsored by the governor of Florida. On our way out, we met Ryan Zinke, the congressman and former navy SEAL who had been nominated as the secretary of the interior. He was accompanied by his wife, Lola, who was a member of the Hispanic and women's outreach team for the Trump campaign. As Ryan shook my hand, he said with a laugh, "Good luck. The president offered me the VA position, but I said, 'Sir, I thought you liked me! That's way too hard a job.' So I took Interior instead."

The next day began with a 9:00 a.m. Medal of Honor breakfast, but here, too, we were basically speed dating. We had to leave before the speeches because we had a meeting scheduled with Ike Perlmutter and Dr. Moskowitz at the Trump International Hotel. We were joined by Lori, Ike Perlmutter's wife; Marcia, Moskowitz's wife; and Tiffany and Scotty Smiley. Scotty is a disabled veteran blinded by an improvised explosive device (IED), and he and Tiffany told us about their difficulties in obtaining VA benefits. Exasperated, Tiffany had just written a piece for the *Wall Street Journal* in which she expressed her concerns. Listening to their story, I felt more confident that I was doing the right thing by accepting this job, and it made me more determined than ever to keep fighting to reform VA programs.

That morning, I also met a woman who worked for the ambassador to Afghanistan. She removed a metal bracelet from her arm that she wore in memory of her husband, who had been killed on 9/11. She paused and then took a moment to stare down at the bracelet before extending it to me and saying that she wanted me to have it. I slipped it on my left wrist and promised to wear it to the inauguration in honor of her husband and the many others who lost their lives on 9/11.

At noon we went down to the ballroom for the leadership luncheon at the Trump Hotel, where each cabinet secretary was assigned to a table of donors. Merle and I sat with a woman from California who owns two hundred wineries and a gentleman who previously had served as an ambassador to the Netherlands. We also spoke with General Jim Mattis (secretary of defense) and met Jeff Sessions (attorney general) for the first time. Having seen images of these people's faces flashed continuously on CNN and Fox News for many weeks, and now seeing them face-to-face, made me feel as though I was stepping into a television show and meeting the cast. But in retrospect, any discussion of Trump cabinet members seems more like the recitation of a casualty list.

After lunch, we went home to change for a Medal of Honor cocktail party hosted by Disabled American Veterans and a black-tie dinner after that. On our way to the first event, traffic was at a standstill, so, much to the dismay of our military escort, Merle and I jumped out of the car and headed for the Metro. She had to navigate the stairs and the platform in her floor-length gown and high heels, but we arrived at the venue an hour before our driver.

Members of the cabinet and other VIPs were once more dispersed and instructed to mingle with donors. I sat next to Scott Walker, the governor of Wisconsin, and I met Sonny Perdue, the former governor of Georgia who would soon be sworn in as the secretary of agriculture.

After several tries to penetrate the ring of Secret Service agents and say hello to the president-elect, I was able to reach him and introduce Merle. He told us, "You know, I watch CNN, and they're all talking about you. They like you, and they think you're my only good cabinet choice."

Then he said, "VA has some prime realty in California, you know. Very expensive real estate." This was an odd statement, especially considering the festivities around us, but it was also true.

The VA owns more than four hundred acres near UCLA in Westwood. The land had been left to the federal government to benefit veterans, and the VA recently had entered into a settlement agreement to ensure that it was being used for just that purpose. I was surprised to hear that President Trump was aware of this parcel, but then again, he was a real estate mogul. I could see the wheels turning in his head but couldn't be sure what he was thinking.

Merle and I got home that evening to our one-bedroom apartment at Fourth and K Street, where we waited for Danny and Jennie to come in from out of town. Our rented apartment had one bathroom and two sofa beds. For this future cabinet secretary, there would be no diamonds or mink coats.

At the inauguration itself, Merle and I were seated next to Ben Carson and his wife, Candy. Reince Priebus and Kellyanne Conway were situated directly behind us. Merle looked down at her phone and opened a text from Jennie with a screenshot of a live broadcast focused on the two of us walking into the ceremony. Merle looked at me and whispered in disbelief, "How did we get here?" Two weeks ago, we thought I was going to be unemployed and that inauguration day would be a very depressing last few hours in office for me.

As the ceremony began, Barack and Michelle Obama, George and Laura Bush, Jimmy and Rosalynn Carter, and Bill and Hillary Clinton proceeded in and took their seats on stage. I give Hillary a lot of credit for showing up. It couldn't have been easy when she had thought she'd be the one taking the oath of office and offering her vision for the nation for the next four years. But the whole country was making that same adjustment to a new set of expectations and a new reality.

After the formal ceremony, we were escorted into Sanctuary Hall for a luncheon with the new president and the congressional leadership.

At one point, I went over to the head table to introduce myself to Senator Chuck Schumer, who was seated next to the president. When he exclaimed, "David, I got your pen!" I didn't know what he was talking about. The senator must have seen the puzzled look on my face and went on to explain that when the president signs the nomination for a cabinet member, it's traditional for him to give the pen to one of the officials standing nearby. President Trump tried to give Schumer Ben Carson's pen, but after the president signed my nomination, Schumer asked, "Can I trade Ben Carson's pen for David Shulkin's?"

When the president asked why, Schumer said, "Because, Mr. President, he's your only good cabinet pick!"

President Trump said, "Come on. You're kidding."

Senator Schumer said, "No, sir, I'm not."

Hearing this made me painfully aware that Senator Schumer and the president were going to have a very rocky relationship at best.

After the festivities were over, I went to the White House to speak with Reince Priebus. I wanted to do whatever I could to expedite my confirmation hearing and subsequent floor vote, because the sooner I was sworn in, the sooner I could get back to work trying to drive reform. He brought me into his office and showed me a large poster board with the names of each of the nominees and proposed dates for each of their hearings and votes. I was last on the list, with a tentative date in late spring. As Reince explained it, so many of the nominees were controversial that, the White House wanted to use all of their political muscle on getting these nominees through first. Reince expected me to be the least controversial of all.

Chairman Isakson disagreed and thought it was better to get a secretary in place at the VA as soon as possible. The veterans service organizations also pushed members of the committee to move quickly. With little apparent coordination between the White House and the Senate, my confirmation hearing was moved up.

At 2:00 p.m. on February 1, 2017, I appeared before the Senate Committee on Veterans Affairs. It's an odd feeling to sit at a table in front of fifteen senators peering down from a raised platform while a dozen photographers kneel in front snapping pictures.

Merle was right behind me—literally and figuratively—and knowing that her face would be on camera for the entire two hours, she tried to maintain a neutral expression. Keeping a poker face was not exactly Merle's strong suit. Glancing around the packed room behind me, I saw Garry Augustine from Disabled American Veterans and Paul Rieckhoff of Iraq and Afghanistan Veterans of America. My brother-in-law, Joe Fetterman, was there, as were friends from Morristown Memorial who made the trip to show their support. This was comforting. I took a deep breath as I prepared to begin.

Senator Isakson began by mentioning the first time he and I met, which was on a Delta flight just before my first hearing for under secretary. On the plane, Isakson told me about a VA anesthesiologist in Atlanta who was concerned about an issue. By the next morning, I had called the anesthesiologist and fixed the problem. The anesthesiologist then called Senator Isakson to tell him how pleased he was. "This is the kind of guy you want running VA," Isakson suggested. This was the kind of comment that prompted NPR to later call my hearing that day "a love fest" between the senators and me.

I made an introductory statement, and then each senator had five minutes to speak, usually about something they wanted me to do for their constituents. Senator Sullivan asked me to return to Alaska. Senator Tester asked me to come to Montana and Senator Manchin to West Virginia.

Since I had already been serving within the VA as under secretary, I was unable to respond to the senators with vague responses like, "If confirmed, I will look into that issue further." I preferred to address the issues head on anyway.

There were a few tough questions about my feelings toward Trump, his new Muslim ban, and ultimately, whether I had sold my soul to the devil. I never took the bait and steered my answers back to the fact that my only goal in taking the job was to take care of veterans. "I don't see what this has to do with veterans" became my catchphrase whenever pressed by a legislator, the media, or anyone else about anything divisive or peculiar the president said or did.

When the hearing ended at 5:15 p.m., the audience erupted into spontaneous applause. I was told it went as well as any hearing could.

Now it was time for me to go meet the senators beyond those who served on the VA committee. I started with the leadership: Mitch McConnell and Chuck Schumer. Having been the CEO at Beth Israel hospital in New York City, where Schumer's children were born, in addition to having a number of mutual friends, I got along well with Senator Schumer from the start. We also had a laugh about one of the president's comments. According to Schumer, the president had asked him, "You know the guy who introduced me to Dr. Shulkin?" referring to Ike Perlmutter. After Schumer shrugged, the president apparently said, "Of course you know him." The senator had to explain, "No, I actually don't know every Jewish person who has spent time in New York!"

But after our very cordial conversation, Schumer leveled with me. "David," he said, "I like you, and you have bipartisan support. But I'm going to have to vote against your senate confirmation because of the president's Muslim ban." Even after having been in Washington for quite some time, I still had a hard time understanding how politics worked.

A few days after the hearing, I received a call from President Trump's office, inviting me to join him for dinner. Madeleine, the president's assistant, told me that Secretary Mattis and Ike Perlmutter would be joining us.

Secretary Mattis and I arrived early, and as we waited in the Blue Room, the general told me about the challenges he had faced personally in getting registered for care at the VA. He pledged his support to all my efforts to improve the system and said I could count on his help. All I had to do was ask, he said, and he kept his word.

Eventually the president entered the room, along with Ike and Lori Perlmutter and Bruce Moskowitz. Apparently, the trio had been visiting with the president in the residence.

This was the first time it hit me just how much the Mar-a-Lago crowd was going to be involved in my new life and in my ability to lead the VA. As Michael Cohen would testify before Congress two years later, Donald Trump did not usually give explicit orders when he wanted something done, but he made it clear through other means exactly what he wanted you to do. I didn't need written instructions to understand this two-tiered social event—the guests who waited downstairs and the guests who were entertained upstairs—as a directive. Essentially, "These people are my friends and confidants, and I expect you to listen to them and make them happy."

I didn't contribute much to the dinner conversation that evening, which consisted mostly of the president peppering General Mattis with questions about which armies around the world were most capable and which nationalities make the fiercest fighters. I found the entire dynamic a little unsettling and mostly pushed my food around my plate. Most of what I was taking in was that, here in the capital, I was going to be in the battle of my life.

The Senate vote was scheduled for Monday, February 13, so Merle and I had a quick dinner and were back at our Washington apartment by 7:00 p.m. to watch the vote on C-SPAN. We tuned in to see Senator Johnny Isakson give an eloquent speech. He put his arms out to his colleagues. "Let's all come together for veterans and show bipartisan support!" he exclaimed. With that, the voting began. My heart raced as I moved my face closer to the television screen.

Each senator walked up to the desk at the front of the room and signaled either a thumbs up or thumbs down while a running tally appeared at the bottom of the screen. Given Schumer's foreboding words, and the contentious nature of the votes for several of my fellow cabinet nominees who had preceded me, I didn't know what to expect. As we watched the vote tally, the number of affirmatives rose quickly and easily to fifty-one, and I breathed a sigh of relief. But then, to my surprise, the votes kept piling up and reached an astonishing final tally of one hundred to zero. Even Schumer had voted for me. The suspense was over, and I was nearly jumping up and down with excitement. I was the only Trump cabinet member to receive a unanimous confirmation. Maybe bipartisanship wasn't totally dead.

Ashley Gunn from White House Cabinet Affairs sent an email informing us that the swearing-in could either be later that very evening in the Oval Office with the president officiating or the next day at 2:00 p.m. with the vice president officiating. I wanted to have my family there, so I chose the next day: February 14, 2017.

Jennie booked a flight from Boston, and Danny booked a train from New Jersey. My sister and her family asked if they could come, as did Merle's brother and his family. Merle's brother, Jon, is an identity-fraud consultant, so he was concerned about having to submit his social security number to the White House in order to gain admission, but reluctantly he provided it. Merle's ninety-four-year-old father and eighty-four-year-old mother also made the trip from Philadelphia.

We all met at the VA at 1:00 p.m., and my new official security detail drove us to the Eisenhower Office Building, where we found our way to the vice president's suite. Joining us there were Chairman Isakson, Ranking Member Tester, Chairman Roe, and Ranking Member Walz. I appreciated the fact that, with the congressional leadership from both parties attending my swearing in, there was yet another healthy sign of bipartisanship.

While I expected the swearing-in to be a mere formality, Vice President Pence presided over what turned out to be a surprisingly meaningful ceremony for my entire family. This was not merely a formality. Prior to the start of the ceremony, the vice president asked for a moment with Merle and the children and me, where he took the time to talk about the importance of the journey we were about to embark on as a family.

After speaking to each of the kids, the vice president complimented Merle's red high heels. They reminded him of Dorothy's shoes in *The Wizard of Oz,* which was quite fitting for the occasion, he said. "You know, I just told this story the other day about your husband, where we looked at dozens of candidates for this job. We looked *all over the country,* and after a long search, we found David—right here at home."

After the ceremony, my entourage of family and friends went back to the VA, where there was a large reception in my honor in the tenth-floor conference room. My staff wheeled in a beautiful rectangular cake, and after some kind words and refreshments, I took the whole family back to show them the secretary's office and my new view of the White House and the Washington Monument.

This was going to be a dramatic life change for all of us. The staff in the secretary's office, for instance, gave Merle a schedule of all the events she was expected to attend, and it was clear that she was going to have to make some major adjustments to her Philadelphia-based medical practice in order to fulfill these obligations.

That evening I sent Bob McDonald an email to let him know I was thinking about him. Bob responded promptly and said he was happy for me and the past was behind us.

15

The New Abnormal

WEDNESDAY, FEBRUARY 15, 2017, WAS MY FIRST OFFICIAL DAY AS secretary, and already I could see that my workload was going to increase by about 300 percent.

Darin Selnick from the beachhead transitional team was insisting that all political appointees have official appointments by that Friday, as per instructions from Rick Dearborn, the senior adviser to the president. I checked with Rick Dearborn, who didn't recall having said this. This was the first of many times that I would wonder about Darin's truthfulness.

As when I became under secretary, I knew that filling key positions with the right people was vital, and no position was more crucial than my chief of staff. Once again, I had the ideal candidate in Vivieca Wright Simpson, whom I elevated from my chief of staff in the VHA to my new chief of staff in the secretary's office.

To replace myself, I asked Dr. Poonam Alaigh, who had been serving as my special adviser, to assume the role of acting under secretary. But even as I was rounding out my team, it became readily apparent that there was a self-appointed coach yelling out plays from the sidelines.

There were days when Ike would call me several times a day. In one of his first calls, he suggested that we travel to VA facilities around the country. He said we should just show up without any notice, to see what was really going on. I tried to explain that I couldn't bring him into VA facilities like that. He said, "Okay, we'll give them ten minutes' notice." I'm not sure he understood that as a private citizen, it wouldn't be appropriate to be part of an unplanned inspection in a hospital. And while I had a better understanding of government, I had to adjust to my new role, too.

Becoming a cabinet member meant getting used to the idea that I was now in the line of presidential succession. A few days before the president's first address to the joint session of Congress, I received a message from the White House military officer that requested I pick up a secure phone that was positioned out of the way near the window. Until this moment, I hadn't even known my office had a special phone.

Adding to my surprise, I was then asked if I would be willing to serve as the "designated survivor" that year. The president's address to this joint session of Congress is one of the few times when almost the entire senior leadership of the US government— both legislative chambers, the cabinet, the Supreme Court, and top military officials—appeared in the same place at the same time. The idea was, should something go terribly wrong and wipe out this entire group of people at once, there would still remain at least one surviving official in presidential succession to provide continuity of government. The White House needed my response right away. Hmmm . . . yes! *Designated Survivor* was my favorite television show, and I had just scored the lead role!

After I agreed, we went over the plan for the following day. I was instructed not to tell anyone, including my staff and my family. Everyone should think that I was attending the address, right up until the moment that people would see that I wasn't walking into the hall with my fellow cabinet members. Not even the White House would be informed until that evening that I wouldn't be attending the State of the Union.

At the end of our conversation on my special telephone, and still in that no-nonsense military tone, the officer asked one last question: "Mr. Secretary, what would you like for dinner?" Wherever they were taking me—and I had no idea except that it was some secret location outside of the city—there was a navy mess hall like the one at the White House, and the chef could make whatever I liked. He suggested steak Diane.

That evening, watching the big event from home on CNN as the cabinet marched in, Merle noticed I wasn't there. Moments later, CNN's Jake Tapper announced that David Shulkin was the designated survivor. In retrospect, I can't help wondering if there wasn't some small irony at work. I survived as long as I could in this administration, but ultimately, I wasn't the last one standing.

There was far more security with me on the night that I was the designated survivor than on a normal day as secretary, but I still traveled with a few security agents everywhere I went on an every-day basis.

As under secretary, I had enjoyed much more personal free-dom. While the VA had provided me with a driver to take me to official business functions, I almost always rode a bicycle to and from work. As secretary, though, I had a full security detail, and riding my bike was no longer an option. My new security team consisted of VA special agents deputized by the US Marshal Service. I traveled with a designated lead agent who sat in the passenger seat of the car, followed by a "chase car" containing one or two additional agents. Almost everywhere I went, so did these two black Suburbans—usually double-parked as they waited for me, often displaying flashing lights. Another advance agent scouted out anyplace we were heading and would be there when we arrived. Depending on the agent's risk assessment of the venue, additional agents might be added.

When I traveled by train or plane instead of by car, I was usually surrounded by several men—each seemingly twice my height and weight—walking in unison with me, which made me feel awkward and conspicuous. Shortly after being sworn in, I was in New York City for the weekend. As my security agents and I were getting off the train, an Amtrak police officer trying to be helpful handed me a black suitcase. A man came running up to me and, eyeing my security detail, huffed, "Sir, you look very important, so if you need my bag, you can have it." Embarrassed, I gave it back to him and found my own.

Having a security detail meant that my family and I had to plan our schedules well in advance. There was no more "Where should we go for dinner tonight?" or "Want to run to the mall?" While this may seem trivial, always having to plan ahead where we were eating out and which errands I had to do on the way home became a nuisance. Spontaneity was no longer a possibility.

Being with security also meant there was no longer any such thing as an entirely private conversation, either in person or on the phone. Even going for walks, visiting the restroom in a restaurant, or just venturing outside of my office suite at VA headquarters meant bringing along a team. When I was with Merle, I was never just with Merle. We got used to using hand signals and whispers in the back seat of a Suburban when we wanted privacy, but for the most part, we embraced our agents as extensions of our family. While Merle didn't travel with security agents unless she was also with me, she was expected to play her part to help keep me safe by making sure I followed the rules. On my first day as secretary, the security team briefed Merle for several hours to make clear to her what *I* could and could not do going forward: no driving, no taking taxis, no visiting friends or doing errands outside the house on my own. Most of the errands fell to her as a result—not that she hadn't been doing most of them for the duration of our marriage anyway.

A couple of times in the beginning of my tenure as secretary, I took a rebellious walk around the block alone to exercise a freedom I no longer had. My security detail caught me most times and scolded me. In contrast, Merle lived a sort of double life. When she was with me, she experienced the level of security and planning that I dealt with every day. When she was alone, she was alone— no security, total privacy, and the ability to take a run or go to a museum without letting anyone know or planning it in advance.

Each security agent had his own style and personality, and since I spent so much time with them, I soon learned their different approaches to the job. Some were more diligent than others—scanning our surroundings when they walked with me, searching for risks. Others seemed oblivious, as if they were just along for the ride. Some engaged me in conversation and joked around; others were totally silent.

I certainly had my favorites, and among those was Ira Bradford, or Brad, as we called him. Brad was almost as wide as he was tall and had already lived about seven other lives. Specifically, he was previously a bouncer, a personal security guard for celebrities, a state trooper, a military police officer, a lawyer (who still took a couple of medical malpractice cases each year), and briefly, a pro football player for the Dallas Cowboys. Brad talked a lot about the Cowboys, perhaps as a strategy to make other people feel more at ease with his intimidating physical appearance. Within a minute, he could sweet-talk most anyone, which made it possible for him to move us through crowds easily and inconspicuously. At airports and train stations, he usually made friends with the police and gate agents so that it was always a smooth experience once I arrived.

The security team was overseen by the Office of Security and Emergency Preparedness, which was run by a political appointee at the VA central office. Since President Trump assumed office, a palpable tension had grown between the new leadership and the security detail itself. What had worked well under the last administration was disrupted by the new administration when the central office removed several agents.

During my time as secretary, many of my most experienced agents retired or left, including Brad. Those who remained grew more distant. By the end, Ty, an agent who had at one point been highly interactive and engaging, barely talked. More troubling, another agent began to take pictures of me when I was out doing errands, documenting everywhere I went and no doubt reporting back to central office. Another frequently sent emails commenting on where I was going, even sending my itinerary to people outside the agency, which exposed me to unknown security risks. One agent did his own amateur analysis of whether the trip we took would have been more cost-effective had we traveled by car rather than by train. Over time, the tension within the team became obvious, and it was increasingly unpleasant to spend time with my agents. More experienced agents were replaced by new people, and any sense of camaraderie and trust was gone. The toxic environment responsible for these changes will become clearer as I continue telling my story.

16

Team Chaos

WHILE IN THE CITY, I MADE ROUNDS AT THE MANHATTAN VA with the medical team, where not much had changed since my days in training on those same wards. Seeing patients was one practice I refused to sacrifice to my new round-the-clock respon- sibilities. Working in Washington or Philadelphia might have been more convenient, but the DC VA was continually besieged by offi- cial visitors, and the last thing they needed was the boss popping in on a regular basis. Similarly, I thought Philadelphia was a bad idea because I didn't want to give the impression that I might drop by at any moment just because I lived nearby. So throughout my time as secretary—just as I had as under secretary—I continued seeing patients in New York City and sleeping on the couch in my son's apartment to save the government money.

On this particular trip, I also did a segment for *Fox and Friends*. The interview was to be live with Pete Hegseth, the former exec- utive director of Concerned Veterans of America (the anti-VA and pro-privatization Koch brothers organization). Moreover, there was speculation that Hegseth wanted the VA secretary job for himself. During the Obama years, VA officials wouldn't appear on Fox, but this new White House loved Fox News, so I thought, *Let's give it a try*. Hegseth had some hard questions for me, but overall the interview wasn't hostile and actually went pretty smoothly.

Attitudes for and against Fox News were hardly the only difference between the old administration and the new. The first thing you noticed about the Obama people was how young they were. The second was how professional and competent they were. In the Trump White House, the more typical attributes were being smartly dressed, loose-lipped, and without any prior government experience.

When I was under secretary, most of my White House meetings had been with a deputy chief of staff, Kristie Canegallo. In her midthirties, Kristie had a degree in international relations and a master's from Johns Hopkins in strategic planning. She had worked at Goldman Sachs for a number of years and then spent five months at the US embassy in Afghanistan before joining a marine unit in Anbar Province in Iraq and then working with the National Security Council. Kristie knew her stuff, always did her homework, and came to meetings knowing exactly what questions to ask. She also followed up and was responsive whenever I brought issues to her attention.

In the Trump White House, I had no single point of contact. Moreover, there were no clear rules of engagement. This meant that I'd receive very different answers to the same question depending on how many people I asked. All too often, there was no answer at all because it was unclear who was leading any particular initiative.

After running the VA for a little more than a month, I still had vacancies on my team that I needed to fill. In addition to career civil servants, every cabinet-level department takes on political appointees—usually campaign workers or contributors—with some direct link to the new administration. Most administrations take care to appoint people who have some understanding of and alignment with a specific department's mission. But given that this president had no government background himself and neither did many of his cabinet secretaries (actually, some had been selected to run departments they had spent their entire careers opposing), Trump's political appointees were not the usual sort.

The VA absorbed about thirty of these people, which was actually a comparatively small number considering the size of the agency. Typically, they were sent over from the Presidential Personnel Office at the White House, and I was instructed to place them in appropriate spots within the agency.

The first one to come to my office was Darin Selnick, whom I've already mentioned a couple of times. Darin previously had served as a special adviser to Concerned Veterans for America (CVA), the lobbying group backed by the Koch brothers. It was there that he worked closely with the CVA executive director who would go on to become a Fox News correspondent, Pete Hegseth.

As previously mentioned, Darin had been one of fifteen members on the Commission on Care during my time as under secretary. This group was ably chaired by a seasoned health care executive, Nancy Schlichting, who had been CEO of the Henry Ford Health System from 2003 to 2016 and was one of the most respected and admired leaders in the field. Nancy possessed the temperament and skill to keep the group focused on the task at hand—except for Darin. An outspoken critic, he pressed his arguments hard.

Whenever I presented to this body, most of the commissioners listened attentively and asked probing questions. I had confidence that Nancy was leading an objective and fair process. The commission approved a report with eighteen recommendations, but then something unusual happened. Two of the commissioners, Darin Selnick and Stewart Hickey, issued a minority report calling for the creation of a federally chartered nonprofit system that would allow veterans open choice for using the private sector. While it was highly uncommon for a committee to have dissenters go public, this would prove to be Darin's signature way of doing business. He came with many preconceived notions, and the art of compromise was not in his toolkit.

Darin was viewed by many other commissioners and by the traditional veterans service organizations as disruptive and often difficult to work with, although I admit that I initially enjoyed my meetings with him. I liked being challenged by the presentation of ideas that might shake up the status quo. But when he showed up at the VA as a member of the VA beachhead team (the first set of permanent political appointees to arrive at the agency), I realized that he was capable of doing some serious damage.

Whereas most of the members of the landing team planned to return to their normal lives, Darin wanted to stay on full time at the VA—but only as senior adviser to the secretary. When I floated this idea by other members of my team and by the VSO community, it was a nonstarter. The only people Darin worked with previously who trusted him were members of the new political team just arriving. These newcomers saw Darin as a knowledgeable confidant who could help them navigate a complicated new environment. Even with all the baggage he carried, I felt that my hands were tied, and I reluctantly decided to move forward with Darin's request to be my senior adviser. This would soon become one of my biggest regrets.

Another political appointee placed at the VA was Jake Leinenkugel, a former marine whose previous administrative experience was running the Leinenkugel Brewing Company in Wisconsin. He was involved in the Trump campaign and was the White House's choice to be the VA's senior White House adviser. Jake saw his role as giving direction to the other political appointees in carrying out the White House's agenda. That, of course, was precisely the role I saw for myself as the Senate-confirmed secretary of the Department of Veterans Affairs and as a member of the president's cabinet. Jake's rather grandiose view of his role would prove to be a source of much tension.

Jake was pleasant enough, the type of guy you might want to get a beer with—which makes sense, considering he owned a brewing company—but I don't really drink much beer. More importantly, Jake had absolutely no experience in health care or human services. I think it is fair to say that running a small family business is very different from running a large government organization, but Jake didn't always appreciate this. Each day, after my morning meeting, which included the political team and the career leadership, Jake would take the politicals behind closed doors and "translate" my instructions into action points. While supposedly "secret," the fact that these meetings occurred was well known to the entire organization.

This sent a strong message to everyone that there was the "secretary's team" and the "political team." In my view of the world, there should have been only the "VA team."

The existence of these two factions put some of the other political appointees in a tough spot. They did not want to participate in the "secret" daily meetings, viewing them as counterproductive political scheming. Several of these nonparticipants shared with me their discomfort with the type of discussions taking place behind closed doors. They also warned me to watch my back.

In addition to Darin Selnick and Jake Leinenkugel, the following people participated in the closed-door sessions: Brooks Tucker, another former marine, became the assistant secretary for congressional and legislative affairs; John Ullyot, a former marine sniper, became the assistant secretary for public and governmental affairs; Peter Shelby, another former marine was appointed as the assistant secretary of human resources; and Peter O'Rourke was appointed as a senior adviser to the secretary. Peter expressed his desire to become the under secretary for benefits, but after a few meetings with him, I was unconvinced that he had enough experience or expertise to run such a large part of the department. Furthermore, the career people who had worked with him in the past didn't feel he was a team player. After I recognized an urgent need to create an office on accountability, I decided Peter would be a better fit taking charge of that. I thought he seemed more suited to firing people than to working with them.

A later addition to the political team was Camilo Sandoval, who was originally assigned to the Department of the Treasury. But Treasury Secretary Mnuchin supposedly was said to have put him in the basement and ignored him, after which I received a call from Ike Perlmutter saying that Camilo would be a good addition to our team. He assured me that Camilo came highly recommended by Jared Kushner. Camilo had worked with Jared on the social media data during the campaign, and he was supposedly technically skilled. I confirmed this with Jared and then inquired internally whether any of our VA teams needed additional help. The VHA expressed an interest, and they brought Camilo in to work with them in building our new integrated operations center. He was not a great fit. After only a short time, no one in the VHA wanted to work with him, so we moved him to IT, where he was asked to assist the acting assistant secretary with our data systems. There, too, the team felt that Camilo was not a team player and was too committed to his own political agenda.

On most days, Jake, John, and sometimes others from this political group went across the street to the White House for meetings. I never heard anything about what was discussed, and I assumed that if it was something important, they would let me know. They never did. In retrospect, I wish I had paid more attention to these intrigues, but I had a great deal on my plate. I didn't want to waste time worrying about their political agendas and political games, and at the time, I didn't think they presented a personal threat to me.

The most atypical member of the beachhead team was Lynda Davis, a former army signal officer who had previously served as the deputy under secretary for military community and family policy in the Bush Department of Defense. She had worked as the executive vice president at the Tragedy Assistance Program for Survivors (TAPS), and she was the mother of a veteran. Lynda was all about mission, and as far as I could tell, she was there for all the right reasons. I asked her to take charge of our Veterans Experience Office, where she focused on the job and tended to stay away from office politics.

My relationship with the politicals was complicated. I understood that I needed them to support our reform initiatives, yet I knew I had never been their choice to be secretary. I also understood that they believed many of the VA's career leaders were part of the problem. The feeling was mutual; the career leadership didn't trust the politicals or want to work with them. I often found myself in the middle, trying to steer these two groups toward some semblance of progress.

In the same way that I had to forge some kind of relationship with the politicals, another important part of my job was maintaining a personal relationship with the president. At least he and I were never hard-pressed for conversation. The president's mind moved quickly, and he was just as likely to ask me about VA issues, health care, drug pricing, a solution for North Korea, or moving the embassy to Jerusalem. It was not unusual for him to call me at night to ask about something he'd just heard on television. Frankly, since the news did not always get the story right, I appreciated him reaching out to me to get my perspective.

Both privately and in public forums, the president often referred to me as the "100–0 man" and "my David." At many public events, he announced what a good job I was doing. Whenever he saw Merle, he made sure he told her she should be proud of me and that I was making a big difference at the VA. His trust and support enabled me to get a lot of important work done in my first year as secretary.

So while the president and I seemed to have a great working relationship, he often raised questions that I knew came either from the inside political team or from the outside VA "experts" at Mar-a-Lago. Once he said, "I hear the electronic record system you're pushing may not be so good." Another time it was, "I hear there are some really bad VAs out there. Why haven't we fixed them yet?" Again, I valued him telling me what he heard from others, because that gave me the opportunity to set the record straight on the facts. I never doubted the president's intention to do the right thing for veterans, but I was very concerned about where he was receiving his advice.

I certainly did not like the back-channel information on the VA that was circumventing me and getting directly to him, but it seemed I had no better choice than to keep Ike, Bruce, and Marc informed on the progress we were making so that when they communicated with the president—which they did very frequently—they could at least relay more accurate information. Keeping them in the loop was also necessary to minimize the number of calls I received from the White House, scolding me for not being in sufficient touch with the Mar-a-Lago trio and letting me know that they weren't happy. Maintaining close communication with the president was an essential part of my job, and I simply had to accept the terms and the mechanisms he chose.

On March 6, 2017, I met with the president and Jared Kushner, among others, in the Oval Office. Trump asked me first about Ike and if I was keeping him informed. He then asked how many people use the VA for health care. "Nine million," I answered. The president asked whether we should begin to close the VAs that were in poorer condition. Current legislation prohibited us from closing such facilities, but I informed him that we were working with Congress to implement a facility assessment and a process for addressing quality issues. "But this takes time," I explained.

He exclaimed, "So let's just do an executive order!"

"Mr. President, this is a legislative issue, so I don't think we can do that."

Then he offered, "Can't we just declare a national emergency?"

At that point, Jared chimed in, "Yes. We're still in a war, so we could."

I glanced around the room, hoping there might be someone else there who understood separation of powers, but to no avail. If anyone else did understand, nobody spoke up.

The following week, the White House sent over a candidate for the deputy secretary position named Sam Clovis. He had been a career air force officer, then worked in the defense industry, and then served as cochair of the Trump campaign. I interviewed him and thought he provided all the right answers. But I had heard of some troubling issues surfacing when he ran for statewide office in Iowa. After we had worked so hard to restore the reputation of the VA after 2014, I knew we could not afford to bring in someone who might do further damage.

Shortly after the interview with Clovis, I received dozens and dozens of unsolicited letters campaigning on his behalf, which only increased my concern. I dug a little deeper and made a number of calls. While I didn't learn anything specific, the awkward silences in response to my questions told me what I needed to know. I hit the pause button. Clovis ended up going to the Department of Agriculture, where, despite having few scientific credentials, he oversaw scientific research. After a few months on the job, he returned to his home state of Iowa.

The next man (and they were almost always men) the White House sent over for me to interview was a candidate to become the chief legal counsel for the VA. He had no management experience, and aside from having been a staff lawyer in a branch of government, he had no qualifications for such a complex job. The meeting lasted less than ten minutes, after which I notified the White House that he wasn't the right fit.

Each time I rejected a candidate sent by the White House, I could sense the politicals' growing displeasure. Apparently, they felt entitled to fill these positions with the people they wanted, regardless of my concerns. Clearly, we were using different selection criteria. They wanted like-minded partisans and usually people from the campaign. I was looking for candidates with knowledge and competence. The political appointees still couldn't figure out why I was secretary in the first place, and they were dead set against letting me add more "outside" players to the team.

In the hyperpartisan atmosphere of Washington, there was also friction among the veterans service organizations. In particular, the more traditional VSOs did not see Concerned Veterans of America as one of them but merely as a lobbying arm of the Koch brothers. In the Obama administration, CVA was not welcome at the table. Shortly before I arrived at the VA in 2015, I was told that Secretary McDonald once agreed to meet with the group, but it didn't go well, and there was no formal contact after that.

When I became secretary, I decided to take a different strategy. First, it was clear that the Trump administration found CVA congenial. I saw CVA representatives consistently at White House events, and in many cases, they were the only group chosen to represent veterans. Of course, Darin Selnick, a former CVA staffer, had made it clear that he planned to stay and take on a significant role.

For my part, I viewed the traditional VSO community as a valued partner but one that in some cases fell prey to groupthink. For that reason, I welcomed new ideas to challenge my thinking, even when they came from CVA.

I invited Dan Caldwell, the CVA executive director, along with other staff to meet with me. I told them I wanted to hear their ideas and work with them to reform the VA. I did not, however, invite them to join my regular VSO meetings, and I did not use them for formal input on policy initiatives or to distribute information to veteran audiences. I opened the door for them, but I was clear that they needed to earn a full seat at the table. I knew this was a risk, but I thought it was the right approach.

Like many risks, this one seemed to pay off at first but less so later on. I took CVA suggestions and input seriously, hoping they might help us make better decisions. Many of their ideas were reform minded, and I thought, when balanced with other points of view, might move the VA in the right direction. With the passage of time, though, it became all too clear to me that their approach was strictly "my way or the highway." I thought they had little interest in hearing other groups' perspectives and even less interest in compromise. From my perspective, they presented two choices: get on board with them or become the target of their next political attack.

For whatever reason, CVA's leadership often failed to take the time to understand the complexity of a situation or the background of an issue. Instead, they raced to be out in front giving opinions, even when their facts were wrong. I think it was a reflection of a young organization with less seasoned leaders trying hard to be relevant. Often, I found their public position on issues misguided and harsh, only to have private conversations with the same people who expressed a more moderate and reasoned point of view.

In early 2018, during the debate on renewing the legislation that provided more choice for where veterans could seek treatment, CVA characterized me as representing the status quo. This was, of course, far from the truth, and when I challenged them on it privately, they acknowledged that I was right. In public, though, their position remained unchanged. As a result, I perceived them less and less as allies working with me for positive change. I still thought their point of view deserved to be heard but wished they were more transparent about their genuine agenda and their source of funding—the ultraconservative Koch brothers.

17

Getting Through to the President

A NOTHER IMPORTANT UNDERCURRENT IN THE CHANGING ATMOSPHERE at the VA had to do with the degree of choice veterans would be allowed to exercise in their health care decisions.

I've already mentioned the problem in timely access to care that had reached crisis proportions at the Phoenix VA. Partly as a result of that crisis, Congress passed the Veterans' Access, Choice, and Accountability Act of 2014 ("Choice Act"). This legislation authorized any veteran unable to schedule an appointment within thirty days, or any veteran who would otherwise have to travel an unreasonable distance to be seen at a VA facility, to receive care from approved providers outside the VA system.

The Choice Act had been authorized for only three years, and it was scheduled to expire in early August 2017. Without a continued authorization of funding, I feared a return to long wait times for veterans. On March 7, 2017, the House held a hearing on reauthorization, during which I advocated for continuing Choice and for other reforms to make the program work better. I sensed a good amount of support.

The next day, I flew to West Palm Beach to speak at a conference on developing new therapies for mental health disorders. Merle flew down separately, and we were picked up from the hotel to have cocktails with Ike and Lori Perlmutter at their apartment.

President Trump had told me about the Perlmutters' 360-degree views of the ocean and instructed me to make sure we saw their aquarium. The Perlmutters collect exotic species of fish, gathered from the Red Sea to Australia, but so much special equipment was required to maintain their survival that it looked like they were operating a fish intensive care unit.

The president's relationship with the trio of Ike Perlmutter, Bruce Moskowitz, and Marc Sherman—and by extension their relationship with me—had been reported extensively by the press, which further politicized debates over the future of the VA, including highly charged issues like Choice. In just about every conversation I had with him, though, the president asked if Ike was "happy" or "helping." It was still not clear to me exactly how Ike should be "helping" me. I was aware that the three men met with the president or with White House staff to discuss VA issues without me, much as the political appointees did. I often heard about these private sessions from senior White House insiders ranging from Jared Kushner, to Avi Berkowitz and Stephen Miller, to John Kelly, Reed Cornish, and Andrew Bremberg. Again, this reinforced the idea that I should pay attention to the advice of these Mar-a-Lago men. But the clearest insistence came from Perlmutter, Moskowitz, and Sherman themselves. They reminded me again and again that I had better move fast, because the White House was impatient with the pace of reform.

With so many different voices demanding my attention, trying to follow the president's policy agenda became somewhat of a guessing game. During the campaign, Trump had released a ten-point plan for VA reform, which I took as my marching orders, and I made sure to address each point. The last item on that list was the twenty-four-hour White House hotline, which we implemented in early 2018, with a fully staffed call center dedicated to addressing veterans' concerns. As I ticked off each item on the list, I felt confident that we were further along than anyone could've anticipated. Each time I saw the president, he told me himself just how proud he was of the VA's progress and how we

were doing more to help veterans than any previous administration. By the end of my first year, the VA had more legislation
passed by Congress and signed by the president than almost any
other agency. Yet Ike continually hammered the point that we
were not getting the job done and that as a result, according to
him, I was on thin ice.

There seemed to be a large disconnect, but knowing that Ike,
Bruce, and Marc had the president's ear in ways that I did not,
even as his cabinet secretary, I made efforts to be responsive to
their advice and feedback. These gentlemen were, in my opinion,
well intentioned, even if sometimes off base with their advice. I
never felt that they pursued anything for personal gain. Truthfully,
I think they mostly wanted to feel useful and that they were making a positive impact.

On the other hand, I also knew the limitations placed on private citizens meddling in government affairs, and I was always cautious to make sure that these three did not cross the line. At least
in the beginning, I was appreciative of their input because each of
them appeared to be committed to making progress and addressing problems that would result in improved care for veterans. I
didn't take advice or recommendations from them as a group, but
only as individuals, because they otherwise might have constituted
a "federal advisory committee," which required public oversight.
I also tried to be the primary point of contact with them, serving
as a buffer to limit their involvement with VA personnel, because
I feared others might interpret their suggestions as orders from
the president. Still, I knew if I didn't promptly respond to them,
the next call would be from the White House, asking why I hadn't
been in touch.

My biggest complaint—at least in the beginning—about having to work with these three men was simply the amount of my
time that was eaten up dealing with them. Ike often called several
times a day, and I demonstrated earlier just how insistent he can
be on the phone. Jared Kushner joked that Ike had become my
adopted father. Adding to that sense of wasted time was the fact

that often their advice was unusable, because none of these men seemed to have much of an understanding of how the VA worked, nor did they possess any health system management experience. Bruce was a physician and knew a great many people in health care around the country, but he was a solo practitioner whose knowledge of management practices was arguably dated. The others clearly had good general business knowledge and plenty of street smarts, but this was often inapplicable to the complexity of running the VA. Most concerning was that these VA "advisers" had never even been to a VA facility (which was also true of the president and his senior staff). Because of this, while I was always responsive to their communications, I felt no obligation to follow the trio's advice and often did not. There were certainly times when their advice was helpful, but primarily I saw our relationship as a way to update and inform the individuals who supplied much of the president's information to him. In this way, I hoped to ensure that what the president was hearing was at least reasonably accurate. Personally, I would have preferred to communicate with the president directly, but I knew that multiple meetings were conducted without me, and I had no choice but to work within that established framework.

I was reminded of this bizarre dynamic on March 17, 2017, during a televised meeting, when the president asked me on air if I was coming to Mar-a-Lago over the weekend to discuss the VA. This was the first I had heard of this VA meeting. Confused and unsure what to say, I smiled widely while shaking my head, indicating that I would not be attending the meeting. The press got a kick out of this. "Why, and with whom, was the president having a meeting about the VA if the VA secretary wasn't going to be there?" was essentially their question. Later, my daughter, Jennie, texted me that my wide smile and shaking head had become a meme and had gone viral. Once I figured out what a meme was and googled the meme she was talking about, I admitted that it was pretty hilarious. But more importantly, the incident made clear to me once again—this time publicly—that there was a "second track" of VA decision-making led by the president's alternative advisers that didn't include me.

As I mentioned earlier, Ike had never visited a VA. I decided it was time to change that if he was going to be offering advice on veterans' issues. So while I was in West Palm, I took him and his wife to a local VA, located just a few miles from their home. They seemed genuinely surprised at how beautiful the facility was and how well it was operating. Ike asked all of the veterans he passed, "Do you like it here? What don't you like? What complaints do you have?" He seemed adamant about finding dissatisfaction, or better yet, horror stories. "Come on, tell me the truth," he'd say, "I want to know." But all he encountered was consistent praise for the services and care received. When he pressed VA staff, they uniformly reported that VA care was far superior to that of the private sector, because the VA was able to focus on the patient without the distraction of managing insurance and other business aspects endemic to private care. I got the distinct sense that Ike was perplexed to see the VA working so well. For him, I think, it was an unsettling clash between what was and what he imagined. To my knowledge, that was the first and last VA facility he ever visited.

18

Dark Clouds in the Sunshine State

W HILE THE CONDITIONS IKE SAW AT THE WEST PALM VA WERE
far better than he had anticipated, not everything there was
in order. The week after our visit, a recently elected first-term Florida congressman, Brian Mast, showed up at the facility with a ham-
mer, nails, and poster-sized framed portraits of President Trump
and myself, which he proceeded to hang in the VA medical center
lobby. Security stopped him and removed the pictures, but not
before Fox News covered the story.

Congressman Mast, a Republican representing Florida's Eighteenth District, had been a bomb-disposal technician in the army
when he lost both his legs to an explosive device. A staunch Trump
supporter, he was upset that, two months into the administration,
no official portrait of President Trump hung in the VA lobby. He
blamed this on a lack of cooperation among union members who
opposed the president.

After the Fox News coverage of Mast's guerilla picture-hanging,
calls and letters piled into my office, exploring conspiracy theories,
including one that the absence of a portrait was because an Obama
holdover was in charge of the agency. The implication was that I
didn't recognize President Trump as our legitimate leader.

What Mast and Fox News didn't know, however, was that my
staff had contacted the White House about hanging an official

portrait of President Trump in VA headquarters immediately
after his inauguration. We tried again now. After making renewed
requests for an official picture of the president and getting no
response, I directed all VA facilities to print a copy of the presidential photo from the White House website, blow it up, frame
it, and hang it in the lobby. Even after this extra effort, the media
stories continued. Out of curiosity and concern, I went to the
lobbies of other government agencies in DC—Interior, Agriculture, Commerce—and found that they too had no pictures of the
president, again because the White House had not supplied them.
Even so, it seemed that only the VA was targeted in this story. I
continued to request the official photo, but it was not until September that we were able to replace our unofficial pictures with
the official ones.

A wounded veteran himself, Congressman Mast was very
involved in issues affecting his local VA, and I met with him on
several occasions. During one of these conversations, he suggested
that he should have an office at the local VA medical center, which
he said would allow him to be of greater help to veterans. Our
lawyers were concerned that this accommodation might indicate a
political preference and therefore wouldn't be legal. After discussions within the agency, I was able to get the lawyers on board—as
long as there was equal access to all political candidates, the space
would be shared by any elected official who wanted access, and
there was no political activity of any type occurring on site. Congressman Mast became the first elected official with an office at a
VA, and since then, others have followed suit across the country.

But there were other problems in the Sunshine State. Before
leaving Florida, I made a visit to the Miami VA, which was bustling
with activity. When I met with the team and reviewed their statis-
tics, it became clear that the number of individuals they served was
declining year to year, which made no sense in a place like Miami,
which had a growing population of retired veterans. It turned out
that the reason for the decline was that the facility had very limited
parking, and it was hard to reach the VA via public transportation.

The city had an empty plot of land adjacent to the VA, though, and the VA had been trying to purchase it for quite some time in order to expand their parking lot and be able to accommodate more people. Apparently, the city knew they had a captive buyer and wanted to extract a premium. So there it sat. Vacant.

I was not happy with this impasse, so I called Congresswoman Wasserman Schultz. She and I then contacted the mayor's office, where a staffer promised to look into the matter. A flurry of activity followed, including a number of meetings with the city, and for a while it looked like things were moving. But despite the congresswoman's efforts, the plot of land remained vacant as of the time I left government, and Miami veterans were still struggling to find parking spots.

19

Unconventional Cabinet Meetings

O N THE FRIDAY EVENING THAT MERLE AND I WERE PLANNING TO fly home from Florida, we got a call from the White House saying that the president would like us to join him for lunch the next day at his club in Virginia. The president spent most weekends in West Palm Beach, and yet the one weekend we were in Florida, he wanted us to join him back near Washington! I was traveling on a government ticket, which is always changeable, but Merle had bought her own nonrefundable ticket. All the same, this wasn't an invitation we could refuse.

Our new flight was delayed due to a malfunctioning onboard computer, and I was getting anxious that we were going to be late for the lunch. To save time, Merle changed in the airplane bathroom.

We raced to the club and went upstairs to find Wilbur and Hillary Ross, John and Karen Kelly, and Steve Mnuchin and his fiancée, Louise Linton, already there. When it was announced that POTUS was arriving, the Secret Service informed us that the president was not wearing a tie, so we all removed ours. The president then came up the steps to say hello before showing us his golf course and the view of the Potomac where he'd cleared all the brush away.

In addition to the secretaries and their spouses and the chief of staff, Steve Bannon and Sean Spicer joined us for lunch. We had not yet had a real cabinet meeting, but with five cabinet members and the senior staff, this felt like a dress rehearsal. Trump asked Spicer to let the press corps in, and suddenly we were swarmed by fifty reporters and photographers. Before dismissing the press, the president jokingly asked if any of them wanted membership applications to his club. He then proceeded to launch into an informal first meeting of the cabinet, throwing out a wide range of seemingly unrelated topics and going around the table to get everyone's responses. This interactive style would foreshadow future meetings with the president.

Calling the first few months of the Trump administration disorganized, even chaotic, would be kind. Absent regular meetings with the White House, each cabinet secretary pretty much found his or her own way of communicating with the president and getting things done.

Prior to being sworn in, my only meeting with Reince Priebus was our brief lunch prior to my *SNL*-esque experience at Trump Tower. But I got to know Reince better after inauguration, when he officially became the White House chief of staff. I wanted to be respectful of his role in controlling the president's schedule and access to him, so I tried to coordinate my communications with the White House through his office. But Reince appeared overwhelmed, as almost anyone in his position would be. The only way to ensure that he would return my call was to label my message "urgent," but not wanting to be the cabinet secretary who cried wolf, I tried not to do this often.

I also learned that if I waited to be invited to White House meetings or events, I might be waiting a long time. So occasionally I simply stopped by, relying on my cabinet secretary badge that granted me White House access. Reince appeared generally comfortable with my unexpected arrivals. Sometimes, after an informal drop-in to talk about issues, the president would ask me to come into the Oval Office and participate in subsequent conversations. He seemed to like having me around, though quite frankly, he may have simply enjoyed having a larger audience. Occasionally, he asked for my opinion on topics completely unrelated to my areas of expertise, but mostly I just listened, fascinated. Other cabinet members and senior staff could often be found doing the same thing.

Obviously, I had more than enough work to do back at my office. But I, like my fellow cabinet members, was trying to figure out how this White House was going to work and how we were supposed to fit into it. Comparing it to the Obama White House, I thought the Trump administration would've benefitted from more structure and formality as well as fewer colorful characters. Given the lack of order that I saw during these visits, I wasn't surprised when the press began to report a steady stream of leaks coming from 1600 Pennsylvania Avenue.

The first official meeting of the cabinet was not until March 13, 2017—nearly two months after inauguration—and it too became a lightning rod. The Cabinet Room is adjacent to the president's suite and the Oval Office, with windows overlooking the Rose Garden. It has a large conference table with oversized brown leather chairs. Seating is assigned in order of presidential succession, and each chair displays a small plaque indicating the agency of each respective secretary. It's customary for each secretary to pay a premium to purchase his or her respective chair at the end of his or her service. Because seats for senior staff also line the walls, the room is often so crowded that it's hard to move around.

Prior to the president's arrival, there was often a short briefing by a senior White House official. For example, Don McGahn, White House counsel, might speak to us about clearance for participating in outside events, or Marc Short, director of legislative affairs, might provide an update. Because of concern about leaks, we were always instructed to leave our cell phones outside the room in a wooden box located near the entrance.

When the president entered, everyone stood and remained standing until he took his seat. At this first meeting, the president let the press corps into the room, and suddenly thirty reporters were clustered in front of the president. The president began the meeting with some remarks and then asked each member of the cabinet if he or she wanted to say anything, starting to his left with Secretary Mattis.

We had not been prepared for this. As we went around the room, most of the cabinet members used their time to thank the president for the opportunity to serve him and our nation and to praise his leadership. The media reported this comically as a kind of fulsome lovefest where secretary after secretary referred to the "blessing" of being able to serve the president. I kept my comments focused on the millions of veterans I served, not the person I report to. Still, we as a group were widely mocked, and I could understand why.

Nevertheless, I looked forward to cabinet meetings. It was one of the few times the department heads got to see each other. Many of us arrived twenty or so minutes early to mingle and catch up. Each cabinet meeting started the same way, with the president speaking to the press corps, after which one member of the cabinet opened the meeting with a prayer.

There was almost always a prepared agenda for the meeting, often accompanied by handouts with supporting information. But we rarely followed the script. President Trump doesn't follow a script. Instead, he used the time to talk about whatever was on his mind. Most often this was something that just appeared in the news. Occasionally, toward the last half of the meeting, we got to the formal agenda. Usually three cabinet members presented a summary of their most important issues. The president often interjected or asked questions. Meetings typically were scheduled for an hour but frequently lasted longer.

Sometimes the cabinet met on the weekends to discuss issues in a more relaxed setting. One weekend, the president invited us to Camp David. That Saturday afternoon, we were driven to an army base near Washington, where two Osprey helicopters landed. Merle and I loaded quickly through the back of one of these aircraft. When it took off, its rotating blades lifted us vertically, but once in the air, the blades rotated to move us horizontally like an airplane. A marine was positioned at the back door, which stayed wide open the whole ride. We arrived at Camp David fifteen minutes later. By comparison, when my security detail had driven me to Camp David several months earlier, it took an hour and forty-five minutes.

Merle and I were assigned to share a cabin with the director of the Environmental Protection Agency, Scott Pruitt, and his wife, Marlyn. Called Rosewood, our cabin contained two bedrooms and a small shared living area with a rustic but contemporary flair. Each couple was assigned a golf cart, which displayed our names on the front. A military aide was available to drive for us if we wished, although I chose to drive. Since becoming secretary, I missed the freedom of driving my own car. I happily settled for a golf cart.

That afternoon, I went out to shoot skeet with Vice President Pence and Secretary Mnuchin. I had never done it before, but somehow I hit six out of ten of the clay disks.

On another trip to Camp David, we all gathered in the private screening room to watch a movie. It was there that the president told us how he brought the bust of Churchill back to the Oval Office after President Obama removed it. The president sat in the front row of the screening room, and I sat two seats away from him. As we watched the movie, *Darkest Hour,* I could not help but notice some similarities between Churchill and the president. Both went against popular opinion at times, and both were leaders who followed their gut, even when unpopular. It didn't surprise me that when the president donned a Churchill-like hat during his state visit to London in June 2019, the press had a field day comparing the two men.

The movie finished at midnight, and we all retired to our cabins. For some, the night wasn't over. It was so cold that most of us used our fireplaces to keep the cabins warm, but the Carsons and the Purdues each neglected to open their chimney flues. This triggered the fire alarms, which kept the marines busy for a while, and there was so much smoke in the Purdues' cabin that they had to relocate at 12:30 in the morning.

20

Rallying for Trump

O N April 26, THE PRESIDENT WAS COMING TO VA HEADQUARTERS at 4:30 p.m. to sign an executive order that would allow me to establish a new Office of Accountability and Whistleblower Protection. This new office signaled that we were serious about changing the culture at the VA. It was a precursor to the accountability legislation that would pass a few months later and enable the VA to terminate employees who violated their duties to the agency.

I tried to get the president to sign the order at a VA hospital because I thought it was important for him to see veterans and talk to them about their experiences. But after multiple requests, the White House informed me that the president preferred to visit VA headquarters.

It was unusual for a sitting president to come to VA headquarters, and we worked closely with the Secret Service to guarantee his security. For aesthetic purposes, we rented special blue drapes to cover the walls of the hallways Trump was going to walk through, as well as a big white awning to cover the entrance on H Street where his motorcade was going to drop him off. We used a lottery system to select VA staff to attend, and we invited key congressional and VSO leadership, along with the press.

By the time the president and vice president arrived, Merle and I were standing at the curb to greet them and escort them to a green room stocked with the president's favorites: Tic Tacs, Hershey bars, Lays potato chips, and Diet Coke. The Secret Service took Merle to a seat in the front row alongside Ike and Lori Perlmutter, who had flown in for the event. A lot of veterans were seated along the walls. I entered and made a few remarks before introducing the vice president. The vice president said a few words before introducing the president. After the president spoke, he signed the executive order and gave Ike the pen.

After the presidential motorcade left the VA, traffic was tied up for an hour, but the day wasn't over for us. We attended a reception for the Bob and Lee Woodruff Foundation at the St. Regis Hotel, where I was asked to speak. Bob is the TV journalist who, not long after being named coanchor of *ABC World News*, sustained a traumatic brain injury while covering the war in Iraq. His foundation does research on brain injuries and provides support for post-9/11 veterans who have experienced them. Several members of Congress were present at the reception. I gave a short speech, after which a disabled veteran gave me a small copper statue of a bicycle with square wheels—a symbol of what it's like to live with a disability.

The president made it clear that he did not want cabinet members to attend the White House Correspondents' Dinner scheduled for the following weekend. Not subscribing to this type of partisan boycott and knowing that the event would be hilarious, I was planning to attend anyway. That is, until I got a call from the White House. The president was inviting Merle and me to travel with him on the evening of the dinner to one of his rallies in Harrisburg, Pennsylvania. Before the rally, we were going to visit a manufacturing plant that employed a number of veterans. I was told that the VA secretary was a key asset on this trip. The timing, of course, was almost certainly engineered to distract media attention from the Correspondents' Dinner, where the jokes were likely to be at the president's expense.

Merle and I were picked up at our apartment at 3:30 p.m. and driven to Andrews Air Force Base. Once aboard Air Force One, we were greeted by the pilot and then escorted to our seats in the conference room, where we encountered Safra Catz, the CEO of Oracle; Hilary and Wilbur Ross; Steve Bannon; Kellyanne Conway; Hope Hicks; and Stephen Miller.

When the president boarded the plane, he went directly to the conference room to find the group and asked, "Have you guys seen this plane? Anybody want a tour?" Everyone said yes, and he was delighted. "Come on, let's go!" he said with an inviting wave of his hand. He took us upstairs to the cockpit, where the pilots were in the process of taxiing. There was one empty seat behind the four air force officers, so the president pointed to Merle and said, "Why don't you sit there?" Somewhat surprised to have visitors during takeoff, the pilots obliged and gave Merle a set of headphones so she could listen to the tower giving instructions as we were lifting off.

Leaving Merle in the cockpit, the president and I returned to the conference room, where, sitting by his side, I had a nice lunch of Maryland crab cakes. (As per government regulations, I received a bill a few months later. In fact, passengers receive a bill for the meal whether or not they decide to eat it, so I figured I might as well.)

It was only a forty-minute flight from Washington to Harrisburg, where we were met by a VA security team who drove up to supplement the presidential convoy. We then traveled by motorcade to the Ames Company in Camp Hill, Pennsylvania, with state police leading the way and people lining the streets, either cheering or protesting.

The Ames Company produced approximately 85 percent of the wheelbarrows sold in the United States, which made it a perfect place for the president to talk about his America First policies of bringing back manufacturing jobs. The factory workers chanted,

"USA . . . USA!" as we began a tour of the facility, after which the managers gave the president a golden shovel. He promised to keep his new trophy in the Oval Office for the next eight years and then bring it back to New York City. Merle and I visited with the veteran employees. Then the president signed two executive orders, one calling for a review of all existing trade agreements, the other establishing an Office of Trade and Manufacturing. He read a prepared statement in which he noted the company's history helping "to build our nation." Apparently, they had produced tools used to construct the Statue of Liberty, the Empire State Building, and the Hoover Dam. Then we were all whisked away to the car to head to the rally.

The green room at the Harrisburg arena was stocked with Diet Coke, potato chips, Hershey bars, and Tic Tacs, as per usual, but this time there were also "Make America Great Again" red hats for the president to sign and hand out. The president spoke for forty-five minutes. Given the political nature of the rally, Merle and I stayed backstage, but we could hear the cheers, except when he mentioned the Democrats, which elicited boos. The crowd was wild for whatever the president said. Three fights broke out.

Once back aboard Air Force One, the president came into the conference room beaming and asked, "What did you think?" He was high on the crowd's energy. Everyone told him he gave a great speech. Then the stewards wheeled in a cake with the presidential seal on it to celebrate the first hundred days of the Trump administration.

As he cut the cake, the president said, "Isn't Air Force One really something? I mean, we all have our own private planes and have for years, but this is something else."

Merle and I exchanged looks. Not only were we some of the only ones who didn't own a private plane, but we had never even flown on one.

My security detail met us at the airport, and we got home at 10:20 p.m. I was up the next morning before dawn to start another busy day.

21

Beyond Health Care: In the Shoes of a Cabinet Secretary

ONE AFTERNOON IN THE SPRING OF 2017, A MEMBER OF MY STAFF barged into my office, almost out of breath. "Secretary Shulkin!" she huffed. "We have an urgent call from the White House. They are gathering the cabinet now. There's no time to get you to the Situation Room, so you'll need to connect from VA."

I logged on to the secure line to the Situation Room from the designated location at the Department of Veterans Affairs. I could literally see the White House from my office window, but we couldn't spare the few minutes it would take for me to get there.

The emergency involved cyberattacks originating from Europe and directed toward hospitals worldwide. Fortunately, by working across government agencies and taking some quick preventive actions, we were able to contain this series of attacks.

As secretary, my portfolio had expanded beyond health care to include situations like the one I just described, all of the benefit programs, and the management of cemeteries. Fortunately, the National Cemetery Administration (NCA), with 135 facilities across the country, was exceptionally well run. More than four million veterans are buried in the VA's cemeteries, and the NCA is consistently ranked higher than other government organizations in customer service by J.D. Power.

Even though complaints and controversies concerning NCA were rare, one emerged in early 2017 regarding the Crown Hill Cemetery in Indianapolis. The VA had purchased a 14.75-acre wooded lot, where it planned to build a columbarium that would hold approximately twenty-five thousand urns. The problem was that the trees on this new acreage were in some cases three hundred to five hundred years old. The Indiana Forest Alliance and some other environmental groups were strongly against the VA destroying any of these trees. On the day the land was scheduled to be bulldozed, protesters climbed the trees and strapped themselves onto their thickest branches. I learned about this when my mailbox flooded with angry residents demanding that we stop the project. Although each protest typically brought out at most 250 protesters, the email campaign expanded the group's impact to a far greater number. Many of those involved were veterans.

I met with the NCA team, which was dead set against accommodation. They were adamant about having "every legal right to proceed with the project and not letting a bunch of protesters tell us what to do." I didn't like the idea of bad blood between us and the community, so I asked Ron Walters, the acting under secretary of memorial affairs, to find a solution. Ron went out to Indianapolis and spoke to the activists in community forums and to local landholders. He brought back a plan involving a land swap with another cemetery that would allow us to build our columbarium on their land while maintaining the wooded acreage. It was a win-win. Some thought it made me look weak to give in to the activists, but I was pleased to find a solution acceptable to both sides.

That same month, I had dinner with the heads of several of the veteran organizations. In addition to keeping them informed about what VA headquarters was planning and wanting them to update me about pressing issues veterans were experiencing, I thought it was important for each of them to hear from the other organizations. I was really heartened when, the next day, these VSOs made the statement that "David Shulkin is not just the president's secretary of veterans affairs, but *our* secretary of veterans affairs." That's exactly how I wanted it to be.

While I experienced satisfying moments like this, not everything was smooth and harmonious. The political appointees were beginning to show their muscle, and more than ever, it was becoming evident that they wanted Trump loyalists in place, regardless of their qualifications. For example, they let me know that they weren't supporting Dr. Poonam Alaigh as the nominee for under secretary of health. This was after the commission had interviewed her and moved her name forward. I knew Poonam to be an incredibly competent professional, but even more importantly, I knew her as someone I could always count on to focus on the veterans' best interests. She had demonstrated her commitment and effectiveness throughout her time as acting under secretary, and in my opinion, she was the best candidate for the job. None of that seemed to matter to these narrowly focused Trump partisans.

Still in the month of May, I flew to Boston for an event called the Brain Trust, a collaborative forum started by Secretary McDonald that brought together the VA, academia, and industry to find ways to help veterans who had experienced brain injury or mental health issues. Soliciting help from industry was still something new for the VA, but I felt it was essential for us to make progress in areas such as brain injury, where effective therapies were scarce. The Brain Trust reception in Boston was held at Fenway Park and was well attended by just the kind of people we needed to advance the cause. I was able to meet committed corporate leaders such as Jeff Immelt, CEO of General Electric, and Joe Robinson, senior vice president of Philips North America.

As under secretary, I had visited the Bush Institute in 2016, and while there, I had the opportunity to seek input and partnerships with industry (mostly pharmaceutical companies) and ask for the kind of focused effort on brain injury and PTSD that the country made in response to the AIDS crisis and is currently directing at cancer. The Bush Institute had gathered about a hundred pharmaceutical leaders to meet with me and discuss possibilities. President Bush was expected to address the group, so I waited for him at the front of a receiving line, hoping to speak with him before he was engulfed by the crowd. When he appeared, I tried my best not to laugh. We were all in suits, and he was wearing shorts, running shoes, and a sweatshirt.

"Sorry I underdressed," he laughed. "Didn't get the memo." Apparently, he was going to an SMU basketball game that night and wanted to be comfortable. "Why don't you take off that tie and unbutton your shirt?" he suggested to me. In my many encounters with President Bush, he was always like this: humble, informal, and able to relate to people on a human level.

I don't think you can be commander-in-chief, or even secretary of the VA for that matter, and not be forever affected by the many brave men and women under your watch. With a special burden of sending soldiers into harm's way, I believe that all presidents have a unique understanding of these issues. As I got to know President Bush better during my time as secretary, I witnessed him perform several acts of kindness outside of public view. It didn't surprise me that he took the time to send me a handwritten note of gratitude for my service after I left the VA. The note is framed and hangs in my family's home outside of Philadelphia.

A few days after the Brain Trust event, I was scheduled to appear on MSNBC's *Morning Joe*. To prepare, I watched the program's episode from the previous day and saw a clip of President Trump saying that the Russia investigation was the worst witch hunt ever suffered by a politician. One commentator said that anyone associated with the president should refuse to be a soldier in his administration and get out now. I felt a little uneasy, as though the television was speaking directly to me, but I reminded myself that although I was serving "at the pleasure of the president," the people I was really serving were the nation's nine million veterans.

After *Morning Joe,* I flew to Ohio to give the commencement address at the University of Cincinnati Medical School. From there, I wanted to go home to Philadelphia, but the VA travel staff said it would cost $400 more to fly directly from Cincinnati to Philadelphia rather than back to Washington. Wanting to be above reproach, I flew from Cincinnati to Washington and then paid for my own train ticket to Philadelphia.

Over the weekend, I went to the park next to our Philadelphia house with my kids to practice throwing a baseball, because I had been invited to throw the first pitch for the Washington Nationals' home opener on May 25, 2017. At first, my aim was pretty bad. However, with Jennie leading the practice, critiquing my throwing motion, and commanding me to do better, I quickly improved. In my defense, I hadn't thrown a baseball since the late 1990s, when my batters were my two children under the age of ten. (By the next week, when I practiced with my security detail in Washington, I was much more confident in my pitch.)

Then, within two days, I went from the playground to a house-warming party at the luxurious home of Wilbur Ross, the secretary of commerce. His wife, Hilary, is a major player in Washington society, so *everyone* was there. But even in social settings like this, I often found myself having to defend the VA from unfair criticism. Dr. Susan Blumenthal, a former rear admiral in the Public Health Service and wife of Massachusetts senator Ed Markey, approached and pulled out her phone to show me a *Boston Herald* front-page story. At issue was the Boston VA's supposed misdiagnosis of the cause of a marine veteran's seizures until a doctor at Massachusetts General Hospital pointed out a mass on a brain scan. I already knew about this and had requested that the image be reviewed by independent radiologists, who found that the "mass" was merely an artifact of the technology. I thanked Susan for raising the issue and explained that I often dealt with situations like this where the media ran with stories without the full set of facts. I also mentioned how hard it was for me to fix the VA when I was always getting pulled away from the real problems in order to manage manufactured problems like this.

On Tuesday, I met with a number of senators on the Hill before Merle and I headed to dinner with Jake and Jennifer Tapper. Jake, the CNN anchor, had gone to the same small high school outside of Philadelphia as Merle, and she and Jennifer had recently become friends through their membership in International Club One—a Washington women's group for spouses of ambassadors, members of Congress, cabinet secretaries, Supreme Court justices, and prominent media figures. Jake and I were friendly to each other despite our own sometimes conflicting positions. Just a few days earlier, he had given a scathing report on the VA. We didn't discuss that at dinner. Merle and I always enjoyed the time we spent with the Tappers. Still, this purely social occasion had a slightly "covert operations" feel to it, especially because of the administration's concern about leaks and its hostility toward CNN in general and Jake in particular. I made sure never to give him privileged information, either on or off the record. What I didn't realize was that my schedule was being shared with the politicals at the VA, who in turn shared it with the White House.

Thursday, May 25, was Federal Workforce Day at Nationals Park, but rain was in the forecast, so my big moment throwing the first pitch was moved up from 4:15 to 12:15 p.m., which meant that my whole schedule had to be rearranged. Jennie was starting as a summer associate at the law firm of Skadden Arps down the street from the VA, so I took her to the ballpark with me. My practice paid off, because I managed to nail a strike right over the plate! Afterward, I met with veterans attending the game.

This was the week leading up to Memorial Day weekend, but Merle decided to stay in Philly a little longer to attend her Bryn Mawr reunion. This was unusual because, knowing how important it was for veterans to see that my family was also dedicated to them, she was almost always by my side at public events.

Merle and Danny arrived on Saturday to spend the weekend with Jennie and me. Our first big event for the holiday in Washington was a motorcycle ride sponsored by Rolling Thunder, an advocacy group working to account for prisoners of war and those missing in action from all US conflicts. The event began in 1988, with 2,500 participants following a preset route through the capital—leaving the Pentagon parking lot at noon, crossing the Memorial Bridge, and ending at the Vietnam Veterans Memorial. By 2017, ridership reached 350,000.

I was asked to attend the event, but I didn't want to just give a speech. I wanted to ride with the veterans. When I was a teenager, I owned a small 125-cc bike and was excited about the chance to ride a Harley for a good cause. Fortunately, one of my security guys, Joe Futch, was a rider and was happy to take me out to practice before the event. Of course, there were six security agents with me in the empty VA Medical Center parking lot, making sure I didn't hurt myself while practicing.

On the morning of the Rolling Thunder ride, my security detail and a team of veterans on motorcycles greeted us outside our apartment building. There was a Harley waiting for me. Merle and Jennie had leather jackets and bandannas to wear, and we all sported boots and Rolling Thunder T-shirts. I thought we were going to start riding from the Pentagon, but apparently the plan was to start from our apartment. Merle was very nervous about this, since it meant I would be riding on the highway. I hopped on my bike, and Jennie wisely chose to ride with a veteran in his midsixties, figuring that he was almost certainly a better rider than I was. I loved this kind of day, where I could spend time with the veterans and my family at the same time.

When we got to the Pentagon, there were masses of bikers sporting long hair, tattoos, cigars, and denim jackets with military patches. We got off our bikes for a few moments to meet some of them, and Jennie and Danny cracked up when a line formed to take pictures with me. It never became less weird to them that their dad was now a celebrity in some circles. I said a few words to the group gathered around me, not realizing that I was standing next to Rex Tillerson. Given that he was decked out in biker gear like everyone else, I didn't recognize him. My security guy later told me, "I thought you were being awfully unfriendly to Tillerson." Then again, Rex had said nothing to me either, which in retrospect was not surprising. Rex was never terribly interactive.

When the ride from the Pentagon started, I was at the very front, right behind the motorcycle police, with my security detail following in their cars. The route was lined with people cheering and waving American flags. At my level of motorcycle proficiency, I was concerned about staying upright while using one hand to wave, but the crowds were so enthusiastic that I couldn't help myself. Somehow I managed not to fall off. By the time we got to the end of the route, the clear skies had transformed into buckets of rain, and I still had to deliver a speech out on the mall about the meaning of this event.

Fortunately, the rain lightened a bit as we made our way to the reflecting pool by the Lincoln Memorial. There was a tent for Gold Star Mothers (those with a son or daughter killed during active service) and for Blue Star Families (those with a close relative serving in the armed forces). We walked through both tents, and I was swarmed by people with issues to raise and favors to ask. It's always been important to me to hear directly from veterans and those close to veterans in order to understand what issues are most important and to focus on resolving them.

After this, we changed clothes and proceeded to Speaker Paul Ryan's reception at the Capitol to greet veterans and join them for some hot dogs and American flag cookies. Then we stepped out on the West Lawn and took our seats for the Memorial Day concert. It started to rain again, but staff handed out ponchos. The concert was a moving tribute to the veterans, complete with songs and clips from documentaries. *What a difference a year makes,* I thought. Last year, Merle and I were invited to this concert only at the last minute, and this year I was the speaker. After the concert, we stopped at the after-party, where I had been asked to speak to veterans and their families. We then went home to get some sleep before an early-morning pickup the next day.

Memorial Day itself began for me with another appearance on *Fox and Friends* with Pete Hegseth. I was starting to feel almost comfortable with Pete, and I even thought he might stop his public attacks on the VA. On the air, he asked me about the president's first trip abroad and then about wait times at the VA. I was able to respond candidly about the improvements we'd made. I was home by 8:00 a.m. with forty-five minutes to spare before heading over to the vice president's residence at the Naval Observatory. Having this kind of down time was rare for me, and I paced the small apartment, making conversation and getting in my family's way as they tried to eat breakfast and get ready for the day's events.

At the vice president's residence, we met with a group of disabled veterans from Project Hero who were about to ride bicycles two hundred miles to Virginia Beach. They had all sorts of adaptive equipment to accommodate for missing limbs and other disabilities. Karen Pence said a prayer for them. We were getting accustomed to just how many prayers there were in this administration—especially when the Pences were in attendance. By the time we arrived at Arlington Memorial Cemetery, there was a long line of cars. We got out, and Merle and Jennie each received a military escort to Secretary Mattis's box, where we were seated as guests. The president gave a salute to General Kelly, who was sitting in front of us, and told the crowd how the general had lost a son in Afghanistan. Karen Kelly was not there, telling Merle earlier that she didn't think she could handle it emotionally. At the start of the ceremony, the cabinet officials were lined up, with Merle and me at the front. The VA representatives stood in the first and second position in the front row. The Department of Defense official was on the left and the VA official on the right. John Kelly marched in and stood next to me. There was a twenty-one-gun salute before Secretary Mattis walked in with the president. A bugler played taps while they laid the wreath.

Later that week, Merle and I went to the White House for a reception for Gold Star Families. We arrived early to greet the attendees, each of whom wore a small pin with a blue background and a gold star in the center, signifying that they lost a child, a parent, or a spouse in the war. John Kelly attended, this time accompanied by his wife, who quickly teared up. Karen Kelly was there as a Gold Star Mother and was expected to attend all of these events, but for her, they kept dragging on as though Memorial Day would never end. Merle took Karen aside to get her some water and comfort her as best she could.

At the event, we met the grandfather of two children, ages five and three, whose dad had died in combat, in addition to two families who had lost their sons, both former navy SEALs. We also met a woman who runs an organization promoting hyperbaric oxygen as a treatment for posttraumatic stress. Her husband had committed suicide twenty-three years ago, and her son was killed in combat in 2007. She knew she couldn't bring either of them back, so she channeled her grief into helping other veterans. I heard many stories like this. This kind of courage and commitment is one of the reasons why the VA and the veteran community is so strong.

On the Tuesday after Memorial Day, I took the family to lunch at the White House mess hall, where we ran into Omarosa Manigault. Moving suddenly from the nobility and solemnity of military sacrifice to the pettiness of Washington politics felt like emotional whiplash. She told us about the departure of White House communications director Mike Dubke after only three months on the job. (Dubke was soon replaced by Anthony Scaramucci, who lasted all of eleven days before getting fired.) Giving us the inside scoop, Omarosa informed us that the shake-up in the wake of the James Comey firing was not really the big story. The big story, she said, was the persistence of leaks coming out of the West Wing and the president's determination to stop them.

Rumors began spreading that Health and Human Services (HHS) secretary Tom Price was under fire and that I might be asked to replace him. I had no idea if this was true, but my primary thought was that the VA had plenty of issues to keep me busy, and I didn't want to be distracted by other considerations. Most of all, I wanted to focus on the types of concerns expressed to me by the Gold Star Families I had recently met. Becoming increasingly aware of political undercurrents and the toxic environment, I knew it was all the more important to keep my head down and steer clear of the circular firing squad of a tumultuous administration.

22

Transparency at the White House Press Room

A NUMBER OF MY VA COLLEAGUES SEEMED TO THINK THAT OPENLY discussing a problem invited unnecessary public scrutiny and criticism. I disagreed. I felt it was the responsibility of an agency head to give an accurate and full assessment of the current situations the agency was facing. I also believed that not disclosing problems makes it far more difficult for others to play a role and help solve them.

If I was going to be transparent, I thought I might as well be *really transparent*. In other words, on a really big stage. The biggest stage I could think of was the White House Press Room, and I requested to do a briefing on the "State of the VA" on May 31, 2017.

The Briefing Room at the White House resembled Grand Central Station at rush hour. People were buzzing around, yelling questions, and it was never clear who would say what next. Before I went to the podium, Sean Spicer offered me a few minutes of advice, the essence of which was, "Be prepared. They're really, *really* mean out there." He told me he'd go out there with me and stand to my side. When I told him that wasn't necessary, he breathed a sigh of relief and whispered, "Thank God." Spicer had been the target of jokes and criticism ever since he started as press secretary, and that day, he was still dealing with the aftermath of Trump's "covfefe" tweet, which many people suspected was a careless typo. He seemed thrilled to have the spotlight on someone else.

I had been secretary of the VA for just over one hundred days, and I wanted to report on what we'd accomplished and what still needed to be done. I wanted everyone to know where we were headed, especially with regard to our focus on thirteen key issues. This would be our road map for the next year. I began with the one that had received the most attention: wait times.

A few months earlier, I had proudly announced that VA had achieved same-day services for primary care and mental health at all of our 168 medical centers. In fact, 22 percent of veterans were now being seen on a same-day basis. I also reported that we had instructed all VAs to publicly post their wait-time data for clinical appointments, which no other health system in America had ever done.

But even with this progress, veterans were still waiting more than sixty days for new, nonurgent appointments in at least thirty different locations, which meant we needed more support staff and more space to meet the demand for services. We also needed to expand same-day services to all one thousand of our outpatient centers.

At the same time, we were improving access to care by working more closely with private-sector health care, especially through our Choice Program. We had five hundred thousand community providers in our network, but many were frustrated by delayed payments, some to the point of dropping out of the program. It took the VA more than thirty days to process 20 percent of payments, and the backlog in outpatient billed charges over six months old amounted to roughly $50 million. We needed the private sector to help by submitting more claims online, which in turn would allow faster adjudication and payment.

Another aspect of the problem was structural. Legislatively, the VA was required to administer its care in the community through eight separate programs. This was an inefficiency that led to confusion on the part of veterans, providers, and VA employees alike. It also caused the VA to reject one out of five community-care claims and one out of three ER claims—a rate much higher than that in the private sector.

I felt that veterans needing care in the community should be able to use any Department of Defense (DoD) facility, but only three DoD facilities were part of our Choice Program. Finally, I felt we needed to completely revamp the Choice Program to allow access based on clinical criteria rather than how long a veteran might otherwise have to wait or how far he or she might have to travel. We also needed to make Choice a permanent part of the VA rather than the temporary authorization it was.

The VA had also fallen behind in using metrics to improve quality. We had plenty of data comparing VA hospitals to one another, but it was not as easy to see how the VA stacked up against other health care in the community. That needed to change. We needed to aggressively address specific quality issues at fourteen medical centers that had been given a one-star rating.

Moving beyond health care, we had more than ninety thousand disability claims that required more than 125 days to process; our goal was to cut this time by 50 percent over the next two years. Toward that end, we sought to go completely paperless for claims. We sponsored legislation that would become law a few months later to shorten the time it takes to respond when a veteran appealed a benefits decision. Similarly, we needed to update our scheduling and financial systems, including the VA Loan Electronic Reporting Interface (VALERI) to help veterans with their mortgages. We also needed to modernize our IT systems by using commercial, cloud-based solutions to the maximum extent possible.

Infrastructure, too, was in serious need of an upgrade. VA buildings were, on average, nearly sixty years old, with only half built since 1920. We had 449 buildings from the Revolutionary and Civil War, and of these, ninety-six were vacant. We had another 591 buildings built in the World War I era, of which 141 were vacant. Facility condition assessments had identified critical infrastructure deficiencies totaling more than $18 billion. All in all, the VA had more than four hundred vacant buildings and 735 underutilized facilities that were costing taxpayers $25 million a year to maintain. The VA also had twenty-seven medical facility leases waiting for Congress to authorize in order to provide 2.3 million square feet of much-needed space to support 3.2 million annual clinic visits.

Even more problematic was how we managed our workforce. The law required that we wait at least one month to hold any employee accountable for misconduct or poor performance. At the moment, we had roughly fifteen hundred disciplinary actions pending, meaning we were continuing to pay people who needed to be fired, demoted, or suspended without pay for violating our core values. It took us an average of fifty-one days from the date management proposed to suspend, demote, or remove an employee for the action to take effect. Nothing like this existed in the private sector, but I needed support to change the law.

Staffing was also covered in red tape. The VA had thousands of vacancies it urgently needed to fill. It took the VA an average of 110 days to onboard a nurse and much longer for more advanced practitioners. We needed to revise the hiring processes to help with physician staffing shortages, and we needed legislation to expand graduate medical education training opportunities. In addition, I sought to grant authority to sponsor Public Health Service Commissioned Officers at the Uniform Services University of Health Sciences. This would allow medical officers to serve in VA clinics in exchange for the VA funding their education.

At the same time, low salaries for health care providers and prosthetics professionals were making it difficult to recruit and retain these essential employees. The 2016 median salary for biomedical engineers was $85,620, whereas the national VA average for biomedical engineers was $65,677, nearly 25 percent below the private sector. Mechanical engineers earned $68,800 on average at the VA, $15,000 or 18 percent below the $84,190 they could make in the private sector.

I ordered the VA Central Office to continue its hiring freeze for nonclinical positions until we consolidated program offices, implemented shared services, and reduced our overhead by at least 10 percent. We also took action to eliminate burdensome regulations that made no sense, and we launched new services to make it easier for veterans to engage with the VA. Our vets.gov website made it possible for veterans to learn about, apply for, track, and manage all of their VA services in one place—an efficiency that resulted in eight times more online applications. I also pledged to have the White House Veterans 24-7 hotline in place as soon as possible.

As under secretary for health, I had launched the STOP Fraud, Waste, and Abuse initiative. Through that program, in 2016 alone, we were able to prevent $27 million in fraudulent payments and to identify potential duplicate payments adding up to $24 million. The VA's debt-management center had also referred over $11 million of potentially fraudulent activity in the first quarter of 2017. But there was much more to do, and we needed to seek assistance from other federal agencies and from the private sector to implement a more effective program.

The reform nearest to my heart was also my top clinical priority: preventing veteran suicide. I authorized emergency mental health services for those who had struggled to get access to care, with a focus on those former service members at high risk of taking their lives. We also launched a new initiative, Getting to Zero, to help us end the epidemic of twenty veterans a day killing themselves. But this too would require more focus and more resources. We needed to hire more mental health professionals, utilize predictive analytics, and work more closely with community organizations and other resources.

In my press conference, I made it clear that if we did not tackle these problems head on, we would continue dealing with them for decades to come. Many of the solutions were clear, but most would take considerable political and financial resources to accomplish.

Maybe because I offered a deeper understanding of the issues rather than the usual Washington sound bites, my press conference was generally well received. Some of the tweets I read included things like, "Wow this seems like it's almost a normal administration," and "Maybe Shulkin should replace Spicer as press secretary."

To my surprise, after my presentation, reporters seemed less interested in asking me about veterans' policy than in knowing my opinion on the president's decision to pull out of the Paris Climate Accord and on the use of medical marijuana.

This was the first time I had been asked about the therapeutic use of cannabis, but it would come up again and again, raised by VSOs and by members of Congress. The conundrum was that more than half of the states had legalized medical applications of the drug, yet federal law continued to prohibit its use. I had heard from many veterans living in states where they were legally prescribed marijuana that it made a huge difference in their ability to deal with anxiety, pain, and posttraumatic stress on an everyday basis.

As a physician, I knew that I needed to be open to research that showed the potential benefit of cannabis, but until it was legalized at the federal level, the VA's policy had to prohibit prescribing it. I didn't make the laws, and I knew that the current administration, with Jeff Sessions as attorney general, was unlikely to endorse changing them.

This triggered a strong reaction from a number of veterans service groups. The American Legion in particular strongly advocated making cannabis available for veterans and had asked me repeatedly to change the VA's approach. I felt that we had little flexibility on the issue without a legislative change, but the more I dug into the topic, the more I realized that there were other steps we could take.

Originally, VA staff had told me that the law prohibited VA providers from counseling patients on the use of marijuana, even in states where it had been legalized, and that the VA was prevented from conducting research in this area. It turned out that neither of these assessments was valid. Once I learned that we did indeed have some flexibility under current law, I took a different position. In my mind, the VA has a responsibility to pursue any therapeutic avenue that might bring relief to suffering veterans. My new interpretation appeared to many as a new position, and some accused me of double-talk. In fact, my personal views never changed on this; any discrepancy arose from my staff's failure to fully explain what the law really stated.

I soon found out that the VA had already been conducting research into medical marijuana in Charleston, South Carolina, and had recently submitted an NIH grant proposal to test its use in the veteran population. This was one time I was glad to be proven wrong. I still don't advocate the use of recreational marijuana, but I do believe that veterans—just like the citizens of the more than thirty states that have legalized medicinal cannabis—deserve access to any and all properly prescribed and potentially beneficial therapies.

23

Doctor Secretary

EVEN WITH THE MANY OTHER ROLES THE JOB OF SECRETARY REQUIRED me to play—ceremonial, inspirational, organizational, and financial—and even though I was putting in seven-day work weeks, with official social functions added in the evenings and a lot of travel, I never took off my clinical hat. Whether in administrative or political circles, I looked at things through the lens of a doctor. Sometimes this overlap was accidental, and sometimes it was urgent. One time at an event at the British embassy, a staffer came running up to me and said there had been an accident. I followed her out of the building. On the street, one of the guests had gone through his windshield headfirst and was dazed and bleeding. I assessed his condition, stabilized him, and prepared him for the ambulance ride to the George Washington University emergency room.

Another time, when I was at Arlington National Cemetery for Veterans Day, I heard the familiar refrain, "Is there a doctor in the house?" I rushed over. An eighty-seven-year-old female veteran had passed out, hit her head on the table, and now was only partially responsive. I evaluated her neurologically and made sure she was safe until the ambulance arrived.

Then at the White House, celebrating Black History Month, the president was talking from the podium in the East Room, and an older woman from the choir dropped to the floor. She was diabetic and probably suffering from low blood sugar. I rushed in front of the president's podium and brought her safely to an outer room, where I monitored her while the White House medical team assembled.

Once, on a visit to San Diego, I was waiting for breakfast at a restaurant when I heard a loud scream and rushed over to offer assistance. The man's name was Bob, and gasping for air, he told me that his leg was in excruciating pain. I helped him over to a table, where we sat together for a few minutes. I asked if he didn't mind telling me why he was in so much pain, and he explained that an injury during the Vietnam War had caused tumors to grow on the nerves in his legs. The Columbus VA had tried unsuccessfully to help him, and now he was left not knowing what to do. When I returned to Washington, I researched his condition and found a surgeon at a local university who thought he could help. Bob had the surgery and thankfully is doing much better. We've stayed in touch, and Bob is now an active participant in the VA's adaptive sports program and a strong advocate for service dogs.

Putting on my white coat and taking care of veterans grounded me in the VA's mission and what we were trying to accomplish. Most often, though, I used my clinical knowledge simply to carry out my duties in my traditional role of leading the agency. The VA has a notable history of leading change in health care, and a big part of my push to modernize the system was in hopes of regaining a position at the forefront of the industry. Not only would this be good for veterans, but it would help to reestablish morale and pride within the VA workforce. One of the most promising avenues for creating world-class health care was personalized medicine, which is the ability to offer more precise diagnosis and treatment by tailoring care to an individual's genetic makeup. With the cost and availability of analyzing a person's genome now within reach, I wanted personalized care for all veterans, but especially for those with cancer.

We started with prostate cancer. Under the leadership of Dr. Mike Kelly at the Durham VA, we initiated a personalized oncology program, but the effort was small and underresourced. To expand, I reached out to the Prostate Cancer Foundation (PCF), run by Dr. Jonathan Simons, a leading oncologist who had trained at Johns Hopkins. While working at Emory University, specializing in prostate cancer, he met Michael Milken, a prostate cancer survivor and financier, who convinced Dr. Simons to join him at his foundation.

Getting Milken and Simons to help us at the VA was not a hard sell. With the support of PCF, we dramatically expanded our ability to help veterans throughout the country. PCF also supported a number of research fellows to work on prostate cancer at the VA.

We were soon approached by a health system headquartered in South Dakota, Sanford Health, about an idea to provide testing for veterans suffering from cancer to determine how they would respond to medications tailored to their specific genetic makeup. The CEO of this system, Kelby Krabbenhoft, visited me in my Washington, DC, office to describe the work they were doing in genomics and their development of something called the Sanford Chip, which performed a panel of these tests. He wanted us to use this technology to help veterans.

Standing six feet seven inches tall, wearing cowboy boots and an easy, wide grin, Kelby's enthusiasm for helping veterans was infectious. It was hard for me to break it to him that as good as his intentions were, the federal contracting process was lengthy and complex. I explained that I didn't want to discourage him, however, and told him about people and groups who could help guide him through the federal rules and regulations. Kelby wasn't one to take no for an answer. He said, "There has to be a way. We just want to help."

I said almost jokingly, "Well, Kelby, if you want to donate the Sanford Chip to us and then donate some funding to help us implement the program, that might do it."

A week later, Kelby called me. "Secretary Shulkin, I have some good news. I told Denny Sanford, our benefactor at our hospital system in South Dakota, and he said he would donate $25 million to get this started. Would that do it for you?"

Yes. Yes, it would.

I was continually amazed by the generosity and support we received from individuals, organizations, and companies that wanted to help the VA. There were many days when the VA felt to me like the underdog baseball team with a stadium full of people standing up and cheering for us to win.

Another key area for modernization was electronic medical records, a field in which the VA played a pioneering role. More than forty years ago, in 1977, VA clinicians started to develop a paperless system. The result was VistA (the Veterans Information Systems and Technology Architecture): a single source of data for all veteran-related care and services, consisting of 180 applications for clinical, financial, and administrative functions, all integrated within a single database.

VistA was built by physician-developer teams within the VA. The problem was that VA administrators were dead set against the effort and did all they could to shut it down. But this just made the VA employees and doctors more determined and drove the effort underground. By the time it resurfaced, it was fortunate that the under secretary at the time was Ken Kizer, who overruled the bureaucrats and embraced the technology—making the VA the first major system in the country to go paperless.

Many of the advances in quality seen in the VA are the result of having all of the clinical information for veterans in a single record, which makes identifying gaps in care much easier than it would be using traditional paper-based systems. Given that more than 65 percent of all physicians trained in the United States rotate through the VHA and learn to use VistA, it became the most familiar electronic health record system in the country.

The VA found a way to make this complicated, though, by allowing each of the 130 different medical centers to create its own customized version. One hundred thirty different versions of VistA emerged, which made systems-based thinking difficult. Given the integration of technology with medicine, if the VA wanted to change a business or health care policy, we had to make 130 system changes each time. Other problems developed, and despite hundreds of millions of dollars and eighteen years of calls from Congress and others, VA and Department of Defense records were never made truly interoperable. The VistA system, written in Mumps (a fifty-year-old programming language), was being held together with Band-Aids and chewing gum. Finding software engineers who were both trained in Mumps and willing to work at government wages became increasingly difficult. The cost of maintenance of VistA, now decades old, was increasing each year. The estimated cost to turn it into a truly modern system and to fix its current flaws was estimated to be close to $19 billion.

As under secretary, I heard endless debates about what to do, and as secretary, I was determined to resolve this issue once and for all. I knew that if I called together a committee or even a new outside commission, I would get the pros and cons of keeping VistA but likely no clear direction. I also knew that even if I decided to move to a commercial system and I followed the traditional contracting path, it probably would take several years to wind through the political process and most likely end up in a stalemate. Little did I know just how controversial these decisions would be and the implications they would have for my ability to remain as secretary.

My objective was to turn the VA into a contemporary world-class health care system, and I knew there was no avoiding the decision to invest in the right technology. I could not find a rationale for why the VA should still be in the software business. Other health systems had long ago abandoned these systems in favor of transitioning to commercial platforms.

So I gathered as much information as I could about VistA and then engaged a small team of IT professionals to study the comparative strengths and weaknesses of all the commercial systems. The Department of Defense (DoD) had recently gone through an extensive contracting process to select an electronic health record (EHR), and I studied the process and the data that led them to select their vendor, Cerner Corporation.

In my view, a key consideration for choosing a new system for the VA was interoperability with the DoD system. See, all of the VA's customers came from one place, the DoD, because the DoD takes care of individuals on active duty, and the VA continues their care after discharge. Yet I had heard too many stories of a soldier being on a stable treatment plan for depression or posttraumatic stress but then leaving active duty and running into unnecessary delays in treatment because VA clinicians didn't have his or her medical records from the DoD.

While the VA and the DoD established a technical definition of interoperability in 2016, the agencies had two fundamentally different systems. What we needed was a system in which clinical data would transfer seamlessly between the two health care systems. Given that the DoD was already working with Cerner Corporation, that company seemed like the logical choice for us, but I needed to be sure.

I was convinced that immediate action was necessary, because it was just too risky for clinicians to continue caring for veterans when clinical information was missing. Federal procurement procedures included an infrequently utilized contracting option called a determination of findings (DNF), which allowed the VA to engage Cerner in detailed discussions before making any formal commitment. Using a DNF to make a procurement decision was rarely done in government, and given the unusual nature of this process, I had to document in such detail my rationale for taking this path that it filled several three-ring binders. I knew that what I was about to do would be controversial.

On June 5, 2017, I announced my decision to follow this course of action, exploring, among other factors, Cerner's willingness to work with other EHR vendors to ensure that we achieved interoperability of our records not only with the DoD but with all community providers. My vision was for Cerner to provide the core medical record system but for it to be just one of many companies that would join together to guarantee a system for sharing the health information of veterans to best serve their needs.

Lawmakers on the Hill almost uniformly embraced the decision. After all, they had been asking for the VA and the DoD to work together on electronic records for close to twenty years. But the reaction among VA employees was mixed. Many were used to the VistA system and had adapted it to their local needs. Having used VistA in my clinical practice since I arrived, I too had grown to like it and could understand the general reluctance to leave it behind. I feel like this happens in any office when something as small as the email programming changes. But most employees were heartened that I made a decision—*any* decision. The VA had been floundering over this issue too long.

Among those who objected to my plan, though, were the CEOs of Cerner's competitors, who expressed their disapproval. Clinicomp, an electronic health record company, immediately sued the VA, arguing that my decision was arbitrary. The court disagreed with them and dismissed the case.

Unfortunately, my determination to break through years of discussion and deadlock and move the VA into the modern technology era would only increase the hostility of those who were determined to cut short my term as secretary.

A reporter from the *New York Times* said that Jared Kushner had been pressuring me to pick Cerner, but there was no arm-twisting from Jared or anyone else at the White House. Someone in the meeting with the DoD, Jared, the VA, and me leaked false information, and the reporter ran with it. Leaking had already been a problem for the White House for several months and was soon going to become a more persistent pattern affecting the VA and my own position.

While not feeling pressure from Jared, I was being pushed by other players to act more promptly. By the beginning of December 2017, Captain John Windom, a former DoD employee who came to the VA specifically to work on this project, had worked out the main components of an agreement and was ready to recommend approval. John felt if we waited any longer to sign, our implementation schedule would not be aligned with the DoD's. Congress also showed signs of impatience that we were not moving fast enough. I, on the other hand, was not convinced that the contract was completely ready. If we made hasty mistakes by rushing into it, it would be too difficult and expensive to change later. My biggest area of concern was that we deliver on the promise of interoperability with community providers. But the harder I pushed on this issue, the less convinced I became that we truly had the breakthrough I was looking for.

Creating interoperability among health records has never been so much a technology issue as a business issue. Companies that make these records want to maintain their proprietary edge by keeping their software code protected, and medical centers too often want to keep their patients' data within their own systems. All this works against the patients' interest, which would be to have a full flow of information among all the professionals who care for them.

The Cerner team tried to assure me that they would have interoperable data, but what their plan called for was mostly sharing administrative data with some limited clinical information, coming from a common clinical data set required for government reporting. But I knew that this data set was insufficient to take care of patients. As a physician, I wanted to see other doctors' notes, particularly consultants' reports, and I needed to see the richness of the full laboratory and other clinical details.

I felt that, rather than genuinely trying to achieve something that would really advance the care for veterans, the Cerner team was in full sales mode. When I expressed my disappointment during a meeting with them, my team appeared shocked, but my message was as much for them as it was for the outside contractors: I was not willing to accept the status quo. I wanted a true breakthrough in interoperability. I knew this would be the largest electronic health record contract in US history and that we needed to take full advantage of the opportunity. If done correctly, we had the ability to change the way health care did business—not just for veterans but for all Americans.

I then asked for a meeting with Zane Burke, the president of Cerner. I told him I had instructed the VA team to put a pause on our negotiations until Cerner was willing to seriously undertake a different approach to community interoperability. Zane took the news well. I got the sense that he truly believed this is where the industry needed to go and he wanted to work with us to get there.

Having set a clear goal, I asked the VA team to engage leaders in health care IT from around the country to tell us what they believed needed to occur. In order to do this, we used a convening group, MITRE (a federally funded research-and-development center), to assemble more than fifteen IT leaders from top centers around the country, who then went to work giving us recommendations for how to achieve interoperability. We also received help from the Office of the National Coordinator for Health IT and DoD. MITRE produced a report with fifty-one recommendations that we used as a guide to renegotiate our contract with Cerner.

This process gave me a new understanding of the issues, which we then used to push for changes within the IT industry but also within the provider community. We launched what we called the "VA Pledge," in which we asked industry and providers to support open application programming interfaces (APIs), adoption of a standardized data exchange language, creation of a common clinical data set that would be published in a public format, and prohibition of information blocking. I presented the pledge and what we were trying to do at the Health Information and Management Systems Society (HIMSS) meeting in March 2018.

Initially, eleven health system leaders had stepped forward to endorse the pledge on behalf of their organizations. After my presentation at HIMSS, more than 150 indicated their interest in joining on.

Meanwhile, everything was aligning for us to sign the contract with Cerner and get to work. We had testified before the House

Appropriations Committee, and they expressed their support in allocating the necessary funds. We had worked behind the scenes with staff on both the Senate and House side, where we shared the details of our implementation plans. The Office of Management and Budget (OMB) had allocated over a billion dollars in the proposed 2018 president's budget for the new EHR implementation, and the 2018 Omnibus Bill also provided hundreds of millions of dollars of new support.

We had asked MITRE to engage an outside law firm specializing in electronic health record contracts to review the agreement. The VA lawyers were not happy about this, having already spent a great deal of time on the matter. I assured them this wasn't any indication of my lack of confidence in their work but rather an added layer to ensure that we had not missed anything. We also worked intensively with several leading chief information officers from academic centers such as the University of Pittsburgh, Mayo Clinic, Johns Hopkins, and Sutter Health to review the elements of the contract and give us additional input. We even went so far as to publish the request for proposal on the website so that no information was being shared that was not public, and everyone who provided opinions had the same access to information.

Still I detected rumblings of displeasure, particularly among the political appointees, about the direction we were moving. There were advantages and disadvantages to each of the commercial systems on the market, so some of this displeasure was understandable. The closer we got to consummating the Cerner contract, which was worth billions of dollars, the more pushback we faced. I simply wanted to get this right, so I appreciated the input from skeptics and supporters alike. I knew we would only get one shot at establishing a framework that would affect millions of veterans and the entire health care industry for decades to come.

Contract negotiations with Cerner had now been under way for almost nine months. Most of the pushback ended up at the doorstep of Scott Blackburn, the VA's acting chief information officer.

A disabled veteran, Scott had left a partnership at McKinsey in 2015 in order to make a difference in the lives of other veterans.

Scott quickly got up to speed on interoperability issues and the Cerner contract. By the end of February 2018, he shared with me that he saw no further outstanding issues and recommended we move ahead. I trusted Scott to the point that I felt comfortable delegating negotiations, and I actually never saw the contract myself. (As with most areas I managed as secretary, it was impossible for my eyes to be everywhere, and I was forced to delegate.) I did, however, ask Scott to follow up on a few outstanding items before I was ready to give my final signoff.

Camilo Sandoval, one of the politicals, had started to attend most meetings involving the EHR. It also got back to me that he was speaking regularly with the Mar-a-Lago team and sharing his concerns about the contract and how the VA IT team was handling the process. The debate over Cerner would continue for the rest of my tenure at the VA, as would the back-channel communication and infighting on the part of Camilo and the other politicals. This aspect of being a cabinet secretary in the Trump administration would go from bad to worse.

24

Righting Wrongs

WHEN I WAS UNDER SECRETARY, I RECEIVED AN INVITATION FROM Rick Weidman, executive director of Vietnam Veterans of America, to an event focused on mental health issues. There were a number of speakers, including Congressman Mike Coffman. In my opinion, Coffman offered very little substance (as usual). For him, though, it was a good political outlet to complain about the Obama administration. Next came a panel of veterans, one of whom had received an Other-than Honorable (OTH) discharge from service—after returning from his sixth tour of duty in Iraq and Afghanistan! Arriving home, he discovered that his wife had run off with another man, and he experienced what he called an "emotional meltdown" and went AWOL trying to locate her. When the army finally caught up to him, they put him in jail and then discharged him as OTH.

This young man now found himself without the army, without his wife, without a job, and without benefits. Just from watching him speak on the panel, it was clear that he was suffering from PTSD and other related psychological issues. When he showed up at the VA to seek mental health services, the clerk searched his name in the computer and informed him that he wasn't eligible because he wasn't listed as a veteran. *Six tours of duty, clear PTSD, and he wasn't a veteran?* I was infuriated.

According to its congressional mandate, the VA was not allowed to offer services to those with less than an honorable discharge, but approximately 15 percent of the active-duty servicepeople leaving the service each year receive an OTH determination. Most of these are for minor behavioral issues or infractions often tied to mental health conditions—both of which were exacerbated by their service. Given that there are approximately 250,000 service members discharged each year, an OTH rate of 15 percent means that about thirty-seven thousand soldiers each year leave the military without access to care or benefits. Under the circumstances, is it really so surprising that these service members so often succumbed to substance abuse or even suicide?

I returned to the VA the next day outraged. I talked with our policy people, our lawyers, and Bob McDonald. Each time, I was told that we needed a legislative change. "Nothing we could do about it. Case closed," was the consistent response. While everyone said they wanted to help, they also said that Congress first needed to change the law. As under secretary, I never really knew if this excuse for inaction was true. It seemed to me that even without congressional action, the VA had to have more authority than it acknowledged.

When I became secretary, I wasted no time putting this hypothesis to the test. I told my staff I had decided that we would begin to offer mental health services to those with an OTH discharge. If we were unable to deliver mental health care to those with OTH discharges, I explained, then we couldn't make the progress we needed—particularly in the area of preventing veteran suicides.

My employees' reaction was predictable. VA lawyers repeated themselves like broken records that we didn't have the authority to do this. VA finance staffers submitted a projection that this change would add $500 million a year to the budget, which would require a new authorization of funds from Congress. I told the senior leadership that I understood the barriers, but I was committed to doing this and wanted them to find a way. To their credit, they did.

Taking a second crack at the problem, the lawyers came back to me with one solution: I had the authority to act on an emergency basis if I felt that veterans' lives were at risk. Many of them most certainly were. We developed a program to address the urgent mental health needs of those with OTH for a ninety-day plan of care, where we would treat anyone who sought help at the VA before working to transition their care to community providers. Under this plan, care could be renewed for additional time if a transition to care in the community wasn't feasible after ninety days. The VA's finance department was still concerned, but I had enough experience with financial projections to know that the career professionals often submitted very conservative projections in order to avoid potential disaster, and I didn't believe this program would present the strain on our medical centers that they predicted. I instructed my management team to proceed without a request for additional funds from Congress. We would find a way to pay for it.

Before anyone else at the VA central office tried to stop me, I went public with our decision to provide mental health services to OTH service members. In response to a question at a congressional hearing, I simply slipped the announcement into one of my responses. It was now done.

Over the next few months, as the word got out, we started to see more and more OTH veterans at VA facilities around the country. In the first year, we saw more than three thousand of them. This was far fewer than had been projected in the financial calculations provided to me, but I felt good that we had helped so many who would have struggled without this new policy.

Ultimately, no one raised any objections. VA leaders in the field also appeared supportive. I hoped that the VA saw this as a lesson: prioritize doing what's right; then figure out how to make it happen.

On June 25, 2017, I was en route to Miami when I missed a telephone call from the White House. When I called back, President Trump came to the phone pretty quickly. He was bothered by a CNN story claiming that VA wait times hadn't improved. He lamented, "This is terrible. CNN's ratings have gone down, so they're out to get us. Actually, they're out to get me, not you. But you have to get them to retract the story!" *How was I supposed to do that?*

Around the same time, in another CNN story, Jake Tapper reported that the VA was denying the claims of World War II veterans debilitated by mustard gas. In fact, this story dated back almost seventy-five years. Because the problem resulted from a secret testing program at the time, the records required to establish exposure and validate claims weren't available. There were approximately four hundred veterans claiming to be affected. Each month, a few more of these veterans died. I decided to use my authority to grant benefits to those with pending claims. Seventy-five years was long enough for them to wait.

Benefits issues don't always date back seventy-five years. Sometimes they're just a decade in the making. In 2009, the VA failed to implement a new law that required the agency to pay for emergency-care coverage for veterans when the emergency was not service related and when the individual had additional health insurance. Then, in 2015, a veteran named Richard Staab had a heart attack and a stroke and was treated at a local non-VA emergency room. The incident left him with $48,000 in out-of-pocket expenses, even after his Medicare payments to the hospital, yet the VA denied his claim for reimbursement of the balance. Unsurprisingly, Mr. Staab sued the VA. The court struck down a 2009 VA regulation that exempted the VA from such coverage and ruled that the VA was required to make the payment. The VA lost an appeal in this case in 2016 and was deciding whether to pursue additional appeal options when I became secretary. I saw no reason to make veterans wait any longer, and whether I agreed with the law or not, I didn't see the legal basis for any further appeals. In June 2017, I announced before the Senate Veterans Affairs Committee that the VA was withdrawing its appeal, and I ordered VA staff to begin processing veterans' outstanding claims.

Benefit changes were almost always controversial. During the budget process in February 2017, when I requested that the president's 2018 budget extend funding for the Choice Program, the Office of Management and Budget required that we reduce spending elsewhere by $3.5 billion per year to offset costs. I asked our benefits team to come up with recommendations on how to do this, and they offered several suggestions.

The first proposed budget offset was to eliminate the cost-of-living adjustment for veterans' benefits for one year. Compounded over a ten-year period, this would result in savings of over a billion dollars. The second suggestion was to scale back on a program called "individual employability," which provided compensation for veterans who were unemployed due to a service-related disability. The proposal was to cut off this program when the veteran reached sixty-five years old and Social Security benefits kicked in. Apparently, thousands of veterans were currently receiving this VA benefit well into their eighties. The third recommendation was to reduce educational benefits by capping the tuition benefit for flight schools to the maximum that we paid other accredited colleges and universities, and to cap our payments to for-profit schools to in-state tuition levels. In addition, the VA benefits team recommended looking at reducing disability payments for sleep apnea in cases where we could treat the condition and the veteran was able to achieve a reasonable functional improvement.

VA staff presented these proposals in a matter-of-fact way that seemed hard to argue with, but they didn't address any of the downsides or the pushback we were sure to confront. Naively, I thought the proposals sounded reasonable, and knowing that I needed to find $3.5 billion, I endorsed them.

So I was totally unprepared for the blowback from the veterans groups when we disclosed these proposed offsets. The VSOs quickly informed me that if we didn't add cost-of-living allowances to VA benefits, veterans would be the only group of Americans not receiving cost-of-living increases. (Even Social Security recipients were going to receive an increase.) "Did we really want to discriminate against veterans?" they asked. As for individual unemployability, they reminded me that if a veteran was unable to work in the first place, he or she was probably not paying into Social Security and therefore would receive very little money at age sixty-five. "Did we really want to see more disabled veterans out on the streets?" they pressed. With respect to the caps on tuition, they reminded me that we were fighting hard to expand educational benefits and shouldn't be sending mixed messages. I heard from many veterans directly that cutting their VA benefits would force them into poverty.

Clearly, this was unacceptable, and I needed to rethink my approach. I regretted moving forward on policy proposals without getting the input of the veterans service groups. I also regretted taking the VA staff recommendations at face value and not considering the counterarguments.

I had no choice but to admit my mistakes, apologize, and withdraw my previous proposals. Fortunately, this pivot was met with strong support from both Congress and the veterans groups. It sent the message that the VA was not going to act like a faceless, soulless bureaucracy but instead would be responsive to the needs of those we aimed to serve. We weren't above admitting that we were wrong. With so many issues moving so quickly at the VA, this was hardly the only time I had to admit a mistake, but I felt it was more important to get the decisions right for veterans than to worry about my pride.

I still had to figure out where we were going to find $3.5 billion, and I wasn't really sure where to start looking. I had learned the hard way that making isolated cuts in benefits programs was going to be difficult. I went back to my VA team and asked them to look at better ways to approach the allocation of benefits dollars. I knew that even with well-thought-out proposals, implementing these changes would likely deteriorate into a political battle along partisan lines, and I was looking for approaches that would maintain bipartisan support. Ultimately, if I could not find another way, I would have to bring the issue to the president's attention and seek his support for maintaining the current level of funding for veteran benefits.

With Washington growing more partisan by the day, I tried to keep the VA out of political fights as much as possible. I pushed policy issues and visited with members of Congress on Capitol Hill, without regard to political party. I worked the phones and made office visits to the Capitol to keep the lines of communication open with both Republican and Democratic legislators, and in the spring of 2017, I hosted a regular breakfast at the VA with members of Congress who served on the Veterans Affairs Committee. Most often, these get-togethers had no particular agenda but were still highly productive. Yet I do remember that during the time when Republican efforts to repeal Obamacare were at peak intensity, most Democrats boycotted my breakfast. To his credit, Senator Tester was the exception.

Besides occasional setbacks like this, I was building strong relationships with members of Congress. Being accessible was one way I sought to maintain good relationships. One time, my staff told me that Senator Blunt from Missouri was on the phone. I picked up.

"Senator, this is David Shulkin. How can I help you?"

"Oh, I'm sorry. I must have the wrong number," he stammered.

"Senator, this is the VA. Were you trying to call here?" I asked.

"I was calling the VA, and someone answered the phone and then actually connected me to the secretary. This has never happened before," he chuckled.

Another way I tried to maintain bipartisan support for the VA was to select a deputy secretary who was known to put veteran issues above politics. That person was Tom Bowman. Tom was a Republican but had developed strong relationships with both parties during his time serving as the senior staff person to the Senate Veterans Affairs Committee.

When I proposed Tom for the position, I received a call from the White House informing me that, during the time Tom had been the VA chief of staff in a previous administration, a computer had been misplaced or stolen that resulted in the loss of a significant amount of patient information. Even though there was no finding of wrongdoing, some suggested Tom was lax in not shutting down the system for several days. But I suspected that the real reason for the call was that some of the VA political appointees saw Tom as too independent for their taste. To me, this complaint was more politics than substance. I knew Tom was the right deputy for me, but to ensure that he got the support he needed, especially from the White House, he quickly arranged to meet Ike, Bruce, and Marc.

Bringing on a new deputy secretary reminded me that one of the reasons big issues (like benefits reform) are so hard to tackle is the lack of continuity among the VA's top political leaders. The VA went through six secretaries in four years, and the turnover in under secretaries was similar. Each new secretary and under secretary had to learn about the agency from scratch and establish relationships with VA career leadership, the veterans service organizations, and Congress. By the time they got their feet wet and began to implement policy changes, a replacement was often already on the way. For this reason, I sought input from former secretaries on how we could best address benefits reform, which admittedly was the area I knew the least about. Considering that each morning I walked by a large portrait of each former secretary on my way from the elevator to my office, I felt like I already knew these gentlemen, even though I had never met several of them in person. It was time to change that, and I invited them all to lunch at the VA.

I was pleased that Secretaries Peake, Nicholson, Principi, and McDonald, and Administrator Harry Walters were able to attend. The group understood, better than anyone else, the pressure on a VA leader to maintain the status quo. Each of us had struggled with Congress and the veterans service organizations in our attempt to implement proposed reforms. My lunch guests talked about efforts that began and died under political pressures. (I can't imagine, however, that any of them experienced the levels of ever-increasing political pressure that I did during the Trump era.)

Together, we came to the conclusion that we might have more of an impact in advancing the cause of reform if we made some joint recommendations. To me, part of being an effective leader is not being afraid to ask for help when you need it.

While I spent most of June trying to fill budget holes without moving forward with the previously proposed benefits reductions, there was also new mounting pressure on Choice—the program that gave veterans private-sector options. I invited a number of senators to my office at the VA to disclose that we would soon run out of funds for Choice. Earlier, I had testified that the budget would last through January 2018, but later, my staff corrected their assessment and told me the money would run out six months earlier than that. Predicting spending in government is sometimes more of an art than a science. The Choice Program prediction was particularly difficult because of its many different programs—each with its own separate pot of money. Making sure the funds were allocated appropriately was a bit like conducting an unruly orchestra. Congress eventually extended the funding for Choice. In working with them to get this done, I made many fence-mending phone calls, where I was open with what I knew about the funding shortage and when I knew it. I usually found that when I was honest and transparent, the legislators were quite reasonable people—especially when no cameras were present.

25

Roadblocks to Accountability

AT THIS POINT DURING MY TENURE AS SECRETARY, THE PUSH FOR reform presented me with an interesting dichotomy. To get the VA where it needed to be, we had to become more demanding of our employees while simultaneously becoming more forgiving of our veterans.

Despite the VA's accomplishments, it was still viewed as a bureaucracy that tolerated mediocrity and sometimes even egregious behavior. It was also known for having stultifying rules and regulations that sometimes protected slackers and punished those who deserved better. I strived to root out and eliminate bureaucratic bottlenecks wherever I found them.

Sometimes removing these roadblocks was as simple as a stroke of a pen. On one particular trip to Rhode Island, Governor Raimondo told me how much she appreciated that I decided to eliminate the requirement for states to adhere to federal building codes that were inordinately expensive. Prior to my decision to rescind these requirements, Rhode Island was forced to borrow tens of millions of dollars to finish their construction projects. This new flexibility allowed Rhode Island to move forward without such a huge burden and, consequently, to house many more veterans.

In other cases, though, progress required an overhaul of the organizational culture. This was particularly true when it came to employee performance. The cliché of the slothful government worker did not align with my experience. The federal employees I worked with were just as passionate about their jobs and just as likely to come in on weekends or work nights as any I have ever dealt with. But no organization has 100 percent highly industrious and competent employees.

The critical problem at the VA was an inability to deal appropriately with the worst performers. Our failure to take appropriate disciplinary actions against the bad apples had been an active topic during much of the time I served in the Obama administration. Chairman Jeff Miller, who led the House Veterans Affairs Committee, had made it well known that he did not feel the VA had taken this responsibility seriously.

When a VA employee was not performing up to expectations, the manager would often "detail" the lackluster employee to another position rather than pursue the laborious path of removing him or her. The press made much of several cases of employees remaining on the job after having been found to be completely derelict.

In one of our more notorious cases, a Ms. Rivera, employed by the San Juan VA, allegedly drove the getaway car in a bank robbery. When I first heard about this as under secretary, I was told that the woman was no longer working there. A few days later, while I was testifying at a House Veterans Affairs Committee on an unrelated topic, Chairman Jeff Miller asked me whether Ms. Rivera was still working at the VA. I told him she wasn't, as I had been briefed earlier by my staff that she had been suspended. At that point, Congressman Miller left the room for about fifteen minutes before returning to announce that he had just spoken with the San Juan VA, and Ms. Rivera was, in fact, still employed.

I was embarrassed, but the chairman had made his point. Employee disciplinary actions are dealt with at the local level, and local VA directors too often didn't hold employees accountable to high enough standards.

When I returned to my office, I looked into the full details. Initially, Ms. Rivera was suspended from her job, but she was later reinstated. I issued a statement with regard to my earlier testimony, admitting that I had been misinformed. In that statement, based on advice from VA counsel, I also said, "A federal employee generally cannot be terminated for off-duty misconduct unless there is a clear correlation between the misconduct and the individual's employer." Chairman Miller responded that my explanation was just further proof that the federal government's civil service system was broken, and I had to agree. Ultimately, in January 2017, almost two years after the bank robbery, Ms. Rivera was finally terminated.

I was often frustrated by the restrictions on my ability to make personnel decisions that would be considered routine in the private sector. When I took steps to remove an employee, I encountered strong resistance from VA staff, who had learned from experience that many of these decisions would be futile. I also found that my decisions were often overruled by the Merit System Protection Board (MSPB) judges.

Making matters worse, as under secretary, I couldn't directly oversee disciplinary actions of our senior executive service employees. This fell under Sloan Gibson's purview as deputy secretary. How could I be accountable for the operations of the health system if I didn't have the ultimate responsibility for the personnel decisions within that system?

For example, Deputy Secretary Gibson decided in 2015 to remove Linda Weiss, director of the VA Medical Center in Albany, New York, from her position. This was based on his assessment that Weiss had failed to hold an employee accountable for unprofessional behavior. Weiss appealed this decision. The judge reversed the decision and ordered that she be returned to her job.

The worst example was in March 2017, during my time as secretary, when I was told of a VA psychiatrist at the Houston VA who was watching pornography in his office during an evaluation of a veteran he was conducting. When I confirmed that this had actually happened, I was so outraged that I requested he be terminated immediately. But I was informed this wouldn't be possible, because watching pornography didn't constitute a serious enough offense. (If he had been watching *child* pornography, that would have constituted a felony, and we could've moved for immediate termination.) All we could do for adult pornography was launch a disciplinary process, and the VA was required to continue to pay the doctor for at least thirty days while we waited for the results.

This was the final straw for me. While many people advised me to do exactly the opposite, I decided to go public with this horror story. I went to Congress and told them that I needed the accountability bill passed right now. Grimacing at my story, they said they understood.

In June 2017, Congress passed the VA Accountability Bill, which gave me the authority to reprimand or fire any senior executive through a condensed grievance process. Whereas the earlier procedures favored the MSPB's judgment, this new legislation leaned in favor of the secretary's management decisions. It also allowed the VA to claw back bonuses or relocation expenses if an employee was convicted of a job-related felony. The law further allowed the secretary to directly appoint medical center directors and other leaders in a streamlined manner, enabling us to fill positions more easily with highly qualified candidates.

A few days after the bill passed, I went to the White House for the signing. The president was particularly excited about this—both because he knew how important accountability was to running any organization and because he knew how difficult it had been to get bipartisan support for this legislation. I was proud, not so much because of the VA's new powers but because it signaled a new attitude within the organization. We weren't going to tolerate excuses for why we couldn't do better for veterans.

Around the time the accountability bill was moving through Congress, Brian Hawkins, the director at the Washington, DC, VA Medical Center, was removed from his position following an inspector general report about the conditions present at the Washington, DC, VA. Since the legislation had not yet passed, the old rules for disciplinary actions still applied. Brian appealed the decision, and an MSPB judge ordered that he be returned to his position. Once armed with the accountability bill shortly thereafter, the VHA decided to remove him once again. In March 2019, the VA would agree to reinstate him yet again in response to a suit that Brian filed. Having to remove someone twice, and then reinstate him again, perhaps exemplifies some of the challenges of managing within this government agency.

In response to the IG report on the Washington, DC, VA, I held a press conference to explain the problems and the steps being taken to fix them. Ike called almost immediately after watching the press conference. He said he wasn't happy about the situation and wondered why it was taking so long to fix it. He also told me he would be seeing the president over the weekend at Mar-a-Lago and wanted to be able to give him an update. Soon afterward, Stephen Miller from the White House called to ask me why Ike was so agitated. Evidently, Ike called the White House as well. My regular routine as secretary quickly developed into communicating through many channels to ensure that the correct information was being transmitted.

Despite the bad press on the Washington, DC, VA, the president was overall extremely proud of the progress the VA was making. He was very much a man of instinct and recognized momentum when he saw it. With bravado and pride, he boasted about the work we were accomplishing together.

During the signing of the Accountability and Whistleblower Act in the East Room, the president praised me and even remarked, "We'll never have to fire David!" Then, turning to me, he said, "We will never use those words with you, that's for sure." (The president had already fired several members of his senior leadership.) Making the moment more "meme-worthy," he used his signature "trigger pull" hand motion from *The Apprentice,* which appeared on the news repeatedly for the next couple of days.

The signing was packed with members of Congress, along with veterans and veterans service organizations. Merle and Jennie were given assigned seats in the second row. While waiting for the ceremony to begin, I spoke with Sergeant Michael Verardo, who had lost his left leg and much of his left arm in the Eighty-Second Airborne in Afghanistan in 2010 and waited fifty-seven days for the VA to repair his prosthetic.

Weeks earlier, I had first seen the sergeant's story on CBS News and was so moved that I reached out and got to know Michael and his wife, Sarah. As we sat in my office, I learned that he had undergone 110 surgeries and that his medical treatments were still not over. We got him connected with a VA near his home, and after seeing how the system can work, both he and his wife had become advocates for the VA. I was very glad to have the relationship I'd developed with both of them, and I was pleased to be able to introduce Michael and Sarah to the president. After the signing, the president asked me to whom we should give the pen and I said Michael and Sarah Verardo. They accepted it proudly.

A few days later, I showed the CBS clip of Michael and Sarah to the entire VA leadership group from around the country, which was about five hundred people. Even though I knew their story well by this point, it was painful to hear again about a fifty-seven-day wait to get help. I communicated to the VA leaders that this issue was personal to me. I imagined it was to most of them as well. Michael and Sarah deserved better from the VA, and they represented why we needed to redouble our efforts on access.

While the Verardos' story was a stark reminder of the improvements not yet accomplished, the VA was making important advances in prosthetics. In June 2017, I had the honor of delivering a new type of prosthetic device, the LUKE arm, to veteran Fred Downs. After eight years of research, the Defense Advanced Research Project Agency (DARPA) and the VA had completed the LUKE arm, which provided veterans with the ability to have fingerlike movement and regain other function once thought to be impossible. For the ninety thousand amputees the VA cared for, advances like this represented new hope and a promise for a better future.

26

Visiting Our Allies

IN JULY, WE WERE INVITED TO THE FIVE EYES CONFERENCE IN LONDON, which forty-three times previously had brought together the five allied countries that had fought side by side throughout the twentieth century: the United Kingdom, Canada, Australia, New Zealand, and, of course, the United States. The purpose of the gathering had always been to discuss ways of managing the after-effects of combat, with this year's conference focusing on mental health issues. I had been asked to discuss our work on improving access and quality—issues that also confronted our allies. We had also amassed significant data on stratification of veterans at risk of suicide, and I wanted to see what we could learn from them.

As the highest US authority directly responsible for veterans, the secretary of the VA was an essential attendee. It had been long recognized that meeting the top allied leadership for veterans affairs was an important and appropriate use of the secretary's time. For this particular meeting, Merle had been invited as an official guest; spouses or significant others from several other countries also attended.

We flew from New York and, as per government regulation, in coach. Amazingly, this trip—otherwise not terribly significant—would become perhaps the defining event in my tenure as secretary.

Certainly, it would be used to fabricate a case that I had misused taxpayer funds and should be removed from my position.

With this conference approaching, my staff inquired whether, in response to several official invitations, we might tack on a trip to Denmark at the beginning or end of the trip. While not technically part of the Five Eyes, Danish forces have regularly participated in active combat in Iraq and Afghanistan, where their troops have incurred injuries similar to those suffered by US soldiers.

Denmark has a surprisingly large number of high-tech companies focused on health, and the VA works closely with many of them. In the fall of 2016, the crown prince and princess made a visit to the VA, and we attended a dinner in their honor at the Smithsonian Museum. The next day on their visit to the Washington, DC, VA, the royal couple invited Merle and me to visit Denmark to further explore our collaborative effort to help veterans.

In the spring of 2017, I met the Danish finance minister at an event sponsored in Virginia Beach by Governor McAuliffe, where injured Danish veterans participated in adaptive sports events alongside disabled US veterans. The Danish minister extended another invitation for us to visit, and he offered to assist in setting up a meeting with Denmark's minister of health. They had recently reorganized their entire health system, centralizing hospital care and developing a "center of excellence" approach for specific conditions, all of which were of great interest to us at the VA.

To me, it made sense from both a time and cost perspective to combine the two trips rather than cross the Atlantic twice. Danish officials said in order to get the most from the visit, we would need two full days in Copenhagen. They wanted us to spend time with senior staff at the Ministry of Health and the minister of defense, visit a Danish hospital that specializes in veterans care, visit a soldiers' home, and then meet with researchers and leaders from the biotech industry. With the Five Eyes conference starting on Tuesday and ending on Friday, two full days in Denmark meant being there the Thursday and Friday of the week before. We could then

1. Prior to the ceremony at Arlington National Cemetery on Veterans Day, President Obama hosted a breakfast at the White House for veterans. Here the president and my family share a moment. November 11, 2016. Credit: White House photographer

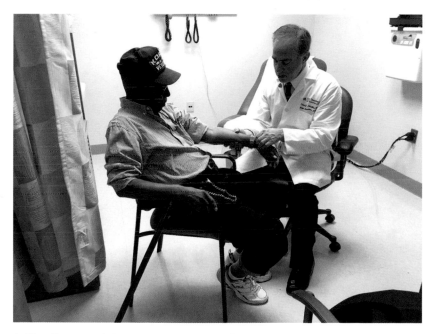

2. Here I am examining a veteran at the Manhattan VA Medical Center. Throughout my service, I provided medical care to veterans in person in New York City and, later, in Oregon from my office in Washington, DC, using telehealth. Credit: Department of Veterans Affairs

3. My grandfather, Joseph Shulkin (left), started as the first full-time pharmacist at the Madison VA in the 1940s. In 2016, I (right) used his original mortar and pestle at the Madison VA. Personal photo

4. First Lady Michelle Obama, Merle, Danny, and I discussed veterans' issues at the Invictus Games in Orlando 2016. The first lady vowed to remain committed to military families for the rest of her life. Credit: White House photographer

5. My swearing-in ceremony as secretary was held at the White House. Gathered with me (seated) from left to right were Vice President Pence; the leadership of the House and Senate VA Committees: Ranking Member Walz (D), Ranking Member Tester (D), Chairman Roe (R), Merle, Chairman Isakson (R); Danny; and Jennie. I was especially pleased to have bipartisan representation present, following a 100–0 confirmation vote in the US Senate. Credit: Jonathan H. Bari, February 14, 2017

6. The first unofficial cabinet meeting in the Trump administration took place at the Trump National Golf Club in Sterling, Virginia. President Trump gathered several of his cabinet secretaries and staff to discuss a number of pressing national issues. Seated clockwise from President Trump were Wilbur Ross, Hilary Ross, Steve Mnuchin, Louise Linton, Karen Kelly, John Kelly, Reince Priebus, Steve Bannon, Sean Spicer, Merle, and myself. Half the table would no longer be a part of the administration by the end of 2018. Credit: Alamy Images, March 2017

7. On National Vietnam War Veterans Day, I took a moment to reflect and honor those fifty-eight thousand Americans who gave their lives in this war and the 6.4 million surviving veterans who served during this time. Now an official holiday, March 29 was the day US troops withdrew from South Vietnam. Personal photo

8. I recognized VA staff for helping veterans impacted by Hurricane Harvey in August 2017. I traveled to Texas and Louisiana with President Trump a few days after the storm to lend support to recovery efforts. I was always heartened by the passion and dedication I consistently observed among VA employees. Credit: Houston VA Medical Center

9. I laid a wreath at the monument to honor fallen soldiers at the Citadel of Copenhagen, Denmark. Forty-three Danish soldiers have been killed in Afghanistan, which is the highest loss per capita among coalition forces. The inscription on the wall reads, "One Time, One Place, One Human." Personal photo, July 2017

10. I gathered with our allies at the Five Eyes ministerial conference on veterans' issues at 10 Downing Street in London. The origins of this conference date back to 1941, with the intent of laying out shared goals for the postwar world. From left to right were the veterans affairs ministers of Australia, Canada, New Zealand, and the United Kingdom. The focus of our European trip was collaborating on best practices to help improve veterans' health. Personal photo, July 2017

11. Veterans Day, November 11, was established by Congress in 1954 and was originally called Armistice Day. The day marks the anniversary of the end of World War I. President William Harding laid the first wreath at the Tomb of the Unknown Solider in 1921. Here, Vice President Pence and I carried on the tradition at 11:11 a.m. on November 11, 2017. Credit: Use granted by C-SPAN

12. In a speech in the amphitheater at Arlington National Cemetery on Veterans Day 2017, my message to the crowd was to recognize each generation of veterans' special contributions to history and to the nation. Credit: Use granted by C-SPAN

13. Medal of Honor recipients were recognized in the Oval Office by President Trump, Secretary Mattis, and me. The Medal of Honor recognition dates back to the Civil War and is the highest US military distinction. It is awarded to those who exhibited extraordinary acts of valor against an enemy force. Credit: White House photographer

14. I spoke at the groundbreaking for the World War I memorial in Pershing Park in Washington, DC. The opening for this memorial had been delayed for years, engulfed in politics of its own; it is scheduled to be completed by November 2021. The memorial honors the 4.7 million Americans who served in World War I and the 116,516 who died in battle. Credit: US Department of Veteran Affairs

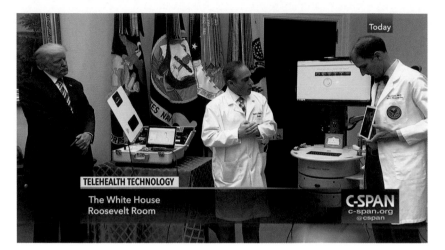

15. In 2017, I brought my telehealth equipment to the Roosevelt Room in the West Wing to show the president how we deliver care to veterans across the country and gain his support in removing regulatory barriers slowing the dissemination of the technology. Telehealth was one of the most important ways that the VA, under my direction, worked to improve access to care for many veterans. Credit: Use granted by C-SPAN

16. During the signing of the VA Accountability Bill at the White House, the president praised me and said, "We will never have to fire my David" while using his signature "You're fired" hand motion from *The Apprentice*. Credit: Alamy Images, June 23, 2017

travel on Saturday from Copenhagen to London and prepare for the conference to begin on Tuesday.

We arrived in Copenhagen and went directly to the Crowne Plaza, which is not in the center of the city but in an industrial area on the edge of town. This hotel was one of the only places where we could find accommodations at a government rate.

The next morning, we went to the Ministry of Defense for a discussion of veterans' treatment in Denmark compared to the United States.

We then went to the Citadel, where I was given the honor of laying a wreath at a memorial for Denmark's fallen soldiers. From there we took the forty-minute drive to Humlebaek, the residence of the minister of defense. Along the way, the minister insisted on stopping the cars to point out the Little Mermaid statue. This would be one of the extravagant "sight-seeing tours" later highlighted by the *Washington Post* in their "exposé" of our trip.

Once at his hometown, a small fisherman's village, we had lunch with about twenty people and discussed health care. The minister presented me with a plaque and thanked me for my contributions to coordinating veterans' health care between Denmark and the United States.

After that, we had just enough time to change before dinner at the Nimb Hotel. The Nimb Hotel is adjacent to Tivoli Gardens, which is the famous amusement park said to have been the inspiration for Disneyland. The dinner, hosted by the American embassy, lasted three and a half hours, and by nine o'clock, jet lag was hitting us. Even so, after dinner, they escorted us out the back door of the restaurant and into Tivoli Gardens. The Danish police spotted our entourage and my security detail and introduced themselves. After we bought tickets to the high swing that offers a view of the city, they insisted on showing us the way and waiting for us until we left the park shortly afterward.

The next morning, we were up bright and early for a meeting with the minister of health, where we discussed the Danish health care system. This involved such issues as data information systems and regional superhospitals. As an official invitee to the conference, Merle, who is also a physician, participated in all of these meetings.

Then we had lunch with about twenty Danish technology CEOs from health-related industries such as pharmaceuticals and medical devices, each of whom gave a summary of the work they were doing to support veterans.

From there we were taken to Royston Hospital for a four-hour meeting and then to a classroom, where we listened to six twenty-minute research lectures from different medical specialties.

The next day, we flew to London's Heathrow, and when I got off the plane, my right leg was numb except for tingling down to the big toe. I had been sitting in an airplane seat that didn't recline, so I hoped the sensation might be temporary. On the other hand, I worried that this was a reactivation of the sciatica that had troubled me in the past.

On Saturday morning, we checked in at the Royal Horse Guards Hotel, where all attendees of the Five Eyes conference had been asked to stay. We did make the most of our weekend to see the sights of London. On Saturday afternoon, we attended Wimbledon, where our friend Vicky Gosling, from the Invictus Games in Orlando, had invited us to be her guests. We had lunch beforehand, then watched Muguruza beat Venus Williams 7–5/6–0 in a blowout women's final that lasted under two hours. We said goodbye to Vicky and her husband and returned to the hotel.

On Sunday, the pain in my back was so excruciating that I wasn't sure I would be able to walk, but we still managed a small bit of sightseeing. That was cut short by a call about a crisis at the Manchester, New Hampshire, VA. The *Boston Globe* had done a Spotlight Report claiming substandard care that had left some veterans disabled. In consultation with the VHA, we recommended that the director of the medical center be removed, and I spoke to New Hampshire's Governor Sununu. Then I sent an email to Reince Priebus and Sean Spicer at the White House, as well as to

Ike, to apprise them of the situation. The White House wrote back, "Good job handling this situation so quickly." This job required putting out fires even when I was out of the country. There was no part about this trip that read "out of office."

Back at the hotel, Vivieca, Poonam, and Gabe (a staff member from the VA's Intergovernmental Affairs Office) met with me in the lobby to continue working on press issues related to the Manchester situation. Afterward, we all went out to dinner at Trafalgar Square. Gabe seemed very excited to be traveling with the secretary, but I also thought he seemed overeager for information. Thirty-four years old at the time, Gabe had previously served in Afghanistan and worked at the Department of Defense, but he still seemed like a kid. In charge of this trip's planning, he had insisted on discussing details with Merle via multiple phone calls and emails each day. Merle also had thought he was overeager, but I assured her that he was just trying to do his job and ensure that security was aware of all of our movements. I asked Merle to cooperate with Gabe, even though it would've taken a lot less time for her to simply plan the trip herself. In hindsight, I can see that I probably should've been more aware of the suspicious undercurrents developing within my own staff and a little less trusting of this young colleague.

By Monday, my back pain was worse, and it was extending down my leg. I asked security to contact the US embassy to see if they could arrange for a doctor to give me an injection. They called me back and said they could get me an appointment in three days but that the consultation would not include an injection. I had to get through hours of lecture and endless events, so I asked for pills to tide me over until I could get home for further treatment. We were driven to the US embassy, where I was given a prescription; I filled it at the pharmacy next door. All the while, I was in constant communication with the VA team in Washington, staying up to date and providing direction.

The next evening, we attended a reception at 10 Downing Street, the prime minister's residence, where we met the other representatives from the Five Eyes—New Zealand, Australia, Canada, and Great Britain. The UK minister of defense, whose agency encompasses Veterans Affairs within it (which is how it works in many other countries) gave a short speech.

Later that night, we were jolted awake by a screechingly loud fire alarm. I thought we should just wait in our hotel room because security would come and get us. I had been trained for situations like this, and there was always the danger that the fire alarm was initiated as a diversion in order to get access to a public official and cause him or her harm. So we got dressed and then waited and waited. Finally, I opened the door and saw two members of my security team out in the hallway. One said he would go check out what was happening. What had he been waiting for? The sirens had been blaring for a good five to seven minutes already.

My security team came back and said that we should go down the stairs. My leg was killing me, so it wasn't easy for me to walk down three flights of steps. But we went outside with the rest of the hotel's guests. It was 4:00 a.m. This was actually one of the scenarios we learned about and were told to avoid in case the whole emergency was a setup. Some hotel guests were panicked. Brad, one of our special agents, opened his door to see a naked woman running down the hall. He quickly grabbed the bathrobe from his room and ran down the hall to throw it around her, which might explain why he was so late getting to our room. The fire trucks came and left, and we were allowed back into the hotel, but we still had to climb the stairs, which, again, was incredibly painful for me.

On Thursday, the conference was at Stoneleigh House, home to three hundred veterans who support themselves by manufacturing poppy flower wreaths for sale to the public. One of these men was an eighty-two-year-old who had been shot thirteen times in the leg during his service in Korea before the Americans rescued him. No one else from his unit survived. He never got to thank the Americans for saving him, so he thanked the secretary as a representative of the Americans who had saved his life fifty years ago. He teared up, and so did I.

Immediately after our long flight home, I went directly to Walter Reed Hospital for x-rays and an MRI of my lumbosacral spine. Then I saw the spine surgeon, who gave me an intralesional steroid injection under radiologic guidance. This was all treatment for the sciatica that had flared up while I sat in coach on the flight from Denmark to London. Prior to this trip, I hadn't had severe back pain in more than ten years. While even simple walking or sitting was painful, I had a packed schedule, so there was no time to rest.

27

Jet Lag

O N MY RETURN FROM EUROPE, I HAD NO IDEA HOW MUCH OF A hornet's nest this seemingly innocuous trip was going to stir up. Judging from the facts I've just provided, it might be hard to see how it could become controversial at all, much less a hugely destructive turning point in my government career. But within just a few months, it would become a major source of turmoil and confusion. It was not as if the pace and complexity of my work—not to mention the larger churning of the Trump administration news cycle—allowed much room for further pointless distraction.

The day I returned from Europe—the same day I visited Walter Reed—I did interviews with the White House press corps and then went to Andrews Air Force Base to travel with the president to visit an AMVETS post in Youngstown, Ohio. Sharing the airborne conference room with me on Air Force One were Secretary Perry, Secretary Zinke, Reince Priebus, Kellyanne Conway, and Anthony Scaramucci, Trump's new—and soon-to-be-fired after only eleven days—communications director.

When we got off the plane, the president requested that I ride into Youngstown with him and Melania. Sitting in the back of his heavily armored limo, called the Beast, the president asked me about a wide range of issues—many far outside the scope of VA business, such as what I thought about Jeff Sessions and what he should do with his now-alienated attorney general. I deflected: "Mr. President, I'm not the one to give you advice on that." White House staffers later told me that this had likely been my interview for the position of Trump's new chief of staff to replace Priebus, but fortunately my response to his question meant that I had failed the test.

We arrived at the AMVETS post, where I introduced the president to an enthusiastic group. They seemed eager to hear from him and clearly supported him. We got back to Andrews Air Force Base late that evening.

I was speaking at the DAV conference when Reince Priebus parted ways with the Trump administration on the tarmac of a Long Island airport. Sean Spicer's exit had occurred the week before. Meanwhile, the president was now publicly chastising Jeff Sessions, so much so that even Republican senators were upset about the unseemly treatment of cabinet members.

The turmoil was unsettling, but not as much as the excruciating pain in my back. I had to leave the conference early, and as soon as I returned to Washington, I underwent another series of injections and began physical therapy at the White House.

The only bright spot came a few days later when we had our first cabinet meeting with the man the president brought in to replace Priebus as chief of staff, General John Kelly. I was pleased by John's appointment, and I thought he would bring much-needed discipline to the White House as well as a strong commitment to veterans issues.

As mentioned, I had gotten to know John during his time as secretary of homeland security, and our relationship was always an important one for me within the administration. Both he and Secretary Mattis were my natural allies, because as career military leaders they understood the importance of strengthening the VA. John shared his knowledge of veteran experiences, and I found his feedback helpful. Karen, John's wife, was also passionate about veterans. She shared stories with me as well and volunteered to help with our work relating to veterans' families and caregivers.

Even though I felt a strong bond with John, I wanted to respect the chain of command, and I reserved my direct contact with him as the new chief of staff to situations that I couldn't resolve at other levels of the White House. As a result, I spent a great deal of time interacting with the Office of Communications, the Presidential Personnel Office (PPO), the Domestic Policy Council (DPC), and the Office of Cabinet Affairs.

Each of these had its own personality, but PPO, overseen officially by Johnny DeStefano, was especially significant because it was the gateway to the political appointees. DeStefano had worked as political director for Ohio Republican congressman John Boehner from 2007 to 2011 and then served as his senior adviser when Boehner became speaker of the House. A few months into the Trump administration, DeStefano was given additional responsibility and turned day-to-day operations of the personnel office over to Sean Doocey, who was all of twenty-four years old. Whenever I saw Johnny, he seemed distracted, and when I tried to talk to him about the status of our appointees, he always appeared to be rushing off somewhere. His constant refrain was that he didn't know the status of whatever I asked but would get back to me. He never did. Sean dealt primarily with our political team at the VA, led by Jake Leinenkugel, who would provide me with regular updates on progress—each of which was limited. Even by the time I left the VA, we still didn't have our top three positions (outside of the secretary's office) filled—the under secretary for benefits, under secretary for health, and chief information officer.

I was also convinced that PPO was applying a political standard in screening of appointees that I had not seen in the Obama administration. On several occasions I had submitted names for key positions only to never hear back or have them outright rejected. When I pushed for an answer, I often received pure nonsense. For the chief information officer nominee, I had submitted the name of a person I had personally referenced and interviewed. I was told that he had previously been court-martialed, which made him ineligible. After hearing about this, I spoke again to the candidate, who flatly denied it. I also spoke to several of his references from the time he'd served in the military, who also said this court-martial never happened. But PPO would not relent.

A commission had been established to identify a candidate for under secretary of health, and I worked hard to find experienced and competent people who might agree to go through the process. When I found promising candidates, I ran their names by PPO. As mentioned before, the first of these was Dr. Poonam Alaigh, the former New Jersey state commissioner of health who was serving as the acting under secretary at the time. PPO pulled her nomination because of what I believed to be clashes with the VA politicals. Then came a respected leader from the private sector who was serving at one of the country's premier academic medical centers. While I never received an outright rejection from PPO, they dragged out the process and never even contacted him, so he eventually withdrew his name. Next was a former CEO of one of the country's largest public hospital systems, a man I had known for well over a decade and thought to be extremely qualified, but PPO did not agree. I was told that he had offered support to one of Hillary Clinton's advisory committees on health care, as if this were disqualifying. And on and on it went. As these positions remained vacant, I assumed even more responsibility. But PPO was committed to having "their" team in place, regardless of what the VA actually needed.

Just to be clear, none of these decisions on personnel were being made at the presidential level or even in the chief of staff's office. Filling forty-five hundred political appointee spots is simply too big a job for a president to manage. At the same time, PPO was being run by people with no significant management experience who did not fully understand, or did not care, how their political screening process would affect a department like mine, or the millions of citizens who might be affected in turn.

Cabinet Affairs, headed by Bill McGinley, was where cabinet officials would go to request information from the White House. McGinley, formerly a lawyer at the law firm of Jones Day, had joined the Trump campaign in April 2016, after serving as the deputy general counsel to the Republican National Committee.

From my perspective, the information we received from Cabinet Affairs was woefully deficient. Even my request for a simple phone directory so I could contact other cabinet members or White House officials never came through.

Respecting the chain of command, I often went to McGinley to seek his input into the behavior of the political appointees. He would listen attentively before telling me that he wanted to discuss the situation with others and would get back to me. He never did. So I would call again, and he would repeat that he would get back to me. He rarely did. We got so used to not hearing back that my staff simply began referring to his office as the "Office of No."

I don't know whether this was a deliberate strategy to avoid the issues or a reflection of the general White House dysfunction. Either way, I know McGinley was aware of the issues going on and provided little support or guidance. If his intent was to let me deal with the issues alone, knowing I had little power against the political forces at work, then he was successful.

After one particular cabinet meeting, General Kelly as chief of staff asked me if I had any ideas about health care reform and then invited me to come to a meeting on proposed health care legislation with the president. This elicited unpleasant looks from Tom Price and his staffers. At the meeting, I told the president that if he let Obamacare fail and didn't replace it with a feasible alternative program, then we would hurt a lot of Americans. I also added that if we did this, the Democrats would more easily be able to blame the president for the country's health care problems. The president said, "No, you're wrong, we'll get our bill passed." *This is not going to end well,* I remember thinking. I saw this as a missed opportunity for the same kind of bipartisan approach to reform that had been instrumental in dealing with veterans' issues.

With no clear direction provided for how I should be working with the White House on any matter, I reached out to the Domestic

Policy Council. One of the more revolutionary ideas I was developing to improve quality in the VA was to make the agency more competitive with the private sector by having the VA compete with community providers for patients. I wanted to do this through a policy called Medicare Subvention, which meant that the VA would get paid for the treatment of veterans with Medicare if they chose to get their care within the VA system. Currently Medicare doesn't pay for a veteran when they are treated at a VA facility, but under Medicare Subvention, Medicare would pay the VA, just as they do other hospital systems. The Department of Defense had tested a similar policy, and from this experience, I came to believe that even if Medicare would pay significantly discounted rates, this policy would provide an incentive for a VA medical center director to bring in more funds through increased patient activity, be more customer oriented, and maximize service offerings to veterans. The current incentives within the VA were the opposite: more patients on a fixed budget meant fewer resources for everyone.

Katy Talento was the senior staffer working on health care at the Domestic Policy Council (DPC). She had come from the Trump campaign, and before that she had worked for Senator Tom Tillis. She listened to what I wanted to do with Medicare and then shut me down. "It's going to have to wait for year two. My priorities are health care reform and infrastructure, not VA." That was my first and only real conversation with Katy, which left me having to seek out her boss, Andrew Bremberg. Andrew was slightly more polished than Katy, but I quickly assessed that the VA was not a priority for him either.

Fortunately, others within the administration were more engaged. Both Ivanka Trump and Jared Kushner at least communicated to me that they wanted to help veterans. Jared felt that the VA could be a cornerstone in his plans to establish the Office of American Innovation. Quite frequently I reviewed the VA's plans with him or his team, which they helped move through the White House. I met with Ivanka on a few occasions to give her updates and try to get her to visit some VA facilities with me, but our schedules never aligned. Jared also remained in close contact with Ike, which kept him close to veteran issues.

The first project the VA worked on with the Office of American Innovation was telehealth, a means of providing health care services to parts of the country where there were few or no health care professionals willing to care for veterans. The problem, however, was that we had no clear authority to practice telemedicine outside of a VA facility. If one of our doctors in New York City wanted to offer a video consultation to a veteran in Idaho, current policy required the veteran to drive into a VA facility to be seen on the screen rather than simply staying in his home and switching on his laptop. In addition, some VA practitioners had legal concerns about practicing telemedicine across state lines. I felt confident that this wasn't an issue, since the Supremacy Clause mandates that federal law trumps state law, but several states indicated that they were prepared to challenge that authority, which made it prudent to coordinate my efforts with the White House.

The process for this was anything but clear. We needed the Department of Justice to commit to defending VA clinicians in case a state challenged the practitioner's authority to practice telemedicine across state lines. We needed the DPC and OMB to review any proposed regulatory changes or executive orders to ensure smooth sailing.

We had numerous meetings of the involved parties with Reed Cornish, who worked with Jared in the Office of American Innovation and served as the overseer of the process. Everyone wanted to cooperate, but the system was not designed for collaboration. Each department representative needed to go back to his or her agency and get permission to proceed through a chain of command, and each agency had its own perspective on the level of risk associated with a new policy. When necessary, we would pull Jared into the conversations to get things unstuck, and that usually worked.

Jared was the ultimate multitasker. He would come into a meeting and sit down, only to be interrupted by a phone call or someone coming to pull him into another meeting. Fortunately, he could always grasp the essence of what we needed him to do and would circle back later.

Ivanka never became very involved in veterans' issues, but I think that's only because she became involved in so many other things first. We worked to coordinate her schedule to allow a site visit to a VA medical center with me, but each time we had a tentative date to get together, a conflict arose on her end. The one exception was when Merle and I joined her and Jared at a David Lynch Foundation event highlighting the work of transcendental meditation in helping veterans with PTSD.

But in the case of telehealth, nothing was moving forward. Each agency seemed to hold firm in its positions, and I was afraid that even Jared might not be able to get this unstuck. So I decided to take my case to the president. I knew that President Trump would not want to read a white paper explaining the issue or receive an extensive policy briefing on telehealth law, so I decided I would show him instead.

I had been "seeing" patients in Grants Pass, Oregon, from my office in Washington using telehealth. Grants Pass was a rural area that had lost its primary-care doctor, so I raised my hand to fill in. Using the computer at my desk in the secretary's office, I could perform a full exam, which included tasks like listening to my patient's heart and lungs. One afternoon in August, I brought my video exam room to the president in the Roosevelt Room at the White House. I consulted with the patient through the telehealth equipment while the president and the press corps looked over my shoulder. The president spoke to the patient, and both the president and patient seemed very impressed by this technology.

I explained to President Trump that we needed telehealth to fix the access issues for veterans, particularly for those who lived in rural areas like Grants Pass, Oregon. I asked him for his help in getting the interagency issues resolved so we could match the needs of veterans with our clinical staff, no matter where they were in the country. The president delivered, and we moved forward with our regulations to fix the telehealth program.

I was now badly limping, the lingering result of the back trouble that had flared up on my trip from Denmark to London. The job required that I keep moving, though, so I did, with some necessary adaptation and the help of my security detail driving me from place to place when possible. On a trip to New Hampshire with a congressional delegation, I was unable to walk from terminal A to terminal B, so when I saw one of the airport carts drive by, I jumped on it, leaving my very surprised security detail behind.

In Manchester, New Hampshire, I met with the leadership team and got their perspective on what was going on. I then met with a group of eight whistleblowers. My impression was that these were thoughtful and caring professionals identifying issues in the operating room that should've been taken seriously and addressed. But in this case, it appeared that their concerns had been ignored.

After discussions with staff, veterans, veterans service organizations, and others, I held a joint press conference with the congressional delegation in which I announced that I was making additional personnel changes, committing to new capital investments in the facility, and appointing a commission to provide me with recommendations on the future plans and role of the Manchester facility.

28

Old Wounds

IN AUGUST 2017, CONGRESS PASSED THE HARRY W. COLMERY Educational Assistance Act, known as the Forever GI Bill. The original GI Bill, passed in 1944, provided more than 7.5 million veterans with educational benefits. After 9/11, there was an expansion of these benefits to allow greater access to higher education and to transfer benefits to dependents, but there were still many restrictions. The Forever GI Bill lifted the fifteen-year time limit on the use of the GI Bill, allowing veterans to seek a second career or opportunities later in life. The bill also allowed for more guard and reserve members to access educational benefits, and it expanded eligibility to all Purple Heart recipients.

Sponsored by Chairman Phil Roe, with 120 cosponsors from both sides of the aisle, the bill would cost approximately $3 billion over the next decade. Due to the strong support of the veterans service organizations, few legislators objected.

On August 12, 2017, the president was signing another important piece of legislation: a bill to extend funding for the Choice Program with another $3.8 billion. At the last minute, I received a call telling me that I needed to be at the president's club in Bedminster, New Jersey, for the event.

That morning, both Garry Augustine from the Disabled American Veterans (DAV) and Bob Wallace from the Veterans of Foreign Wars (VFW) asked me why they had been excluded from the signing event. The White House had invited only a select group of organizations, including Concerned Veterans of America, the group supported by the Koch brothers.

When I arrived at the president's club in New Jersey, I was told that he was playing a round of golf. After about forty-five minutes, I spotted him in his golf cart, with Secret Service and a medical team trailing behind in about a half-dozen additional carts.

As he drove by, the president told me, "I'm going to do thirty-six holes today. Just need to finish up this last nine, and then I'll find you. What do you hear about what's happening in Charlottesville?"

The president was referring to the KKK rally and counterprotest that sparked violence and resulted in at least one death. At this point, the story was just breaking. I heard some very preliminary reports on the radio while driving to Bedminster.

"I heard it's pretty bad," I said. "Looks like it could get out of control."

While Trump finished his last nine holes, I went to the main reception area where they planned to hold the ceremony. I reviewed the setup, which included a podium with the presidential seal and American flags behind it. The press had assembled, and a protocol officer brought in some veterans and directed them to make a line in front of the flags.

A few moments later, the president entered, distracted as he flipped through his notes. He looked up at me and asked, "What else should we say about the bill?"

"Mr. President, I think we should thank the leadership in Congress, especially since this was a bipartisan effort." He cringed at the word *bipartisan*.

"Like who?" he asked.

"Chairman Isakson, Chairman Roe, and also Senator Tester and Congressman Walz," I said.

"No," he said curtly. "I'm not doing that."

I didn't respond, knowing I would lose an argument with the president about the virtue of cooperation with the Democrats. He spent a little more time flipping through his notes and then confidently said, "Let's go!"

President Trump opened with comments about Charlottesville. I was very uncomfortable with the way he discussed this topic, and I found myself ever so slightly inching over to the left (no pun intended), hoping I would not be in the frame of the TV camera.

The president then turned his attention to signing the bill. He talked about the importance of the bill and then paused. He continued, "I want to thank David for all the good things he's doing. Such a great start as the secretary of VA."

He then went on to talk about all of his own accomplishments so far. It seemed out of place, particularly on this day when the nation was experiencing violence and crisis. Then, to my surprise, he looked over at me and said, "David, is there anyone you want to acknowledge or thank that helped with this bill?" The president stepped to the side to allow space for me at the podium.

"Yes, Mr. President. I do want to thank Congress for its support, particularly Chairman Isakson and Senator Tester, and Chairman Roe and Congressman Walz. We couldn't have done this without them."

The president then came back to the podium, looked at me, and smirked. "See. I got it done." He sat down at the small desk that had been set up, pulled out a large black pen, and signed the bill.

Afterward, the press skipped questions about the bill to focus on Charlottesville. The president deflected.

News of Charlottesville now appeared to be much worse than initially reported. The media said that this was the president's worst day in office for not denouncing the white supremacists, and several corporate leaders resigned from the White House jobs panel.

I was horrified watching the news clips. I felt sick that this was happening in our country. Jake Tapper from CNN sent me a text: "I'll save you a bunk in the camps" (since Jews are a frequent target of hate crimes). Following the events of Charlottesville, references like the one Jake texted to me became much more prevalent.

It was a day or two afterward, during an impromptu press meeting in front of the elevators at Trump Tower, that the president created a firestorm by saying that he believed there were "fine people on both sides" of the Charlottesville fiasco. Elaine Chao, who had emigrated from China at the age of eight, was standing next to him. Steve Mnuchin and Gary Cohn, both Jews, were also on the stage. I was thankful to be nowhere near.

I was torn. On the one hand, I felt that the secretary of veterans affairs had no right to get involved in an issue like this. My usual deflection to the press when they asked me questions about anything the president did outside of my sphere was, "I don't see what this has to do with veterans." I also had to consider that the president was my boss—a boss who sees any disagreement as disloyalty. I was afraid that speaking out would jeopardize my ability to continue to do the work I cared about.

In the end, a conversation with my daughter, Jennie, convinced me that I really didn't have a choice here. Because of the podium my position provided, it was my responsibility to speak out and condemn hate. Jennie reminded me that our own family has been so affected by prejudice and hatred that it has become part of our identity as American Jews. While Merle's father escaped from Nazi Germany at the age of sixteen to come to America, many members of both Merle's family and mine were not as fortunate and perished in concentration camps. Jennie said, "This is your chance, Dad, to tell the world that we can't let history repeat itself." She spent the evening developing talking points, including quotes from Elie Wiesel, a famous poem from German pastor Martin Niemoller, and the importance of emphasizing that I did not speak for the president.

As a cabinet secretary, I was never supposed to criticize or contradict the president, but I decided that if this were the last thing I did in public office, it would be worth it.

Amid all this controversy, my new chief legal counsel, a former marine named Jim Byrne, told me he was thinking about leaving after only a few weeks on the job. He told me that Jeff Sessions had called him about possibly taking over the Drug Enforcement Agency (DEA), but regardless, he also had doubts about remaining at the VA for other reasons. Jim told me that there was a target on my back and that the politicals at the VA were intent on bringing me down. I was mortified to hear this, but I focused my attention on keeping Jim on board. He didn't want to be in the middle of the fight, but I asked him to stay, telling him I really needed him to help me navigate the internal politics. Fortunately, he agreed to stay and ended up playing an important role in the department and eventually being nominated as deputy secretary.

A few days later, I was back at the summer White House in Bedminster, New Jersey, for the president's signing of the Forever GI Bill. Before heading to Trump's club once again, I visited the Lyons VA, where I met Frank Gammo, a ninety-four-year-old World War II veteran who had experienced intense fighting with the Nazis on D-Day. Frank risked his life fighting for freedom, and this chance encounter with him inspired me to express my feelings on hate all the more forcefully when my chance came later that afternoon.

The signing ceremony itself was simple, with just the president, me, and a few staffers in attendance. The whole event took five minutes at most. The press had been kept off site at a hotel about ten minutes away from the club.

When I arrived at the hotel where the press was waiting, I walked up to the microphone and began speaking. I talked about the importance of both the GI Bill and the Choice bills. Few of the reporters were looking up from their computer screens, but I could see the red lights of several TV cameras recording my comments. A reporter in the first row glanced up and asked me, "What are your thoughts on Charlottesville?"

So here was my moment. I told the reporter I was outraged by the behavior of the white supremacists in Charlottesville. I made it clear that I couldn't speak for the president, but speaking only for myself, I put no blame on the counterprotesters. "If history teaches us anything," I continued, "it's that we can't stay silent when we see this type of behavior." Then I quoted from Pastor Niemoller's poem that Jennie had typed out for me the night before:

> First they came for the socialists, and I did not speak out because I was not a socialist. Then they came for the trade unionists, and I did not speak out because I was not a trade unionist. Then they came for the Jews, and I did not speak out because I was not a Jew. Then they came for me, and there was no one left to speak for me.

As I thought about my earlier visit with ninety-four-year-old Frank Gammo, I went on to say that it was "a dishonor to our country's veterans who fought in World War II to let the neo-Nazis and white supremacists go unchallenged, and we all have to speak up about this as Americans." I concluded, "Staying silent on these issues is not acceptable," and I pledged to continue to speak up for what I believed was important in the future.

My response was nationally televised, and major media like the *New York Times* and the *Washington Post* reprinted my remarks. I got a lot of feedback, first and foremost from Jennie, who was apparently cringing during my live remarks when, for example, I butchered the name of the German pastor. "Dad! We went over this," she lamented. In some ways, she thought I should've taken a firmer stance against President Trump, but overall, she was very proud of me and herself for the role she played in making sure I stood up for my principles.

I responded with a text: "Thanks. If it weren't for you, I may not have done anything. I agree we can't afford to stay silent. Thanks for being tough on me. That's how I get better. Love, Dad."

I wasn't sure I agreed with Jennie that I had been too protective of the president. I thought it likely that the administration would chastise me—or even worse, fire me—for speaking out on Charlottesville without informing them that I would be, and I was prepared for both. Fortunately, I never heard anything from anyone at the White House.

Soon after, a representative from Baltimore called, saying that they were taking down Confederate statues and wondering if I would put them up in VA cemeteries. I took no time to think about this. "No way," was my only response.

29

A Storm Is Brewing

IN LATE AUGUST, MERLE AND I WENT TO THE HAMPTONS FOR A series of lectures on prostate cancer sponsored by Michael Milken, whose commitment to prostate cancer and to veterans' issues was really amazing. The purpose of the Hamptons event was to inspire billionaires to donate money for veterans and for VA researchers, and Milken succeeded in raising funds to the tune of hundreds of thousands of dollars. As we followed the lectures and other events, we moved from mansion to mansion, eventually winding up at the home of David Koch, the fourth-richest man in the United States.

The Kochs were surprisingly unwelcoming to Merle and me. It was as if they wanted to know how we had infiltrated their home, particularly when we were seated in the front row of arranged outdoor seating. In fact, they tried to move us out of our seats in a less than courteous way.

No one gives you a crash course in political influence when you come to DC, and when I first arrived, I didn't know much about the Koch brothers. A few months later, I read the book *Dark Money*, and I came to understand the grip these two men had on not only the VA but the rest of government. Once I knew more about their mind-set, I could see why they would have treated us—the nonpartisans—with something less than warmth.

Several months later, I attended a dinner in New York sponsored by the Milken Prostate Cancer Foundation that raised $20 million for the VA. The VA Ethics Office had expressed concern that the dinner might be seen as purely social. The evidence to the contrary was the $20 million I brought back to support VA research. Part of the Ethics Office's timidity stemmed from a fear of losing their own jobs now that the IG was monitoring and investigating seemingly everything. But the politicals smelled blood and were giving me a hard time about every event, even events that already had been cleared. Substance didn't matter. Their only objective was to create pressure through negative attention. They had perfected the art of the leak.

At that dinner, I had my picture taken with Whoopi Goldberg. She said, "I don't think you want to have a picture with me. POTUS won't like it." I smiled for the camera and took the picture anyway.

The next storm brewing over the VA was literally a storm, Hurricane Harvey, which devastated the Gulf Coast. I was on the phone with the White House right away, discussing how we could coordinate help for the VA in Houston.

Watching the devastation on television while we experienced beautiful weather in Washington was very tough. The president arranged for an urgent call with the cabinet to make sure that we were doing everything we could. I was concerned about the four hundred thousand veterans caught in the storm's path, and we already had reports of severe damage to some of our medical clinics that were close to the shoreline in Texas and Louisiana.

The Houston VA had remained open, but the water was inching dangerously close, making it difficult for the facility to receive additional supplies. I wanted to get down there as soon as it was safe to travel. I knew the vice president was planning a trip, so I hitched a ride on Air Force Two on August 31, 2017. Also traveling with the Pences were Secretaries Alex Acosta, Elaine Chao, and Rick Perry. We met with Texas governor Greg Abbott and talked about how the federal government could help. We worked with volunteers who were distributing food and other supplies to those in need. Then we boarded Osprey helicopters and toured the devastated area all the way down to Corpus Christi. At one point, we pitched in to help clear some debris, and wearing a VA hat and VA leather jacket, I was told that I looked a lot more like a worker than a cabinet secretary. The Secret Service kept stopping me and asking to see my credentials. Karen Pence repeatedly requested that we gather in a "prayer circle." At her insistence, we must have done about ten prayer circles that day.

I returned to Washington and then returned to the Gulf Coast a few days later with the president and Mrs. Trump. On Air Force One from Washington to Houston, John Kelly pulled me aside to say that people had been talking to him and to the president and that they were not supporting my choice, Dr. Poonam Alaigh, for under secretary. I had already heard this might be the case, but I was surprised that this had been raised to the level of the West Wing. I told John Kelly that she was the best person to lead the VHA and that I had full confidence in her. Kelly said he just wanted me to think about it, but I knew that in Kelly's language, "think about it" meant "don't do it." I couldn't escape the uneasy feeling that things were about to get much worse.

After we landed in Houston the second time, the motorcade took us to the convention center that had been turned into a shelter and a distribution center for supplies. Along the way, I saw signs on the roads saying, "Please do not drop off any more donations. We have all that we need." Apparently, the people of Houston and from around the country had responded very generously. Governor Abbott talked about the lines of people snaking around the building who were not those in need but volunteers. The community and the country as a whole had pulled together to revive Houston.

Inside, uniformed members of the National Guard passed out supplies. VA clinicians had set up a mobile medical unit and a benefits center. The members of the National Guard showed me their equipment and reviewed the list of veterans who had been helped.

We returned to our cars, and the motorcade hadn't gone very far before the president made an on-the-spot decision and we turned down a residential street and stopped. President Trump got out to talk with residents who were cleaning up their yards. When he found out that they were VA employees, he said, "Hold on. I have the VA secretary right here. I'll get him to come over."

They said, "No, Mr. President. Don't do that. He'll make us go back to work."

The next week back in Washington was the first time I recall having doubts about my job as secretary. Amid the whistleblowing and increasing number of investigations, rumors, and political sabotage, it was becoming more and more difficult to keep my focus on the mission itself.

For the most part, a number of the political appointees were unwilling or unable to do the work that needed to be done, and I was left to pick up the pieces. I've always had to deal with some degree of institutional politics, but never of this magnitude. Not only did these people know absolutely nothing about health care or Veterans Affairs, but they had no interest in learning or in making the place better. Apparently, all that mattered to them was their political agenda, which did not include having the VA succeed. Because of that, they spent all their time stirring up trouble. Between dealing with the politicals who wanted to destroy the place and the small minority of career employees who simply wanted to hide out and wait for their pensions, I was facing roadblocks every step of the way.

The way the emergency response team in the VA central office reacted to Hurricane Harvey was a perfect example. They had been waiting for Federal Emergency Management Agency (FEMA) to deploy their assets, and in my view, were not being proactive in assisting veterans in the meantime. I specifically told them they had my permission to move our personnel and assets to the hardest-hit areas and that they didn't have to wait for FEMA's approval. FEMA had plenty of priorities other than taking care of veterans

and VA facilities. The political appointees in charge said to me,
"Sir, this isn't how we do it in the military. We wait for orders."

Frustrated, I barked, "You're at the VA. You work for me. Get
moving." Our Houston VA medical center was only a few hours
away from running out of food and supplies. If our teams had continued to wait for FEMA as they had planned, we would've had to
evacuate the facility.

On the Tuesday after Labor Day, Tom Bowman was confirmed
by the Senate as my new deputy secretary of veterans affairs. On
the sixth, which was also Merle's and my thirtieth anniversary, I
administered the oath to him in front of 175 invited guests.

After the ceremony, Tom's first act as deputy was to meet with
Poonam and inform her that the White House would not support
her as the permanent under secretary. Tom confided in me that
someone from Capitol Hill had called him the night before and
said that VA politicals were working hard to block Poonam from
staying in her role. I knew that what was being said to justify their
position simply wasn't true. But in this environment, and given
how the VA politicals were behaving, it did not entirely surprise
me that people would sink this low and disregard what I thought
was best for the agency. I was disheartened and wanted to fight
back, but I knew that making more of it would end up hurting
not only Poonam but the VA itself. I knew this meant I would be
losing a colleague and confidant and one of the people at the VA I
could always count on.

30

Painful Times

O N SEPTEMBER 14, I TRAVELED TO CLEVELAND WITH THE PRESIDENT'S
Commission on Combatting Drug Addiction and the Opioid Crisis. Governor Chris Christie, who chaired the commission,
succeeded in bringing industry leaders, academics, government
officials, patients, and family members with different perspectives
and fresh ideas. Once there, I invited Governor Christie, Congressman Patrick Kennedy, and Kellyanne Conway to visit the
Cleveland VA Medical Center with me to see firsthand how the
team there organized its opioid-safety program. The Cleveland
VA's opioid prescribing rate, at 3 percent, was the lowest of any
VA in the country, and their medication best practices were worth
studying.

Sixty-five percent of veterans report suffering from pain, and
veterans have 40 percent more severe pain than nonveterans. Veterans are also twice as likely as nonveterans to die from overdose.
In 2010, well before public recognition of the crisis, the VA rolled
out its national opioid safety initiative, which began with a push
for proper prescribing and alternatives to opioids.

Our efforts to combat the opioid crisis throughout the VA were
delivering results. Since 2010, the VA has seen close to a 40 percent reduction in opioid prescribing, and the number of patients
started on opioids has decreased by 90 percent. This meant 240,000

fewer veterans were using opioids in 2017 than in 2013. Many of our medical centers were accelerating their efforts to offer programs in integrative medicine. Leadership focused on educational efforts and monitoring practice patterns, while behavioral health programs worked to offer more medication-assisted treatment.

Still not satisfied, I asked our leadership team to create more aggressive goals to improve prescribing practices. I also proposed a four-part plan to reduce opioid abuse based on the (1) sharing of best practices in medication management; (2) transparency of prescribing practices; (3) finding nonpharmaceutical approaches to pain management such as acupuncture, chiropractic, yoga, tai chi, and mindfulness; and (4) conducting research in nonaddictive pain medications. As part of this plan, the VA became the first health system in the country to publicly release its opioid-prescribing rates for each of its medical centers.

Over the weekend of September 23, I went to Toronto as part of the first lady's delegation to the Invictus Games, but this was a very different experience from the games I had attended in Orlando as under secretary. Mostly, this was because of the inherent differences between Melania Trump and Michelle Obama. Both are pleasant to be with and tried hard to make the veterans feel comfortable, but Michelle was naturally warm, enthusiastic, and interactive, while Melania was reserved and formal.

Merle and I had been planning to go together, but I was told there was no longer any room for her on the first lady's plane. When we boarded, though, I observed plenty of empty seats. In the meantime, Merle had booked a ticket on American Airlines but then was told that even if she traveled on her own, she could not join the delegation once there. So Merle had to cancel her nonrefundable ticket.

The unconventional delegation consisted of Melania Trump; Karen Kelly, the wife of John Kelly; entertainer Wayne Newton and his wife; golfer Nancy Lopez; the deputy secretary from the State Department, John Sullivan; and me. When we arrived in Toronto, the first lady went with her staff to meet Prince Harry, while the rest of us remained at a hotel. We were in Toronto for a total of about six hours, never got to see any of the athletic events, and due to poor scheduling, we were unable to interact with many of the veteran athletes from other countries. When a staff member noted that things seemed to be disorganized, Karen Kelly turned around and snapped, "I lost my son in Afghanistan. I spend every day just trying to get by! So get a good attitude!" We were all stunned.

The staff member mumbled, "Yes, ma'am," and quickly walked away.

The following Monday, I was seeing patients at the Manhattan VA when my staff informed me that there were now requests under the Freedom of Information Act (FOIA) for all emails related to my travel arrangements. The request covered the period from February 14, 2017, when I was sworn in, to the present. Someone—or multiple people—wanted to know how I got everywhere I went, who paid for the trip, and what I did at each location.

A few days later, the other shoe dropped when the *Washington Post* wrote a story about our trip to London and Copenhagen—a story that seemed more appropriate for the *National Enquirer*, with sensationalized accounts of river cruises, a visit to the statue of the Little Mermaid, and tickets to the finals at Wimbledon. Somehow, all those days spent in conference rooms and evenings at official dinners had been transformed into an extravagant jaunt through Europe at taxpayer expense. Given the sensational nature of the article, the real purpose of the trip—attendance at the Five Eyes conference and an intensive visit with leaders of the Danish government—was totally obscured.

Moreover, the *Washington Post* had made it sound as if Merle's trip had been paid for inappropriately, which was entirely inaccurate. Whenever Merle, Danny, or Jennie joined me on a trip, each of them booked and paid for his or her own transportation. This situation was unique in that Merle had received an official invitation to join the delegation, and consequently, as VA staff informed me, her travel arrangements would be handled by the

VA on this one particular trip. In order to comply with the accompanying protocol, Merle actually had to get a new passport—the red-colored kind carried by US government officials. I had never heard of this type of arrangement before, so I asked that everything be cleared by the VA ethics officials. A few days later, I heard back from my staff that these travel arrangements had indeed been given a green light. I didn't want to take any chance of doing something inappropriate, so to be absolutely sure, I asked front-office staff whether other secretaries they had worked for had ever had their wives travel with them as part of the official delegation with expenses paid. Jackie, who had been there the longest and was responsible for the secretary's schedule, assured me that these kinds of arrangements had happened frequently. She physically brought me past itineraries of former secretaries as proof. My security team also confirmed that they had traveled overseas with former secretaries and their wives as part of an official delegation.

Given the indiscretions of some of the other cabinet secretaries, the Washington press corps were all too eager to report another "ethical violation" of a high-level Trump official. But given other currents within the VA and how careful I was about checking into the legitimacy of this trip, I knew there had to be more to the story of how my travels had turned into such an elaborate story. The only way the *Washington Post* could have gotten our detailed personal itinerary was from someone inside the organization. Presumably, the person who released the itinerary would have been someone with an agenda.

Trips like this one usually have two different itineraries. The first is a public document that includes all official business and does not include personal activities or principal movements. The second itinerary, marked for internal distribution only, is a complete listing of all planned activities so that security can do risk assessments and preplanning. This second document is always marked *confidential*, with clear instructions not to be shared outside of the VA, because such a detailed itinerary, if made public, could compromise security. The only purpose I could see in leaking this information was to embarrass me and attempt to get me in trouble for innocuous activity.

The morning the article appeared, Dave Hawkins, a member of my security detail, let me know that he had been contacted by the *Washington Post* about the trip. He said they were mostly interested in our attendance at Wimbledon and why we had stayed in Europe for the weekend between our business in Denmark and the meeting in London instead of flying home in between. They also wanted to know if security always accompanied the VA secretary on trips.

Then Gabe, the thirty-four-year-old staffer helping to plan the trip, came into my office and said that the *Washington Post* had called him as well. By now, the office was in a buzz, trying to understand who would have leaked a confidential document that was meant only for security purposes. General Kelly called me to discuss the article. He was already facing backlash over reports of Secretary Tom Price's spending more than $1 million in government money for privately chartered planes. Secretaries Pruitt and Mnuchin were also coming under fire for travel on private and government planes. Now, rightly or wrongly, he had one more secretary being criticized by the press.

During my time as secretary, Merle traveled almost every week from our home in Philadelphia to either DC or other locations for VA-related events, many of which were not optional. All these trips were at her own expense and required time off from her medical practice. Whenever we could, we encouraged our kids to join us as well. Serving at this level of government is a family affair, and we wanted Danny and Jennie to see firsthand how valuable and fulfilling public service can be. Jennie was in law school a plane ride away from Washington and had less time to take off, but Danny had more flexibility and tried to participate as much as he could. He always paid his own way and was eager to volunteer for events that supported veterans, such as working at our homeless stand-downs.

What made the criticism of Merle even more galling was the commitment she had shown to serving as an advocate for veterans and their families. It wasn't unusual for veterans to call her office and ask to speak with *her* or to stop by our Philadelphia house to drop off disability appeals and talk to her about their struggles. The negative press attention seemed to be yet another instance of the adage that no good deed goes unpunished.

31

Traveling on Low Battery

THE WAY GOVERNMENT PURCHASES TRAVEL FOR ITS EMPLOYEES IS rather complicated. When traveling overseas, employees must comply with the America First Act and only fly American carriers. Then they must adhere to preferred routes called contract routes, meaning that for each city there is a preferred carrier. Government fares actually tend to be higher than fares paid by the general public, because federal officials need flexibility in their schedules, so the government buys tickets that can be changed or canceled at any time. On numerous occasions when Merle traveled with me and my plans changed, she would lose the cost of her original ticket and try to purchase a new one at the last minute or pay the exorbitant change fees. Booking separately meant she also faced the real chance that she would have to travel separately from the official party. On our European trip, as an official invitee to the conference, she had the type of ticket that allowed for modifications.

Merle had already looked into a round-trip ticket to Europe and found that it was going to cost $1,100. She was waiting for final confirmation of my travel plans before booking her ticket when she was notified that she was an official invitee and wouldn't need to purchase her own. The government then paid $4,312 for Merle's round-trip ticket—nearly four times the price almost anyone with access to Google Flights would pay. Note also that the government pays a service fee to a private company, Duluth Travel, to book tickets. Because of this, I would rely on my internal travel team to make arrangements, and then they would have Duluth do the actual ticketing—a wasteful and inordinately complicated process that only a huge bureaucracy could come up with. I would have much preferred to go to a travel website and make the arrangements myself.

At no time did any staff or anyone else object to Merle's joining the trip. In fact, I had cleared our travel and the purpose of the trip with the White House chief of staff, the State Department, and the appropriate security agencies—none of which expressed any concerns. The White House had even explained to Merle during her ethics training for cabinet members' spouses that spousal travel in response to an invitation was not only appropriate but expected.

The implication that our trip was a "European vacation" was perhaps the most infuriating part. Rather than sit in our hotel room when we were not scheduled to be in official meetings, we did occasionally step out to see the sights. But as I've already discussed, we were tightly booked, and given the large number of calls and emails with the VA central office, work always came first, even in my free time.

Immediately after the *Washington Post* story broke, the VA chief general counsel Jim Byrne came to see me. He said that we should have an ethics official give an official opinion on our attendance at Wimbledon. I said, "You do know that we already went, so this would be after the fact." He replied that it was still appropriate to do now in order to address concerns before the problem grew larger. I thought it was a good idea, and within a few hours, the VA's chief ethics official sent me an email with a number of questions. I answered quickly and gave full and complete responses. She replied that the attendance was appropriate and there were no ethical concerns.

Government officials are prohibited from accepting anything or asking for a special favor from someone who qualifies as a "prohibited source." A prohibited source is a person or an organization seeking something from an official or doing business with the official's agency. Vicky Gosling was not seeking anything, and neither she nor her husband work for any company seeking business with the VA. She left the Invictus Foundation a year before we met her at Wimbledon, and regardless, Invictus never had a business relationship with the VA. Guidelines also prohibit federal employees from accepting a gift if the giver may expect to receive a favor later. Vicky met none of these criteria. She was merely a friend. Her invitation to use her sister's tickets after her sister could no longer use them was an act of hospitality and friendship. Even though I tried on a number of occasions to reimburse her, she refused.

In the weeks ahead, many other versions of the story appeared that were even further removed from reality. Some suggested that Merle was given $3,600 as a per diem. Merle never requested or received a per diem. Her only expense covered was the single coach airfare that the VA itself had insisted on.

On the train home from DC, Merle got a call from Vicky Gosling in London, saying that the *Washington Post* had just called her to ask if she had hosted us at the tennis match. She told the reporter that I had attended a conference hosted by the minister of defense in London. She explained that she and Merle had hit it off at the Invictus Games, that they both love tennis, and that she had offered us tickets that would otherwise go to waste. She tried to dismiss Wimbledon as the nonevent that it was, but she was unnerved that a journalist had gotten her name and tracked her down across the Atlantic Ocean.

Confident that there was absolutely no wrongdoing, I asked Michael Missal, the VA inspector general, to complete an investigation as soon as possible. I didn't want this to linger on, and I was sure that any investigation would vindicate us. The sad irony of Washington is that, even though the IG acknowledged that there was nothing inappropriate about the government paying for a spouse's travel under these circumstances and that I had nothing to do with the official approval process of this request, the episode served as ammunition to help my political opponents challenge my integrity, and it remained an albatross around our necks many months later.

I decided that once again, transparency was the best policy, so I posted all my travel details on the VA website for the public to see. In comparison to some of my fellow cabinet members, my private jet travel tally was and remained zero.

Friday, September 29, was the start of Yom Kippur. It was also the day that Health and Human Services secretary Tom Price resigned over $400,000 spent on chartered planes. Merle and I still remained hopeful that our "scandal" would fade into the background. But after we got back from services at synagogue that evening, we turned on MSNBC to find Rachel Maddow mocking the supposed luxury of our trip, tightly woven into the ongoing narrative about Secretaries Price, Pruitt, Mnuchin, and Zinke. We didn't just go to one palace, she said, we went to *four*. And we didn't just go to a tennis match, we went to the women's final at *Wimbledon*.

I lowered my head into my hands and lamented what was to come. "I'm done," I said.

Merle said she had never seen me so depressed. Even so, I knew I had to get the real facts of this trip out there, so I started working on a rebuttal. I must have gone through twenty drafts. Then it occurred to me that nobody had ever given me a chance to respond to the inquiries made by the *Washington Post*. Wasn't it standard practice for journalists to reach out and ask for a response from the person they were accusing? Months later, the *Post*'s Lisa Rein told me that she had, in fact, called the VA Media Relations Office, asking to interview me, but she was turned away and blocked from speaking with me.

I emailed John Kelly, Sarah Huckabee Sanders, and Bill McGinley. Kelly called and said they didn't know who was responsible for the leak of misinformation to the press, but clearly it had been an inside job.

I was still struggling to understand why the politicals would want to sabotage their own secretary. After all, we had already made so much progress at the VA, and we had the enthusiastic support of the president who had placed them in their positions. By this point, we had demonstrated our ability to pass numerous pieces of legislation with bipartisan support. We had also improved access both inside and outside the VA; advanced efforts to modernize the system; expanded benefits in education, disability, and health care; and tackled many recalcitrant problems.

Eventually I realized that it was most likely the success we were enjoying that threatened these partisans the most. There is no doubt that I had not been their preferred choice for secretary and that the president's decision had caught them off guard. The fact that we were reforming the VA, but not in the way they had planned (i.e., privatization), was an increasing problem for them. After all, it would be hard to argue that a smoothly functioning, world-class agency should be dismantled. In addition, the less that I was open to their recommendations, the more critical it became for them to get rid of me.

After the inspector general published an announcement that his office would be doing an official investigation, Donovan Slack from *USA Today* asked if I would do an interview. She said she had tried to get in touch with me through the VA's Media Relations Office but, receiving no response, had finally come directly to me. When the VA media office found out about this, they said she wasn't trustworthy and instructed me not to talk to her.

When we did talk, Donovan was surprised to learn that Merle had not received a per diem and that the taxpayers had not paid for our Wimbledon tickets. She said I should make the *Washington Post* print a retraction. I hadn't known that was a possibility. I was now my own press officer, since my own PR department was no longer supporting me.

I had prepared a rebuttal that I hoped the media would print to set the record straight, but John Kelly said he didn't want me to publish it and that the story was getting buried by other news anyway. But once again, he ended with, "It's your call," which in Kelly language meant "you can do what you want, but you better not."

That same day, the *Washington Post* called and said that a source had told them I made more money than any other cabinet secretary, which was ridiculous but a good indication of just how out of control the rumor mill had become.

My communication with the president continued as before, and he didn't seem too interested in the stories on my travel. One afternoon, just after I'd done an interview on Fox, POTUS called me from the Situation Room. My phone was on 2 percent battery power, so everyone on my staff started scrambling in search of a charger but without success.

I answered, and the president said he'd just seen me on Fox and was calling to tell me that I'd done an excellent job. "I'm proud of you," he said. He was actually in a very chatty mood, and normally, I would have been happy to chat with the president, but not when my phone was about to die and he might think that I hung up on him. I was thinking to myself, *I'm going to lose battery any second, so can you get to the point?* But President Trump follows his own timetable.

He then said, "David, you're doing such good work. Ike says you have to stay. You want to stay, don't you? At VA, right, and not go to HHS?" He was referring to the fact that Tom Price had just resigned and there was a vacancy at HHS.

When I told the president that he was correct, he said, "You're not Tom Price, David. I'll stand behind you," indicating that he was aware of the press reports on my recent travel.

The president then went on about his ratings, how he'd risen in the polls, and how many followers he had on Twitter. He exclaimed, "We should be staying put for seven years!" He then went through a list of other things that had been accomplished, and miraculously, my phone battery lasted through it all.

32

A Growing Tension

DESPITE MY REPEATED DISMISSAL OF THE IDEA AND THE RELENTLESS beating I was taking in the press, reports continued to say that I was one of the two top candidates to replace Tom Price at HHS. I had, in fact, had a very brief conversation with John Kelly and the president about the position, but I had insisted that I did not want to leave the VA until I accomplished what I set out to do: to fix it. Then again, I was finding it increasingly difficult to function within the toxic culture created by the politicals and their malicious feeding of misinformation directly to the White House and the press. Tom Bowman was outraged by their behavior and tried to lay down a new set of ground rules. If the politicals had an issue, Tom told them they needed to come to him first, and he would then speak to me. They were also told not to send inappropriate information outside of the agency. But they neither listened nor followed the chain of command. The weeks that followed were filled with continuous leaks of my itinerary and tracking of my movements. To the numerous inquiries about my whereabouts, my driver Reggie would simply say "out and about," but other members of my security team were more than happy to report details. This was not only an invasion of privacy but a risk to my safety.

I now saw that there was a clear strategy to weaken and eventually get rid of anyone not viewed as loyal to the VA politicals.

They had already succeeded in getting rid of Poonam. Next would be Vivieca, then Tom, followed by any number of others—and finally me.

Even with all this, there were powerful reminders of why the job was worth saving. In October, I went to the Newseum to attend the premiere of the movie *Thank You for Your Service,* based on the experiences of Adam Schumann, who had returned from Afghanistan in 2006 with posttraumatic stress and suicidal ideations. I was asked to give the opening remarks at the reception, and I admitted that I had mixed feelings about the film because of its depiction of the VA. It showed an agency struggling to meet the overwhelming needs of the veterans returning from conflict and in many cases failing. But it also showed dedicated and passionate employees who, despite a broken system, were struggling to help. For me, the importance of the movie was to generate a dialogue about how we as a country could do better, and in that respect, I thought the movie was successful.

The real impact, though, was in the theater, where grown men were openly weeping. The man seated directly in front of me was sobbing almost violently. Joe Futch, another of my long-term security guys, remarked that this was the eleventh anniversary of his friend being killed by a sniper in Afghanistan. Joe told us later that he had been in the back of the theater crying, too.

On October 8, the *Washington Post* ran a story headlined "Traveling in Style: Trump's White House Wrestles with Cabinet Cost," which reviewed the travel controversies surrounding Secretaries Mnuchin, Pruitt, Zinke, and Perry. It also observed that the president himself set a rather extravagant example with his frequent trips to Mar-a-Lago, which involved shuttling the entire presidential entourage back and forth to Florida on Air Force One. With respect to me, the reporters had gone so far as to find a woman from Madison, Wisconsin, who claimed to have seen us at Tivoli Gardens and was offended when our party was whisked to the front of a line—a security measure that had been insisted on by the

Danish police. The woman also commented that she saw a security agent burdened with shopping bags. The agent in question had been holding our cell phones and day bags while we went on a ride, because nobody was permitted to carry loose items on the ride.

On October 13, the *Wall Street Journal* released a report that I was the leading candidate to replace Price as HHS secretary and that I had interviewed at the White House for the position. According to the *Journal,* this had been confirmed by a White House source. This was blatantly untrue, but once the story came out, the phone started ringing with other reporters wanting to follow up.

In mid-October, Vivieca met with the inspector general for two and a half hours and came out physically shaking. The IG also interviewed Jackie, my executive assistant, for three hours, along with Brad from my security team. Shortly afterward, Brad told me that he had decided to "put in for retirement." He said, "This is not what I signed up for. This is miserable. I've never seen anything like this in all my years of service." On his way out, he approached three other security people he suspected of leaking information and stirring up trouble. He warned, "Dudes, get your act together. If you want the secretary to be successful, stop doing this to him." I have no idea what the motivations of these agents were, but I suspected they were simply giving in to pressure from the politicals.

Even more than for her travel, Merle had attracted the IG's attention because of her interactions with my staff—behavior that traced back to instructions we received when I was first appointed secretary. Merle had been told that as the secretary's wife, she needed to email Jackie and Kathryn to tell them all our plans as far in advance as possible. This included even mundane Sunday dinner plans at a restaurant near our house. Then Jackie or Kathryn would send the information to security so they could do the necessary advance work. Jackie and Kathryn also communicated often with Merle about our schedule of official social events. Jackie got all the invitations and emailed Merle to see which ones we were going to accept, which ones we would both attend, and which ones I would attend by myself. They were constantly going over scheduling and logistics.

The IG interrogators asked my staff why Merle was doing this and not me, which showed a fundamental lack of understanding of what the life of a cabinet secretary is like. If I had personally done all the scheduling, I would have had no time to actually run the VA—the second-largest agency in the federal government. Merle had taken on what was essentially the full-time job of managing my calendar—while continuing to run her own medical practice.

Meanwhile, VA was asked to do a comparative study to see if my travel expenses were out of line with those of the two previous secretaries. It turns out that during my first ten months on the job, I had spent $44,000, compared to $37,000 spent by Secretary McDonald and $180,000 spent by Secretary Shinseki. In contrast, other members of the Trump administration were reported to have spent close to one million dollars using private charters and military aircraft. It seems that the only cabinet secretaries who were not under fire for travel expenses were the ones like Secretary DeVos, who traveled via their own private planes, or the ones whose departments owned official government planes, such as the secretaries of Defense, State, and Homeland Security, and the director of the CIA. With VA medical centers to oversee in almost every part of the country, all my flying had been commercial. I tried so hard to do everything by the book. Nearly every weekend that I didn't have an official event, I took the train home from Washington to Philadelphia, even though it meant paying the fare myself, instead of being driven in a government car, which would have been so much easier.

By this time, the tension among the cabinet was palpable. New rules for the White House mess hall were announced by the chief of staff, John Kelly. From this point on, we were allowed to eat there only once a week, and only two secretaries at a time. By the next day, these rules had been leaked to the media. I understood that some greater discipline might be needed, but I felt that this was sending the wrong message—that the cabinet was out of control and needed to be reined in like children.

I still hoped that I could be a moderating influence in the Trump administration and that more bipartisan spirit could emerge. I recall a conversation with Mattis where I told him that his moderating voice was needed. My perhaps naïve optimism was renewed when General Kelly took over as chief of staff, thinking that he would be able to impose more discipline. Ironically, it may have been Kelly's discipline—including limiting direct access to the president—that allowed others to shape the narrative about me and led to the political distortions about my resisting reform at VA. When I had the opportunity to explain directly to the president the reasons behind the decisions I made, I could almost always count on his support.

In mid-October, we were invited by Garry Augustine, the executive director of DAV, to attend a United States Organization (USO) gala. At the table, Garry's wife, Kelly, said something about a river cruise and then turned to Merle and said, "You know what that's like. You've been on one." Evidently, even among those sympathetic to us, the *Washington Post*'s account of our trip was accepted as fact, even when it was far from it.

The infamous river cruise reported in the *Washington Post* was actually a ride on a glorified water taxi to get from one location to another. Hundreds of people joined us on this "exclusive" and "luxurious" trip. To avoid potentially unsafe lines, my security team's recommendation was to purchase the London Pass, which included approximately 120 venues for one price—something we had paid for with our own money. The "river cruise" was included in the London Pass (as were the few other sights that we visited). Even during this short boat ride, I had been on the phone the whole time discussing the Manchester VA issues with the governor of New Hampshire.

After the USO event, each guest was offered a twenty-five-dollar gift bag filled with little toiletries and such, the kind of things that the organization gives out to soldiers. I'm not sure how they knew it was worth twenty-five dollars, but apparently the VA ethics staff checked ahead of time. Given that government officials are allowed to accept only gifts worth no more than twenty dollars, they told us we were allowed to take the bag at the event but had to put back five dollars' worth of items. I decided to refuse the gift bag and buy my own toiletries.

Amid this turmoil, I continued to try to get things done for veterans. After I made it clear to the president that I did not want to move to HHS, he asked me to help that agency from my perch at VA. The president wanted my help to decrease pharmaceutical costs, since the VA was able to purchase pharmaceuticals for the best price available in the country. Between Medicare Part D, VA, DoD, and state Medicaid programs, government was the largest funder of drug purchases by far, so why shouldn't the VA's deal extend to these other agencies? But I didn't want to suggest that we go back to price controls or use our size to drive down price. I wanted to find a way to reduce the price of drugs as a barrier to access to those who needed them and at the same time not starve the industry in a way that would create a barrier to new drug discovery. I believe that the way government buys drugs should be based on episodes of care and outcomes, and with that in mind, I started to reach out to leaders of the drug companies.

I also called together executives from the Center for Medicare and Medicaid Services (CMS), the Food and Drug Administration (FDA), the DoD, and, of course, the VA to put all our ideas on the table. We generated a good list of potential new paradigms for government drug purchases, which for me was further evidence of just how much can be accomplished simply by agencies working together.

After a series of meetings with the FDA and other agency officials, HHS was making some regulatory changes, and the industry had already responded with moderate improvements in drug pricing. The White House was content at the time to simply declare victory.

Still the partisan sniping in Washington continued.

The new rules for security were to record every stop we made on every trip, how long we were at any given location, and who we saw. This meant that as soon as we got in the car, the agents were texting information to their bosses. They spent so much time with heads down, staring at their phones, that they had no idea what was happening around them. This was not exactly the definition of alert security.

Since the story of our European trip broke in September, Merle and I were under ever-increasing scrutiny. On Saturday, October 21, Merle and I were expected at the White House in the afternoon and decided to spend some time beforehand walking around and having lunch in the old part of Alexandria, Virginia. We were there for ninety minutes at most. The following Monday, my security team was grilled for every detail of where we went and what we might have purchased during this time.

On rare weekends when we did not have official functions to attend, I started to cut my security down to a single individual who would multitask as my driver and my bodyguard. This was considered dangerous; at the very least, two agents were supposed to be with me at all times—preferably three to four. Given all the criticism of travel and the use of security, I felt it was just better not to be seen with a big team. This made no sense to Merle, and she did have a point: with all the controversy surrounding us, I probably needed more protection now than ever. But I wouldn't listen.

Now that I could no longer trust my own security detail—and I had no way to know which agents were loyal and which were stirring up trouble—weekends became something similar to house arrest. I wasn't allowed to go out without security, but calling security only led to more scrutiny and issues. After a while, we just stayed home.

Meanwhile, the important work continued. On Wednesday, October 25, Filipino American veterans of World War II came to the White House, including Celestino Almeda, a one-hundred-year-old man who had petitioned almost every past VA secretary for his benefits, but to no avail. When I met with him, he told me he fought against the Japanese invaders, but due to an administrative error in 1948, he hadn't made it on the list of those who helped the Americans. He desperately wanted his family and his country to recognize the sacrifice he had made fighting for the United States. He told me that he wasn't seeking a cash payment; he just wanted to be acknowledged. I met with our benefits department, but once more they said they could not grant his request because he wasn't on the original list. This was the type of circular bureaucratic logic that drove me insane. I decided to grant his petition, and I instructed our people to prepare the paperwork, along with a press release.

That afternoon, we went to the Capitol, where there was a special ceremony. As I finished my remarks, I said, "Mr. Almeda, you have been waiting seventy years for this," and I gave him a check for fifteen thousand dollars for what was owed to him in benefits. It was such a privilege to be part of realizing Mr. Almeda's dream.

33

In the Public Eye

BEFORE LONG, THE INQUIRIES INTO MY FOREIGN TRAVEL HAD expanded to cover trips to New York and Philadelphia. Basically they were investigating every place I'd been for the past nine months.

My staff at the VA assured me they had never done this to any other secretary, yet my travel was no different. In fact, they told me that few other secretaries had paid their own way on trains but rather chose to be driven in government cars. Once more, I felt like this was a targeted political campaign.

By the end of the month, there were more accusations against us, including that Merle had asked the Philadelphia VA Police to provide her with a ride to the upcoming Veterans Day parade in Philadelphia. This never happened. Merle, who lived in Philadelphia, had her own car and did not need a ride. It was Tim, my security agent, who'd pulled me aside to tell me about this, saying that he couldn't email me anymore because people were monitoring all of his communications. "Sorry this is happening to you, sir. You don't deserve this, but they're out to get you," he whispered.

I was supposed to speak at a reception sponsored by the Bob Woodruff Foundation honoring two hundred wounded warriors. The VA ethics lawyers, who had already cleared the event, came back and said that if I wanted to attend, I would have to buy my own ticket. The absurdity continued to escalate, but certainly I was not going to disappoint two hundred veterans because of this pettiness.

Finding new ways to recognize the contributions of veterans was always important to me. I had been working with a local non-profit to create a Veterans Day concert similar to those held at the Capitol on July 4 and Memorial Day. I thought it was a great idea, but the White House Office of Public Liaison shot it down.

In early November, we learned that the president was going to be in Vietnam on Veterans Day, which would preclude him from hosting the traditional Veterans Day breakfast at the White House. While disappointed, we still hoped that the vice president would fill in as host. Then, a week prior to Veterans Day, we were told by the White House that the East Wing reception areas were available only if the president or first lady was present. More red tape. We scrambled and secured the reception hall at the Chamber of Commerce. Through the Office of Community Liaisons, we extended an invitation to the vice president to host, but we were told that he was not available. Veterans Day is sacred to veterans and to the military, so I was concerned that the veteran community would view this as a significant slight. We held the breakfast at the Chamber of Commerce, but without the commander-in-chief or even his second in command, it wasn't the same.

After the breakfast, we went to Arlington National Cemetery, where the vice president was present and was greeted by a nineteen-cannon salute. Merle and I accompanied the vice president and his wife, as well as the commandant of the cemetery and his wife, along a path lined with soldiers in uniform that led to the Tomb of the Unknown Solider. There, in the frigid cold, we presided over the laying of the wreath at the tomb. Merle, Danny, and Jennie stood proudly in the second row.

Afterward, we proceeded to the amphitheater, where hundreds of dignitaries and the public awaited our arrival. Merle sat in box 1 with Karen Pence. On stage were members of the veterans service organizations, the vice president, and me. Each of us addressed the audience briefly. During my remarks, I recognized and told the personal story of one veteran in attendance from each of America's conflicts—starting with World War II and ending with our conflict in Afghanistan. Since Vietnam soldiers in particular experienced mostly resentment when they returned home, instead of the joyful and grateful welcome that all other troops received, I, along with Vice President Pence, made a point to officially welcome home our Vietnam veterans—something they had been denied for far too long.

As many cabinet secretaries and close advisers to the president were being disposed of, and the press had already began attacking me, I had no idea how much more time I was going to have as secretary. As a result, I tried to focus on areas where I thought I could have the most impact, one of which was veterans' treatment courts.

First established in Buffalo, New York, in 2008, but now existing all around the country, these specialized courts allow veterans charged with a crime to seek mental health or substance abuse treatment as an alternative to incarceration. In addition, each VA medical center has a justice outreach specialist whose job is to provide services to veterans in jail or at high risk of incarceration. This may include treatment planning or referrals to VA mental health services. These specialists advocate for alternatives to incarceration and help train law-enforcement officers on posttraumatic stress and traumatic brain injury.

I was very proud of the impact these courts had had, with recidivism among arrested veterans in our justice outreach programs reduced by 80 percent.

Later that month, I was invited to give a talk at Harvard Law School, where many of the students volunteer in their veterans' legal clinic. A number of law schools around the country operate clinics especially for veterans, where students do casework to help veterans obtain benefits and navigate other legal issues. After my talk, I attended a luncheon sponsored by the Disabled American Veterans. At the time, Jennie was a third-year student at Harvard

Law School, and besides engaging with the veteran community in Boston, I looked forward to visiting her. When she was a child, I was too busy running hospitals, so I never made it to "bring your parent to school day." I looked forward to fulfilling that fatherly duty and maybe embarrassing her a little bit by mentioning that in front of her classmates.

On this trip, I also visited the Boston VA, where I spent time with Dr. Ann McKee, who led the VA Brain Bank initiative. Dr. McKee was instrumental in describing chronic traumatic encephalopathy (CTE), a brain condition that leads to early dementia. CTE is seen in football players and in veterans alike who have experienced head trauma. Under Dr. McKee's leadership, the VA had developed the largest bank of brains with CTE anywhere in the world and therefore has been able to do cutting-edge research involving this condition.

The next day, I met with Senators Elizabeth Warren and Ed Markey at the Bedford VA, where the death of a veteran had attracted a lot of negative media attention. This gentleman had been in a local acute-care hospital and needed a defibrillator, but he and his family refused further treatment. So with nothing further to do medically, he was sent to hospice for end-of-life care at the Bedford VA. As is to be expected in a hospice setting, there was no cardiac monitor on this unit, and patient surveillance consisted of a bed check every hour. Unfortunately, the nurse keeping an eye on him missed the bed check between three thirty and four thirty in the morning, during which time he happened to die.

If this mistake had occurred at a private hospital, it would have been handled as an internal matter, most likely resulting in some recommendations for improvement. But as an indication of the kind of scrutiny VA facilities face, members of Congress called for an investigation. The VA had done its own internal investigation, and my hope was to share the details of the case with the elected officials at a press conference that day. But first I took these officials onto the wards, where we met with veterans and their families, all of whom uniformly raved about the quality of care.

Even so, Senator Warren asked why the decedent's family had learned the details of his death from the *Boston Globe* and not from the VA hospital itself. The medical director denied this and asserted that he had called the family himself. We talked more specifics of the case and made sure all questions were adequately and truthfully addressed.

Off camera, Senator Warren was calm and understanding and seemed generally impressed by the quality of care she witnessed at the VA that day. As soon as she got in front of the cameras, though, she went on the attack, saying how badly we needed to fix the VA. I was dismayed once again that so much of what goes on in the context of government is adversarial and partisan rather than collaborative. At some point, the constant barrage of criticism actually becomes counterproductive and hinders progress.

34

Working to Benefit Veterans

THE INTERSECTION BETWEEN HEALTH CARE AND BENEFITS AT THE VA is not always easy to see. Even though both administrations are part of the same VA, in some ways they might as well be on opposite poles of planet Earth. It was only in interacting with veterans that I really began to see the importance of integrating these efforts.

One morning, I arrived at the Manhattan VA to see patients in the walk-in clinic off the main lobby, a facility for any veteran to be seen right away even without having a regular physician. I liked working in the clinic. As secretary, I had fewer opportunities than I would've liked to put on a white coat and practice medicine the way I used to. More importantly, however, this role gave me the opportunity to be undercover in many ways. I never told veterans at the clinic that I was the secretary. This was for two reasons: First, the only thing that really mattered at that moment was that I was their doctor and they were seeking care. Second, not telling them who I was meant I received no special treatment from them. As a result, I was able to see veterans' issues firsthand, without the filter I would've viewed them through had they tailored their stories to what they thought the secretary should hear.

My first patient that day was a forty-five-year-old army veteran with a number of medical and psychiatric issues. I looked at his chart and could see that he had been coming to the Manhattan VA for many years, often to this same clinic. I asked him why he was there that morning, and he told me he needed to get a letter from a physician to support his court case. I took the paperwork from him and reviewed the court document. The veteran explained that he was suing Secretary Shulkin. I blinked, trying not to react. Apparently, he had been living at a homeless shelter for the past eight years, receiving partial benefits from the VA when he felt he should've been receiving full disability, and it was Secretary Shulkin blocking him from obtaining those benefits.

I told him that the VA could help him identify more permanent housing, and he said he was aware of that but did not want it. He explained that if he had an apartment, he wouldn't be able to afford the cost of utilities and food—costs that the shelter covered for him if he stayed there.

I broke my normal rule of secrecy and introduced myself as the VA secretary. When I told the veteran who I was, he wasn't sure if I was joking. I assured him I wasn't, and while I was probably not the right person to write a letter on his behalf, I said that I could refer him to another doctor who would likely be able to help. I told him I'd have his disability file reviewed. I also offered to sit down again and figure out if there was a way to get him into a better living situation and connect him with a regular physician to obtain greater continuity of care. He agreed, and we organized a plan to do just that.

The VA spends tens of billions of dollars annually on service-connected disability payments, but the VA also is the gatekeeper, blocking many veterans from benefits they feel they deserve. Even more problematically, the system rewards disability rather than promotes independence. If veterans receive a disability payment and then improve, they are often reevaluated and lose their benefits. The incentives are backward. I wanted a system that assisted veterans and facilitated their well-being. Any meaningful change would require updating the disability ratings, which were still based mostly on manual labor and failed to take into account opportunities in the growing digital economy. Then, to truly bring us into the twenty-first century, we needed to develop personalized disability payments based on predictive analytics from similar injuries or disabilities. Beyond that, we needed to grandfather in existing benefits so that no veterans would lose anything previously promised to them.

We reached out to Dean Geoffrey Garrett at Penn's Wharton School and asked for help in applying insights from behavioral economics to realign incentives with desired outcomes. We got input from a number of faculty and business students who were themselves veterans and had experience with the VA benefits system.

Unfortunately, my time as secretary was cut short before we could complete this work, but along with our White House fellow who partnered with me in this effort, Dr. Kyle Sheetz, I continued working on the project for many months, even after we both left the VA. Our ultimate goal was to move the VA toward a benefits program that would serve not just as a form of compensation but would help veterans achieve their full postservice potential. Part of this effort was to simplify the benefits process to make it easier to navigate and provide veterans with quicker decisions. I was particularly intrigued by the use of lump-sum payments. Canada has moved toward a tax-free disability system in which veterans choose between a lump-sum payment or an annuity. The lump sum has the advantage of providing enough resources at once to buy a house, start a business, or engage in long-term planning. The obvious disadvantage is that some people receiving a large chunk of cash at once don't apportion their money well.

We worked with Congress to pass the Veterans Appeal Improvement and Modernization Bill, which, when fully implemented, would allow veterans to utilize a new track that would produce a decision on their benefits within thirty days. This was vitally important, because the process of obtaining benefits had been far too complicated, and many veterans felt these decisions were arbitrary and unfair, which led to a great many appeals. There were, in fact, so many appeals that the backlog had grown to approximately 450,000. If a veteran had appealed in 2016, it would be six years before he or she could expect a decision.

On November 6, 2017, at the National Press Club, I announced my intention to revamp the system for veterans to obtain benefits. Big changes were now in motion, and I was excited about our initial efforts, but when I did an hour-long interview with CBS News, I saw how hard continuing the reform effort was going to be. While I wanted to talk about modernizing and optimizing benefits, CBS kept asking me about the Europe trip from four months ago. When I think how much time was wasted on this episode overall—my time, reporters' time, the inspector general's staff's time—I still am appalled.

Another of the most persistent benefit issues, as I mentioned earlier, was the question of who qualified for benefits related to exposure to Agent Orange, the toxic defoliant used by the military during the Vietnam War. This issue has been debated since the 1970s, with no resolution for thousands of veterans.

The law states that the VA should provide benefits where the exposure to an environmental hazard is "more likely than not" to have caused harm or disability. The VA had commissioned studies to determine the specifics of Agent Orange, such as what kind of exposure caused disease and which specific diseases it likely caused. But the studies continued without any further action. With each new study, decisions were again deferred.

Each disease identified as likely to have been caused by the hazard in question is termed a "presumptive condition," meaning that if you develop disease X and you can demonstrate that you were exposed to hazard Y (in this case, Agent Orange), then you are assumed to qualify for compensation. It is not a guarantee of benefits but significantly lessens the applicant's burden of proof. The VA established several presumptions previously, including amyloidosis, chronic B-cell lymphoma, chloracne, diabetes mellitus type 2, Hodgkin's disease, ischemic heart disease, multiple myeloma, and non-Hodgkin's lymphoma.

In 2017, the National Academy of Sciences published a new study on the connection between Agent Orange and bladder cancer, thyroid disease, Parkinson's-like symptoms, and hypertension. I reviewed this new report and assembled a team of experts from the VA to provide me with their recommendations, but they were unwilling to offer a firm opinion.

It seemed like no one was willing to make a decision. The constant turnover of political leadership ensured that no one was ever required to actually make a determination, which meant that some veterans had been waiting for their determination for more than forty years. To me this was unacceptable, so in the spring of 2017, I announced that I would make a decision on these new presumptive conditions by November 1. Panic ensued among the VA old guard. But I saw this not as a political issue but as an objective decision about the government's legal and moral responsibilities to people who had made great sacrifices in service to their country.

After I reviewed the data and the legislative requirements for granting benefits, I determined that three of the presumptive conditions should be granted. My interpretation of the data was that there was a likely association between Agent Orange and bladder cancer, hyperthyroidism, and Parkinson's-like symptoms. The data on hypertension was also suggestive, but additional studies were pending, so I did not feel I could make a true assessment of that condition at the time.

Well in advance of my self-imposed deadline, I relayed my decision to the Office of Management and Budget (OMB) at the White House. This was the normal process, and they needed to look at my recommendations, my rationale for making them, and the economic impact of these decisions. For a while I heard nothing, but after some prodding, they informed me that they were not recommending approval. I wasn't sure how they could argue with the data, but they found a way.

I was warned by VA career staff that when the OMB denied a secretary's recommendation, the action could not proceed. But I didn't like losing to red tape, so I requested a meeting with the OMB staff and asked that Mick Mulvaney, the head of the department at the time, be present. At that meeting I made my case, both in terms of the data that supported them and my congressional mandate. The OMB team listened intently before telling me that the VA was wrong.

I went back and clarified the standards on which I needed to make these determinations; I reviewed the data again, and I looked at possible financial offsets. But I didn't change my opinion, which left us at an impasse. One of my biggest regrets is that this wasn't resolved before I left the VA.

The other seemingly endless debate was over Agent Orange benefits for Blue Water navy veterans, which I discussed earlier as an issue in my first confirmation hearings. Along with Senator Gillibrand, one of the more vocal champions of the ninety thousand men and women affected was John Wells, the director of the Military-Veterans Advocacy. Commander Wells had served in the navy from 1972 to 1994 before becoming an attorney and suing the VA to get benefits for Blue Water navy veterans. VA lawyers advised me not to meet with him, but I was not interested in how a meeting might affect a court battle. I was interested in doing the right thing for veterans.

More than that, I never felt that I was getting the whole story from the VA's internal experts. So I met with Commander Wells and other proponents, and each time I did, I learned something. After hearing from all sides, it was clear to me that the elapsed time since these sailors served meant that we would never have enough scientific data on which to base a decision. That left me with only two choices: do nothing and continue to neglect the needs of these veterans, or base a decision on moral grounds. I favored the latter.

The other group I spent time with during this period was the National Gulf War Resource Center. Their president was Ron Brown, who had served two combat tours in the army. After his service, he had spent thirteen years battling the Veterans Benefit

Administration to address his own condition, during which time he decided to devote himself to helping other veterans.

It had been more than twenty-five years since Operation Desert Storm, in which the United States led the liberation of Kuwait. More than seven hundred thousand US military personnel served in the Persian Gulf between 1990 and 1991, and as many as 30 percent of these veterans became ill with what has since become known as Gulf War Illness, a disease that is difficult for inexperienced physicians to diagnose and thus meant that many veterans weren't well served. Even in terms of the VA's own disability and compensation systems, fewer than 20 percent of those who applied for benefits were approved for a service connection.

Ron was particularly focused on getting a presumptive condition for brain cancer in Gulf War veterans. He met on many occasions with Secretary McDonald, and after a thorough review with independent experts, the secretary had forwarded his recommendation to the White House, saying that this presumptive condition should be approved for disability benefits. But here again, the OMB did not agree, and it couldn't move forward. In typical fashion, the VA announced that yet another study group would be formed to look at the association with brain cancer.

Ron reengaged me to see if I would consider adding my support. There were about four hundred veterans known to have had brain tumors associated with Gulf War service. The Institute on Medicine reported on two published studies showing that those exposed to environmental toxins in the Gulf War had a two- to threefold increase in brain tumors. However, there were reasonable concerns raised about the validity of the modeling used in making these conclusions, and therefore it was argued that there was insufficient data to make a final determination.

My feeling was that our system had it backward. We made veterans and their families wait without the proper support or assistance while we spent decades looking for irrefutable scientific validation. This simply fell short of what I believed our commitment was to those who suffer as a consequence of serving our country. I understood that we could not offer compensation to all who claimed it, but there had to be more latitude given to the secretary when veterans weren't being treated fairly. I agreed with Secretary McDonald in his decision on brain cancer presumptive for Gulf War veterans, and I told my team at the Veteran Benefit Administration that I wanted them to prepare my recommendation to also support this and engage with the OMB to begin this process. Unfortunately, this was another initiative I didn't have enough time in office to see through.

35

Nasty Surprises

D ESPITE THE DISTRACTIONS OF THE MEDIA CIRCUS AND THE POLITICAL infighting that increasingly ate up my time, I continued to try to do my best for America's veterans. On November 7, 2017, I went to Wall Street to ring the closing bell on the New York Stock Exchange, an event intended to bring attention to our efforts to prevent veteran suicide. Alex Gorsky, the CEO of Johnson and Johnson, and I had been on the road doing media appearances to get corporations to reach out to veteran employees who were struggling emotionally and needed help. Being part of this Wall Street ritual was just another way to increase awareness of this critical issue. One of the politicals, Camilo Sandoval, was involved in making the arrangements for the VA's participation. When I got to the trading floor, I saw Marvel Entertainment characters parading around. This was odd, to say the least. Later, allegations arose that I was involved in promoting Ike Perlmutter's company at this event, yet another indication of how out of control the rumor mill had become.

The controversy over my European travel had hardly abated. Back in Washington, I met with David Cox, the head of the American Federation of Government Employees, to ask him about his recent comments to the press. Significantly, those comments included, "I think Shulkin owes us and the nation an explanation about his and his wife's European trip." I told him that if he wanted an explanation, all he needed to do was to call me; he didn't need to go through the press. But this was the Washington way, posturing in front of the media instead of genuinely working toward solutions. Especially considering my good relationships with unions and the near guarantee that whoever replaced me would be likely far less receptive to unions, I didn't understand this betrayal. In fact, approximately one year after I left, the VA announced plans to reduce union time and to eliminate twenty-eight provisions in the bargaining agreement, making it almost impossible for the union to continue business as usual.

John Ullyot, the assistant secretary for public affairs, then arranged for me to do a *Washington Post* live interview in front of 150 people. He assured me that the interview would focus on VA policy issues only and that the organizer had agreed not to ask about the Europe trip. But once I was on stage, all of the questions were about the trip. I took the opportunity to set the record straight, and while I was talking, a reporter sitting in the audience repeatedly yelled "Bullshit!" My career in medicine certainly hadn't prepared me for this. The moderator asked if I would like the reporters who did the story to reinterview me. I said they never interviewed me in the first place; they had simply picked up unsubstantiated rumors and run with them.

When it was all over, I turned to John Ullyot and asked how this ambush had happened. John shrugged. "I don't know what happened. They promised me they wouldn't ask about Europe."

Not long after, I got a call from one of the reporters, telling me that my own media relations staff was setting me up. Various members of my staff confirmed that the leaks were coming directly from the VA press office and the political appointees.

At the White House, the Domestic Policy Council (DPC) was looking to add some expertise in veterans' issues. The DPC had its hands full with the focus on health care reform and infrastructure, and the VA issues seemed to be of secondary importance. Andrew Bremberg felt the solution would be for us to "detail" an expert in VA issues to the DPC. After going through a list of potential candidates that Andrew Bremberg rejected, I reluctantly recommended Darin Selnick. Darin was knowledgeable about the VA, and moving him out of my office solved a lot of other problems for me. Besides, I thought that Darin and I had established a good rapport, and he could be helpful in attracting more attention for the VA's agenda within the DPC. This decision may have been my biggest mistake as secretary.

When I first became secretary, Darin and I met on a regular basis, and he always sought my approval before moving forward with a plan or proposal. From my perspective, he challenged the traditional thinking, and we needed more of this at the VA. However, Darin's strength was not consensus-building, so he preferred to deal with me one-on-one or with a few other select people who shared his perspective. Soon he became a problem for members of my management team, who told me that they found him disruptive and difficult to work with. Increasingly, I found myself acting as referee.

Once over at the DPC, Darin started to run with his own agenda. The DPC was glad to have their VA "expert" and gave him plenty of latitude. But soon Darin was representing himself as "the White House," calling regular meetings with VA staff, giving orders, and moving policy in new directions. This new aggressiveness by the "White House" set off alarms both inside and outside of the VA. Not only VA staffers but also veterans service groups felt that Darin was simply dictating terms to them. Making matters worse, VA pushback always conveniently coincided with a leak to a reporter from anonymous "White House sources," expressing "White House" frustrations with how the VA was handling something.

36

Pushing Forward Toward Reform

ONE PART OF MY JOB I ALWAYS LOOKED FORWARD TO WAS WELCOMING participants from honor flights, where ordinary citizens took World War II veterans on a trip to DC. They toured the World War II Memorial and sometimes scored an invitation to the White House. On one occasion, I met a large group in the Indian Treaty Room at the White House and then introduced Vice President Pence to the group. On another occasion, Merle and the kids and I were touring the monuments on a weekend when I saw an honor flight of veterans gathering. I took the opportunity to approach and greet them. The group, averaging age ninety, thought it had been prearranged for the secretary to meet them there, and they were all pretty excited.

I also looked forward to Medal of Honor ceremonies. I had not known much about this distinguished group of Americans until we met one young man at the 2016 Army-Navy Game. Florent Groberg, or Flo, was born in France thirty-three years earlier to an American father and a French Algerian mother. He became a naturalized citizen in 2001 and joined the US Army in 2008. He served in Afghanistan, and in 2012, when he saw a suicide bomber approaching a group of fellow soldiers, Flo ran toward the terrorist and pushed him as far away from his men as he possibly could. He saved some lives, although he was unable to save everyone. He himself was severely injured and still struggles to hold on to one of his legs, which doctors had recommended amputating. President Obama awarded him the Medal of Honor in November 2015. There are approximately eighty Medal of Honor recipients alive today, only eleven of whom served in Iraq or Afghanistan, which puts Flo in a pretty select group of individuals. I kept in touch with Flo and saw him regularly at events around Washington.

I wanted to fix the system for all veterans but especially for those who, like Flo, were severely injured but, unlike Flo, lacked the podium and resources that a Medal of Honor provides. Toward this end, I met regularly with veterans and families who were struggling to get the help they needed. One day when I met with a dozen veterans and their caregivers, a mother talked to me about her son, who was now a quadriplegic. He had no bladder function and required urinary catheterization three times a day, yet the VA would only dispense thirty catheters a month. Fortunately, his mother often found VA staff who looked the other way and let her take more, but each month she was anxious about securing the equipment she needed. Other stories I heard that day also reflected a system that too often prioritized rules over following through on our moral obligation to take care of our veterans. I told my staff that I wanted an "easy button" to simply cut through the red tape. For these men and women, it shouldn't be so hard to get the help they deserve.

On November 13, 2017, I joined Senator Elizabeth Dole and former first lady Laura Bush at a conference to highlight the importance of those individuals who personally care for the veterans in their life. As I came to know more of these caregivers personally, I saw how important they were to maintaining the dignity and quality of life for our most severely injured veterans. I also got a glimpse into just how difficult their lives are—sacrificing their personal aspirations to care (often full time) for someone else.

One year earlier, I established the first VA Committee on Caregivers and Family, which I asked Elizabeth Dole to chair. I knew it was unfair to ask someone whom I thought was already far too busy, but I also knew she was unlikely to say no. She hesitated for about ten seconds before agreeing.

During the next several months, I grew quite close to Senator Dole. An octogenarian, she had more energy than almost anyone I'd ever met. Caregivers were really important to her, in part probably because she was one herself.

In 2010, Congress approved legislation to provide comprehensive caregiver support for veterans who served after 9/11. This program serves approximately twenty-seven thousand caregivers and has been critical to helping them provide the right care to those in need. However, while there was an intention to expand the program to veterans in other generations, that never happened.

The program, like many approved by Congress, had good intentions but did not necessarily lead to the desired outcome. VA research actually showed that caregiver support added to costs rather than reducing them. I believed the reason for this was that the program was legislatively restricted to exclude many veterans who needed caregivers the most, and therefore the full potential impact of caregivers was not seen. This belief gave me even more reason to advocate for expanding the caregiver program. As originally authorized, the program was only for post-9/11 veterans, and therefore older veterans—those most likely to get benefit from caregivers—were ineligible. As a result, caregiver support, while clearly beneficial, was not being optimally utilized.

The largest groups of veterans today are Vietnam veterans, whose average age is seventy. As these veterans age, they use more health care resources, and if projections are correct, will soon require significantly more long-term care. The budget for long-term care is expected to increase by hundreds of millions of dollars over the next twenty years. The VA is one of the few health systems that offer long-term care benefits, and taxpayers are obligated for this expense.

I was among those who advocated for an expansion of the caregiver benefit to the pre-9/11 veteran population, and while there was strong support for this among veterans service organizations and many members of Congress, once again the Office of Management and Budget was not supportive. I felt that the OMB did not understand the cost offsets associated with caregivers in the older population, and I was convinced that the expansion of caregivers to older veterans would save money in the long run. I also took a public position that we needed to change the eligibility criteria from a single deficit in activities of daily living to three. This would focus the program on those who were most severely disabled and would be more aligned with industry standards.

As secretary, I announced a "VA moonshot" meant to deliver on a promise that veterans could remain at home in a safe and secure environment as long as they wanted. Through the VA's extensive telehealth infrastructure, home health aide and attendance programs, remote monitoring technology, home delivery of drugs and durable medical equipment, caregiver programs, and home-based primary care and specialty care programs, we could help veterans avoid ever having to involuntarily leave their homes to receive care.

This was not only the right thing to do, it was also in the best interests of taxpayers. The cost of caring for a veteran in a long-term care facility averaged more than $130,000 per year, while the cost of comprehensive service in the home was about $75,000.

After I left office, I was pleased to see, as I had advocated, that Congress incorporated the caregiver benefit into the permanent benefits package for veterans who served before 9/11.

37

Rumors Flying

REPORTERS WERE NOW CALLING ME TO TELL ME THAT THERE WAS A new rumor, from sources they trusted, that the Mar-a-Lago crowd not only wanted me removed but had been talking to Jared Kushner and the president about replacing me with Toby Cosgrove. This was hardly surprising, nor was the fact that the politicals had been feeding Ike, Bruce, and Marc misinformation about what I was trying to do to improve the VA.

But I was also suddenly under fire from the opposite direction. Some of the VSO leaders thought I was aligned with the Koch brothers in wanting to privatize the VA. The VSO leaders communicated to people within the VA that they were not going to let me shut down the VA and privatize it. When I reached out to explain that this characterization couldn't be further from the truth, several of the VSO leaders told me that Darin Selnick had told them that he and I were aligned in our goal of privatization. I was livid. This was typical Darin, not only representing that he spoke for the secretary of VA, as well as the "White House" when convenient, but completely misrepresenting my position.

Later that day, the president's budget came back with far less money for the VA than I had requested. Fortunately, I had taken the opportunity to tell President Trump that I thought the OMB's plan to offset the Choice Program and the expansion of the GI

Bill with billions from discretionary VA spending was a mistake. The president looked at me and said, "We shouldn't do it, right?" I nodded. Then he turned to Kelly, "Let's make sure this doesn't get cut."

Over the Thanksgiving weekend, I spoke to Ike for more than an hour one day, and he let me know as always that he soon would be speaking with the president. In a particularly serious yet eerie tone, Ike predicted, "You're going to be gone in six months." I shuddered, knowing exactly how much influence Ike had—in general and with the president. When he wanted something, he got it. Ike suggested that I was already negotiating a $5 million per year job in the private sector. If only. I didn't bother to ask where he was hearing this completely false information, but I suspected it might have come from one of the politicals. Certainly Camilo Sandoval was known for bragging about his close contacts with Ike. During one of his conversations with Ike, he once held up his phone so others in the room could hear and see just how close they were.

The president continued to get advice on the VA from a variety of nontraditional sources. I knew he was holding a meeting with his VA advisers over Thanksgiving weekend. Upon his return from the holiday break at Mar-a-Lago, the president asked to see me. When I got to the Oval Office, the president immediately tried to reach Ike, but Ike did not answer his phone. The president then said to me, "Why can't you negotiate a better deal with Cerner?"

I was taken aback because I had no information at all about the financial arrangements being discussed with Cerner or any of the specifics of the contract, so how could anyone at the White House know that it was supposedly not being negotiated appropriately?

Soon afterward, there was an event in the Oval Office to honor the Navajo code talkers—Native American World War II veterans who allowed the United States to convey secure messages by speaking over the radio in Navajo, a language largely unknown outside the American Southwest. Only eleven of these men were still alive, and one of them was ninety-seven years old and in a wheelchair, but he stood up when the president entered the room.

This was the first time that I had been in a room with the president when he did not make eye contact with me or acknowledge me publicly. Afterward, I spoke with Kelly, who said that President Trump was very upset with me because of what his friends in Florida told him. I responded, "You must mean Ike?"

Kelly said, "Yes, that guy tells POTUS what to do despite not knowing what he's talking about."

I was pretty concerned, so I called Ike and blurted, "What did you do?" I asked him how this type of talk was going to help the VA, but Ike refused to respond.

38

Choosing Choice

I F THERE WAS AN ISSUE THAT LOOMED LARGER THAN ALL OTHERS AND persisted throughout the entire time I was at the VA, it was how freely veterans should be able to obtain medical care from private providers at government expense. In the original 2014 legislation—the Veterans Access, Choice, and Accountability Act—Congress approved an appropriation for $10 billion to fund Choice for a three-year period. By law, the money was due to run out in October 2017. We all knew that Choice needed to be a standard feature of the VA system, so in early 2017, working with the Office of Management and Budget, we included Choice as a permanent program in the 2018 proposed president's budget. This would change the VA's direction for decades to come.

But along the way, I sought to incorporate some major reforms. As set forth in a 2014 law, Choice had been difficult to administer, and in three years, we had learned a significant amount about how it could work better. The most problematic feature was the number of different funding sources, which VA was not allowed to merge, making it almost inevitable that we would run out of money in one account while still having funds going to waste in another.

In working to pass new Choice legislation, I wanted to move all funds for community care into a single funding source. I also wanted to redesign the program so that the onus of paperwork would be on a third-party administrator and direct interface with the veteran would be left to the VA. We had learned the hard way that any successful, customer-driven organization doesn't outsource its interface with its customers.

I also wanted to get rid of the 40/30 rule that determined eligibility. The 40/30 rule provided that a veteran had to live more than forty miles from a VA primary-care provider or wait more than thirty days for an appointment in order to access Choice funds. I didn't believe that any health care system should be based on arbitrary, nonclinical criteria like this.

Before the Senate committee, I testified how our new design for the Choice Program could improve clinical outcomes while maintaining fiscal responsibility to taxpayers. We proposed replacing the existing Choice system with something similar to what most nonveterans experienced with their health care. In our proposal, a veteran would contact his or her provider, who would then make a clinical determination and prescribe a service. If the service was available in a clinically appropriate timeframe at the VA, the veteran would be seen there. If not, the veteran would be sent out into the community. Additionally, a veteran might be asked to wait for a VA appointment for something elective, such as a routine eye exam or an annual physical but would never be asked to wait for an urgent clinical need. I also proposed that if the local VA was not performing at a standard equal to or above the quality of services elsewhere in the community, this alone should allow the veteran access to community providers. After my testimony, I met separately and on several occasions with many of the key committee members to make sure they understood why we proposed what we did and to address their specific questions and concerns.

Based largely on our proposal, on November 28, Chairman Isakson introduced bipartisan legislation to give veterans more options for private health care when the VA couldn't meet their needs. This plan would expand use of Choice well beyond the fewer than one million veterans who were previously able to avail themselves and would make the benefits available to all nine million users of the VA system.

Senator Moran was the only member of the committee who opposed the bill, arguing that it didn't go far enough. He was from Kansas—a rural state where staffing at VA clinics had been inadequate, particularly in the least-populated areas. Consequently, the senator became an advocate for unfettered choice so that any veteran would have the ability to visit a VA facility or a facility in the private sector whenever he or she wanted. He believed that our proposal still left the VA with too much control over the veterans' decision to seek care in the community.

I met with Senator Moran and his staff and told him that I was not philosophically opposed to his approach. That is, I supported giving veterans more choice over their health care decisions. But I also told him that, as a practical matter, this was just not something we could do in the immediate future. For one thing, economists working with the Commission on Care estimated that the cost of unfettered choice would be over $21 billion more than what we were currently spending. (I thought this was a very conservative estimate and would likely cost much more.) Unlike in the private sector, many who use the VA system don't have copays and deductibles; veterans' use of the private sector would result in the VA having to cover these new expenses. I told Senator Moran that we needed a multiyear plan if we wanted to move in the direction that he proposed. I further told him that the plan that Chairman Isakson had introduced would lay the groundwork for opening up the system for greater choice while simultaneously strengthening existing VA facilities. But I also told him that implementing the changes he wanted too quickly and all at once, as he was advocating, would in our opinion have a devastating effect on the health of veterans and the future of the entire VA system.

Senator Moran ignored my advice and made a number of proposed amendments to the bill, including new language expanding access to the private sector, but he found no other supporters on the committee. The vote was fourteen to one for Senator Isakson's version of the bill, with Senator Moran as the sole dissenter. I supported Isakson's version, and the plan was to submit it to the floor for a full Senate vote. But even in the face of this lopsided defeat, Moran went ahead and introduced his version with his language that had just been voted down by the committee. Twenty-six VSOs signed a letter of support for Isakson's version of the bill. The representative for the American Legion created a short video clip of him lighting a match to the Moran bill and watching the flames destroy it. Veterans by and large felt that the Moran bill would dismantle a system that they fought hard for and on which they had come to rely.

In mid-January, I was asked to testify before the Senate VA subcommittee, and for the first time ever, I was asked to take an oath. In the past, it was always assumed that I would be truthful. But this new wrinkle wasn't simply the atmosphere of suspicion stirred up by the inspector general. Senator Moran was, in fact, planning an ambush. He personally attacked me, calling me "two-faced" and accusing me of saying different things to different people.

I was offended, but I kept my composure and stuck to the facts, setting forth very clearly where I stood on the issues, particularly on the matter of Choice. Moran continued to push for an approach that had been overwhelmingly voted down by the committee. The big story from the day was Moran yelling at me. One headline read: "Secretary Lying." This was a stark break from the civility and respect that I had always experienced at congressional hearings until now.

I suspected that Darin Selnick was behind this. Darin was close with Senator Moran's staff and was meeting with them on a regular basis. I had been told that he was feeding them completely misleading information. If Senator Moran's objective had been the truth, he might've had the decency to talk to me before coming into a hearing and slinging public accusations. But he was still pushing to get his own version of Choice approved, and if getting rid of me via slander helped, so be it.

To be generous to Senator Moran—and given the way he went from zero to sixty and politicized the issue at a public hearing without giving me any warning—I have to conclude that he was simply playing the Washington game, grandstanding in the hope of scoring some points and maybe convincing some of his colleagues on the far right to follow.

The political appointees, supported by the Domestic Policy Council at the White House, however, were very much in favor of Senator Moran's version that called for unfettered access to private care. To me, this seemed like a more politically acceptable way of saying they wanted to privatize the VA. They also refused to support the caregiver provisions. The White House didn't seem to understand that Senator Moran's version not only would put the VA system at risk of harm by diluting its delivery capabilities but would cost the US Treasury billions more each year. It seemed to me that the White House's enthusiasm was pure political ideology, detached from any rational understanding of how health care actually worked. Aside from the very wealthy who can afford to pay out of pocket, there is no other group in the United States that can access whatever care they want without copays, deductibles, or some system for managing utilization and costs. Chairman Isakson and others on the committee were frustrated with me for not speaking out in full support of their version of the bill, but my hands were tied. I couldn't speak out publicly against the White House. But everyone, especially the political appointees at the VA, knew exactly where I stood.

With John Kelly now limiting access to the president, I needed to reach out to others in the administration. Rick Dearborn responded that he would check on why there appeared to be such a disconnect between this Republican committee chairman, Senator Isakson, and the White House staff. I also spoke to Marc Short, the legislative head for the Trump administration at the time, who affirmed that the secretary should be in charge of making policy decisions. But that didn't seem to matter. Andrew Bremberg from the Domestic Policy Council called me back and said that the White House was concerned that I did not support the type of VA system that the president campaigned for. I saw

Isakson's proposal, and now the Senate Veterans Affairs Committee's proposal, as a major reform, but force-fed information by Selnick and Bremberg characterized it as hardly a step above the status quo. Meanwhile, Senator Moran was working closely with Selnick and Bremberg to sabotage this measure that had passed in the committee by fourteen to one. These guys were always all or nothing—no compromise—and it seemed pretty clear to me that their ultimate goal was privatization of the VA.

John Ullyot pressured me to send out a press release saying that neither the White House nor I was fully supportive of Chairman Isakson's bill. The press release became public before I even had the chance to carefully read it, because I was in a cabinet meeting and wasn't allowed access to my phone in the West Wing. When Senator Isakson and Senator Tester read the press release, they were furious. Isakson—a Republican committee chairman feeling like he was thrown under the bus by a Republican president—called the president to ask for clarification on his position.

For days I was forced in the middle of a political fight over the future of veterans' health care that seemed stuck in the Washington swamps. I had a meeting with the White House about Choice, where Darin Selnick told me he spoke for the president. I flashed back to Darin saying that he spoke for the secretary. Now he spoke for the president, too.

At this point, I was eager to talk to the president in person. The White House press team, under pressure from Darin Selnick, was not allowing me to put out a new press release that offered my support for the committee's version of the Choice bill that passed fourteen to one. The veterans service organizations were increasingly upset that I was not publicly supporting it. They didn't understand the kind of battle brewing between me and the White House staff.

While the VA staff had been working hard to develop our approach, Darin Selnick had been saying that the proposed legislation I supported was really just the "status quo" and that the White House needed to support Moran's bill. Darin had effectively created two separate voices on veterans' issues for the administration—the secretary and the White House. Before this, we had made good progress with a strong bipartisan approach to veterans' issues. But now the dissonance between these two dueling power bases threatened to derail it all.

Chairman Isakson held a meeting at his office with me, Senator Tester, Senator Moran, Darin Selnick, and Andrew Bremberg from the Domestic Policy Council. Isakson said he wanted to work things out but if we couldn't come to a resolution, he would move the bill (as voted out of committee) forward to a full Senate floor vote. Everyone seemed open to a compromise except for Senator Moran. But in the end, he agreed to sit down and see if we could work out a mutually agreeable approach.

The real issue boiled down to the criteria we used for allowing veterans to seek care in the community. I wanted it to be a clinical approach—a joint decision made between the doctor and the veteran. Senator Moran wanted the access standards to be fixed and posted so veterans wouldn't have to rely on a VA doctor. He communicated that he simply didn't trust VA doctors to do the right thing.

Several times I thought Senator Moran's staff and my staff had worked out a compromise that would satisfy everyone and that the compromise legislation would move forward. Ultimately, though, there just seemed to be too much bad blood.

With a delay on the Senate side, the House started to pick up steam in mid-March. Working to get something into the omnibus, Chairman Roe had proposed a slimmed-down version of the Senate bill to keep the Choice Program funded. I supported Chairman Roe's effort, and I was in contact with both Republicans and Democrats in the Senate and House. It was clear to me that it was essential to include some expansion of caregiver benefits—an important issue to many Senate Democrats as well as a number of Republicans—yet the White House refused to support this provision. Despite my best attempts, the bill died before getting to the omnibus. The veterans service organizations told me that the politicals blamed me for the failure to achieve a legislative solution.

I continued to look for a way forward. Both Chairman Isakson and Chairman Roe were willing partners. The ranking members were also supportive of the original bills, but I understood that they weren't enthusiastic about bills that stripped out all of the additional support for the VA and did not include a caregiver expansion.

Ike Perlmutter, Marc Sherman, and Bruce Moskowitz flew up from Florida for a meeting about the VA with Jared Kushner in the West Wing. Once again, I wasn't invited. My sources suggested that the topic was Isakson's approach on Choice versus Moran's more extreme version. Senator Isakson told me that he had been trying to get in touch with John Kelly about the status of the White House support for his bill. I spoke to Kelly and told him that Isakson had called the White House multiple times but no one had returned his call. This was just one of many times that I wondered if the White House phone lines had been cut.

Hearing that Ike was in town, I called him. Ike suggested meeting at the Trump International Hotel. At the hotel, he mentioned his meeting with the president earlier, and while he would not give specifics, he kept repeating, "The president is not happy with you." Ike seemed to think I was intent on signing the Cerner contract imminently, even though I had repeatedly told him I wasn't going to move forward until I fully resolved any outstanding concerns, especially related to achieving data interoperability with the private sector. I didn't share any private details of the contract with Ike, of course, and he never pressed me on them. He just felt that I was rushing. Once again, I suspected that these concerns were generated by the politicals spreading inaccurate information.

Soon after, it was finally my turn to meet with the president in the Oval Office. I explained that we were at a critical point with the Choice bill and told him that my recommendation was to support the committee-approved bill. Unaware of the political roadblocks his appointees were constructing daily, Trump said, "Sure, whatever you need. Let's get this bill through." Then he said, "Do you want me to call Isakson?" Without waiting for my response, he picked up the phone, called the senator, and put him on speakerphone. Isakson, not knowing that he was on speakerphone or that I was in the room, told the president how much he enjoyed working with me and how much he appreciated having me as the secretary. The president relished this praise, because praise for me was praise for him, but he was finished with the conversation. He said, "Look, Johnny, just get the deal done. Make it great and get it done," and hung up.

The president never asked me to delve into detail on Choice but consistently instructed me to push hard for effective reform. He seemed to understand that we had a good opportunity to make progress, but at the same time, moving too rapidly would be disastrous for the VA, fiscally irresponsible for the government, and politically unpredictable. Clearly there were some short circuits in the transmission of information among me, the president, and the White House staff. The White House staff was still not issuing a statement of support from the president for the bill that passed committee or allowing me to release one from my office. They remained firm in their commitment to Senator Moran's version of the bill rather than Isakson's. This rogue group seemed to do whatever they wanted, regardless of whether their perspectives were aligned with the president's. This may be one of the reasons why we often see the White House come out with a policy that the president then contradicts almost immediately.

39

The Interrogation

THE INVESTIGATION INTO MY EUROPEAN TRAVEL WAS NOW IN FULL swing. The IG met with many of my staff before coming to meet with me at VA headquarters. I obtained my own legal counsel as soon as I realized that the IG investigation had taken on a life of its own, so there with me were my attorney, Justin Shur, and Eric Nitz, Justin's associate. Even though I was 100 percent certain that I had done nothing wrong, everything was out of control and being twisted, so I was advised not to navigate this alone.

Justin was a well-polished and mild-tempered attorney with a great résumé. He was previously the deputy chief of the US Department of Justice's Public Integrity Section of the Criminal Division as well as an assistant district attorney at the Manhattan district attorney's office.

My meeting with the IG's staff was hostile from the start. "Who is Barbara Van Dahlen?" the lead investigator began.

"Barbara is the head of an organization called Give an Hour," I said, wondering where this came from.

"Well, isn't it true that you never met Vicky Gosling until Barbara Van Dahlen introduced you to her in March of 2017?"

"No, that's not true. I met Vicky in 2015 at the British ambassador's residence."

"Well, then explain this!" he countered, throwing an email in front of my face and shaking it wildly. This was more like a page from a bad legal thriller than the dignified meeting with a cabinet member that it should've been.

I took the email and read it. It contained several paragraphs from Barbara Van Dahlen, thanking me for attending a Give an Hour event. At the end of the email was an offer to introduce me to Vicky Gosling. As I recall, the entirety of my reply to her several paragraphs email read "OK."

As secretary, I had received several hundred emails a day. Many of these were multiple pages in length. Given the volume alone, on top of calls, letters, and a packed schedule, my practice was to rapidly skim emails for important information and then respond when possible with a single-word answer: yes, no, or OK. These one-word answers were often more acknowledgments that I had received a message rather than an indication to take an action. It was simply a matter of time management and survival, but it often meant that my communications were distracted and unclear. I explained to the investigators that my "OK" to Barbara was simply an acknowledgment of her email.

"Well, if you already knew Vicky Gosling, in a subsequent email, why did you ask Barbara Van Dahlen for her email address? Isn't it true that you didn't know Vicky Gosling at all?"

In fact, Merle and I had seen Vicky at Barbara's event at the Canadian embassy a few days before Barbara's email arrived. Vicky and Merle spent most of the event catching up as I worked the room. Vicky told Merle that she had left the Invictus Foundation after the prior year's Orlando event. Merle told Vicky of our upcoming plans to go to the United Kingdom in July, and Vicky said that we must get together and wanted Merle and me to meet her husband.

After receiving Barbara's email where she mentioned Vicky, I realized that I only had Vicky's Invictus Foundation email address, which I assumed she no longer held. So I wrote back to Barbara and asked if she had Vicky's current email address.

I tried to explain all of this, but the investigators just shook their heads and proceeded with even more aggressive questioning.

Placing another email in front of me, one of them said, "Why did you ask Vicky Gosling if she could get you Wimbledon tickets?"

I reviewed the email, in which I let Vicky know that we were indeed coming to London and asked her if she knew where I could buy Wimbledon tickets for Saturday, the day we were scheduled to arrive. She responded that it was perfect timing, since she had bought four tickets, and her sister just told her that she and her husband were unable to attend. Vicky asked if Merle and I would join them and use her sister's tickets. I responded, accepting her invitation and asking how much we owed her for the tickets. I had no expectation of not paying for them. Vicky didn't respond to my question over email, and even though I asked her on several other occasions for the price of the tickets, she always responded, "Oh, I'll let you know later." It was very similar to that awkward moment at the end of a dinner when each person reaches for the check and says, "You can pay next time." This is what friends do.

It was later, after the IG report exploded, that Merle pushed Vicky for the cost of the tickets and told her that we really needed to reimburse her. If not, even though there were no government funds involved, we were instructed to reimburse the US Treasury for the cost of the tickets. In actuality, it was more of a donation to the Treasury than a reimbursement.

At that point, Vicky said, "You want to know why I never responded to any of David's requests to pay us for the tickets? I get a military subscription series to all the Wimbledon matches, which comes at a big discount. It's buy one, get one free. But there's a strict set of rules, one of which is not to resell any tickets under any circumstance, even to family and friends. I actually got two of the tickets free and didn't know what to say. You were my guests, as friends, and I wanted to leave it at that."

At one point in the interview, another investigator chimed in. "Dr. Shulkin, after Vicky Gosling emailed you that you could join her at Wimbledon, you immediately emailed your wife to let her know. Now why did you do that?"

I let the absurdity of the question sink in. "You realize that my wife and I live in different cities during the week. I often email her with new information," I replied.

Now yelling, she asked, "But why did you consider this important enough to let her know right away?"

Justin, who had been silent during the entire interview to this point, spoke up. "I don't think you're treating the secretary with proper respect."

Both investigators yelled at Justin in unison, "You are not allowed to speak!"

Justin started, "I have the right to—"

Justin was cut off by a harsh warning that if he continued to speak, he would be asked to leave the room. Justin and I decided it was best that we both leave the room and let the investigators' tempers cool down. We returned ten minutes later, but the investigators picked up with their same aggressive style and accusatory line of questioning.

Justin and I were taken aback by the outright hostility we experienced. So much of what they asked was misguided, and their every interpretation was twisted and completely off base. We wanted to clear the record, so we prepared a written response, complete with emails, pictures, and other supporting documentation.

Meanwhile, the IG had started in on a second front, this time focused on whether or not I made inappropriate use of my security detail.

My approach to security had been to simply follow the recommendations of the professionals. On the same day that I was sworn in as secretary, the Office of Emergency Preparedness and Security team requested a meeting with me. They told me their job was to assess the risk to the secretary and that they highly recommended we continue the security protocol of past secretaries, which was to have a team to protect me whenever I was in public and to have all locations checked in advance for risk. They handed me a written recommendation and asked if I agreed. Knowing the least in the room about security risk and protocols and having no reason to question their practices, I agreed.

"Did you have the security team take you to Home Depot?" the investigators began.

"Yes." As per my security protocol, my agents accompanied me whenever I left my home. Merle and I had just purchased a small one-bedroom condominium in DC and needed some new fixtures from Home Depot. I wasn't sure where this line of questioning was going.

"Did you have them carry a toilet to your home?"

"No," I said. "We chose a toilet for our bathroom, but our contractor picked it up from the store, delivered it, and installed it. We paid the contractor for all that. I have the receipt."

"Did you have your security detail load other packages into the car?"

"Not that I recall, and this may seem strange, but I actually have pictures right here on my phone from that day. Merle loves to take pictures, and she snapped a picture of the scene because she thought it was funny to watch me and the Home Depot guy struggling to get things into the trunk of the car with my big, burly security team standing by, just watching."

"Did security accompany you to the supermarket or the drug-store when you went out?"

"Yes, I was told that they had to."

There was no reply from the IG.

I left the meeting somewhat puzzled. I thought the security protocol for cabinet secretaries was black and white: security at any and all times outside the home.

I spoke to John Kelly about all of this. He was sympathetic but didn't offer any particular advice or help. This surprised me, since he knew that as a cabinet secretary, he had security with him at all times and that all cabinet secretaries had similar or even greater security arrangements.

Not knowing who to turn to, I called my general counsel and my assistant secretary for security into my office and said, "Look, I don't know what to do at this point. I want to make sure we are doing things properly. I have this sheet of paper you gave me the day I was confirmed as secretary. It says that I require protection at all times outside my residence, but I guess it doesn't specifically spell out that I should be accompanied on personal errands. I want a clearer document on when I need security and when it's appropriate. Can you do that?"

A few days later, they produced a document that specified I was to have security on any occasion that I was outside my residence, including personal errands.

The irony was that while I liked many of my agents, I hated having security following me around. Suddenly strangers had to be included in everything my family and I did. I felt like I had no freedom and no privacy.

I now understood why several of my staff had left their IG interviews shaking and why tough guys like Brad and others had decided to leave the agency after this experience. The IG's approach led me to believe that his office had an agenda and was determined to prove some negative version of events, regardless of whether the facts supported it.

During the lull between Christmas and New Year's, I decided to take a quick break from the Washington rancor and go to Florida with my family, but I cut the trip short to meet with Ike and Lori Perlmutter, Bruce Moskowitz, Marc Sherman, Tom Bowman, and Jared Kushner. The Mar-a-Lago trio scolded me for not communicating enough with them and informed me that they had lost trust in me. With all the Washington craziness I was dealing with, as well as the real changes I was trying to drive, I had neglected to be as accessible to them as I was in the past. It's also true that while I had no official obligation to them whatsoever, this level of contact almost certainly fell below their expectations.

40

New Year's Resolutions

As we entered the new year, and with my time very likely running out, I knew I needed to redefine priorities and focus even more sharply than before. With the Choice legislation still pending, I felt it was essential to describe a vision for what the VA health care system should be.

In March 2016, I detailed a road map that was published in the *New England Journal of Medicine*. Central to my vision for honoring our commitment to veterans was my belief in sustaining a dedicated VA health system. Many of these men and women required services that were simply not available in the private sector. But I also believed that many VA services were either readily available or done better in the private sector. The reformed system I envisioned needed to be a hybrid. We needed to make full use of the private sector where it made sense but at the same time strengthen the services that were central to the VA mission—the so-called foundational services that included traumatic brain injury, spinal cord injury, blind rehabilitation, hearing centers, posttraumatic stress, prosthetics and orthotics, polytrauma, and centers focusing on the environmental hazards of war. In this category I also included general primary care and behavioral health services.

But achieving that hybrid system was going to require more creativity, so I asked each medical center director to participate in a brainstorming exercise in which they had to present a plan to move 5 percent of their budget from routine services to foundational services. While 5 percent may seem like a small amount, 5 percent of a $70 billion budget adds up to $3.5 billion per year—which, over three years, is more than $10 billion.

Over videoconference, each of the network directors presented a plan that was thoughtful and comprehensive. Almost uniformly, they recommended that money be moved from specific purpose funding sources to unrestricted general funding. Because Congress often appropriates money for particular programs rather than allowing the heads of the facilities to determine where the funding is needed most, medical centers frequently have a surplus in some accounts while other necessary programs are deficient. Technically, the VA can redirect moneys from special purpose to general purpose after notifying Congress. One of the programs that many network directors suggested moving some funds away from was assistance for the homeless, since in many parts of the country, the allocated levels of funding for it were no longer needed.

Of course these directors supported ending veteran homelessness, yet Congress kept increasing the funding for this program, which now stood at close to $1.5 billion per year and was sometimes more money than we requested. Some areas of the country had already made good progress, and some had ended veteran homelessness altogether. Other medical center directors wanted to increase their efficiency and effectiveness by further integrating their social work and counseling programs into their homeless program and other behavioral health services.

Clearly we were just at the first stage of a lengthy discussion. In Washington, almost any change that results in fewer resources for a specific program is controversial. But my new policy to allow money to shift from the central office to local medical centers and to allow them to make their own spending decisions signaled that we were starting to listen more to our leaders in the field instead of dictating to them from VA headquarters. It was certainly not targeted to reduce our efforts in ending homelessness.

Yet some leaders in the VA central program offices who stood to lose control reacted swiftly. Rumors began to spread that the VA no longer cared about homeless veterans. Others said we were completely eliminating research programs. These rumors quickly reached both advocacy groups and congressional staff members. Soon I started to receive letters from Congress and inquiries from the press about my lack of support for homeless veterans.

Then an article came out reporting that I had recommended cutting support for homeless veterans by $680 million. This was ridiculous. Few people knew just how important ending veteran homelessness was to me. I would attend events where the goal was to identify homeless veterans by walking inner-city streets after midnight. My family and I would work at the homeless stand-downs, giving out food and clothing to veterans in need. This issue was personal to me, but as happens so often in Washington, rumors and news reports reinforced each other until they spun out of control. This kind of intense and distorted overreaction is one of the reasons why some career staff chose never to take any risks. Challenging the status quo in Washington is not for the faint of heart.

Given the misrepresentation of my policy to move funds from DC to the field, I decided to temporarily suspend any of the proposed changes to the program. Washington had already taught me that changes can't be rushed. These events reminded me of a quote by George H. W. Bush's chief of staff, John Sununu: "You can get in trouble for doing something right in such a way that your enemies can make it look as if you did something wrong."

Over the weekend, we found an unmarked envelope in our home mailbox that contained articles about my cuts in the homelessness program and referred to my European trip with some unflattering and disturbing comments. Security said that Merle should never have opened it. They also recommended that we install panic buttons and cameras in our home.

41

Leaks Turn into Floods

Darin Selnick, one of the most persistent thorns in my side, continued to meet with the VSOs without my knowledge, and he continued to tell them his version of what the administration was thinking. I tried to stay focused on my priorities, one of which was preventing veteran suicide.

Knowing that the highest incidence of veteran suicide was in the first twelve months after a soldier left the military, I worked on a bold plan to eliminate the gap in medical coverage from the time a soldier was discharged until he or she gained access to care. Although this was going to be expensive (with 250,000 soldiers discharged each year), I did not want this initiative to get held up by the Office of Management and Budget, so I asked for no additional dollars to get it done.

The president was delighted with this effort and signed an executive order to increase mental health benefits for veterans during the twelve months immediately after discharge from the military. After the signing, I walked out to Pebble Beach on the White House lawn, hoping to address the media, but reporters were focused on the administration's hardline immigration policies and the border wall. So with the press still at the White House, I went up to Leo Shane, the *Military Times* reporter, and asked him why he hadn't asked me about the executive order. Shane said, "Mr. Secretary, I already broke the story twenty-four hours ago." I was stunned and asked him how he'd gotten the information. His response: "Darin Selnick told me."

Toward the end of January, I was told that the IG report on the trip to Europe was soon to be released. In early February, even before its release, I received calls from reporters who had already obtained a copy of the draft report and told me it was pretty negative. I was shocked. Why did the press have a copy of the report when I didn't? And given the facts and the evidence that I provided, how could it possibly be so bad?

My lawyer, Justin, contacted the IG about the leak. The IG's office assured him that no such thing had happened. But if that was true, how did the IG's report get into the hands of reporters?

At roughly the same time, a national publication informed the VA press office that they were prepared to run an article on the extravagance of my domestic travel. They said I'd stayed in a hotel in Indianapolis that cost $239 per night and a hotel in Chicago that was 300 percent over the government rate. These reporters never took into account that I had little or no control over my travel arrangements. The VA has a travel team that arranges all hotels, airline tickets, and train tickets, and everything has to be approved in advance. I usually wouldn't know which hotel I was staying in until security dropped me off at the location and I checked in. The reporters also wanted to know why I stayed at the Ritz-Carlton during the Invictus Games in Toronto. I had been in Toronto for a total of six hours and didn't stay overnight. As mentioned above, I was at the Ritz only because the entire delegation had to wait for Melania Trump while she met with Prince Harry, and the hotel provided a room where all of us could answer emails and complete other work. This space was made available, gratis, by the State Department. Nevertheless, in a 24-7 news cycle, the facts never stood in the way of a good story.

These new allegations once again could only have originated through leaks from within the VA. The amount of time and energy wasted on this nonsense was absurd. While the media certainly serves an important role in society, its rapacious appetite for scandal does not always lead to constructive outcomes or a more open democracy. Clearly, I had adversaries within the VA who understood how to manipulate reports, exploit the media, and use them against me. This wasn't a game I had any experience or knowledge of playing.

Meanwhile, tension continued to build over the Choice bill. I was getting calls from a number of the organizations saying that Darin threatened the VSOs that if they didn't support Moran's version of the bill, they wouldn't be invited back to the White House. Apparently, Darin had also gone off on a screaming diatribe against Verna Jones, the executive director of the American Legion. Verna, previously outspoken in her opposition to any policy weakening the VA, suddenly lost her position at the American Legion a few months later. That evening, I spoke on the phone with Andrew Bremberg to inform him that Darin was out of control and hurting both the VA and the administration. Andrew said he would look into it. As usual, there was no follow-up.

Shortly afterward, I had a meeting with John Kelly to discuss the trouble being stirred up by Darin and other political appointees. Unknown to me, Kelly also invited Jared Kushner, Andrew Bremberg, Bill McGinley, and other aides. I assume they'd hoped I would be intimidated by the large attendance, but I wasn't. I laid out the evidence to Kelly, step by step, while he shook his head in disbelief.

I told the assembled group that with this level of interference, progress was at a standstill. I said that if we want to move ahead with reform, they were going to have to let *me* be the secretary and stop the Domestic Policy Council from acting as if they ran the VA. Kelly told me he agreed with me. If cooperation didn't improve, Kelly promised to raise the issue with the president.

Soon after, I got a note of apology from General Kelly, expressing his regrets for not having better controlled the White House staff. I was hopeful that Kelly was genuine and that he and the president were going to be more clearly on my side from this point forward, but I also doubted that Kelly was going to be able to flip the very intentional and malicious behaviors of the politicals. It seemed to me that the White House staff followed their own intensely partisan instincts, no matter who instructed them to do otherwise, and this was all deeply discouraging. This was no way to run the VA. This was no way to run the agency. This was no way to run the country.

42

Out of Control

SEAN DOOCEY, THE TWENTY-FOUR-YEAR-OLD WHO HAD BEEN entrusted with day-to-day operations of the Office of Presidential Personnel (PPO) by its head, Johnny DeStefano, sent messages to Tom Bowman and to the new under secretary of Memorial Affairs, Randy Reeves, reminding them that they served at the pleasure of the president. Tom Bowman had already been told that he was not allowed to fire political appointees because that decision rested with the White House. I requested a meeting at the VA with PPO to discuss these veiled threats to my management team.

I started, "Okay, tell me what the problem is."

Sean said, "I'll tell you what the problem is. The problem is *him*." He pointed dramatically at Tom. "We don't like him because he doesn't support the president's agenda. We think he's still working for Isakson's bill." Sean continued on to their issues with my chief of staff, Vivieca, all stemming from the fact that she was a career person and not a political appointee.

The next day, I called in a group of politicals, including John Ullyot, Brooks Tucker, Jake Leinenkugel, Darin Selnick, Peter Shelby, and Camilo Sandoval. I said, "Why did this twenty-four-year-old have to tell me what's going on? Why didn't you guys let me know directly that you had concerns about Tom?"

They told me that when Tom arrived, he called them into his office and said, "Game over. You're going to do things our way from now on." Ever since, they said, relations had only further broken down.

The fact is, this group targeted my acting under secretary, then my chief of staff, and now my deputy secretary. Obviously, it was a strategy of attrition. If they could get rid of everyone around me—everyone I trusted—it would be harder for me to survive as secretary. I told them they had to work together with Tom and that we had to address the issues jointly. But I might as well have been talking to a brick wall.

On Sunday, February 5, I received an email with a copy of the draft IG report attached, and when I read it, my heart sank. These inquisitors twisted every fact, no matter how innocent, into an indictment of my character. The cover stated that while this was merely a draft, no changes would be considered except to correct typos or grammatical errors. Compounding the absurdity, they were giving me two business days to review the report. Two days is an insanely short amount of time to review something so complex and so important—especially considering that they took several months to write it.

The report was sloppy. On page 14, it said that the VA had paid $4,312 for Merle's airfare, but by page 45, it was $4,326.95. They were thorough enough to subpoena Merle's telephone records but conveniently left out the forty hours of lectures and meetings I attended in Europe and the hundreds of emails I sent during my time away. They also said that Merle had used Gabe, the overeager young staffer from the VA's Intergovernmental Affairs Office, as a "personal travel concierge," perhaps hoping that the awkward term they'd conjured up would catch on with the media. In planning the trip, Gabe had insisted that Merle provide all of our logistical details in order to coordinate with my security team. What exactly did the IG expect the staff person handling the logistics for the trip to do but to handle logistics? It was a hurtful and direct attack on Merle's reputation in addition to mine.

On Monday morning, the VA's chief legal counsel, Jim Byrne, came into my office and said, "Look, I don't think this is so bad for you. When it's released on Wednesday, you'll have a couple of bad days, but you'll get through this."

I said, "Wait, how do you know it's being released on Wednesday?"

Byrne didn't even realize that he had slipped and said something I wasn't supposed to hear. He reluctantly admitted that he knew because the IG had promised Senator Moran that he would release it on Wednesday. Byrne said that the politicals knew about it from Senator Moran's office and were giving each other high-fives over the news. My mind raced: the politicals . . . Senator Moran . . . Concerned Veterans of America . . . could they all be working together to spin the intricate web closing in around me?

It was beginning to make sense to me—I had not seen or heard from these political appointees in several days. My office usually had contact with them, especially with the media staff, several times a day. Now, with this report about to be released, they were nowhere to be found. In any other agency, the Office of Media Relations would be developing a full-blown communications strategy in response to such a report, starting with an official press statement. In this case, there was complete silence. It was clearer now than ever that I was all alone.

On Friday, February 9, the *Washington Post* released a story that the White House was firing my deputy secretary, Tom Bowman, later that day. According to "anonymous sources" in the administration, Tom was being fired for his failure to adhere to the president's agenda and as a *warning shot* to me. The all-too-clear implication was that I better support all things Trump, including the politicals and Senator Moran's Choice bill, even if a Republican-dominated committee had already rejected it. Most outrageously, according to the article, my major sin was talking to Democrats and maintaining a bipartisan approach!

Tom Bowman came into my office looking pale and asked me what I knew about this. I told him I knew nothing and assured him that he had my full support.

A few hours later, in the Oval Office with the president, I asked him if he was aware of any upcoming changes, especially regarding Tom. President Trump's reply was innocent enough. "You and I are the only ones who could fire your deputy. If neither of us is planning to, it can't be true. It can't be true."

When I conveyed this to Tom, he was reassured, but the damage was already done. People saw it as a direct attack on our authority to manage the department. With the draft IG report about my "lavish" trip to Europe having just been released and the political appointees clearly aware of my increased scrutiny in the press, the timing seemed more than coincidental.

Prior to becoming deputy secretary, Tom had been the staff director for the Senate Veterans Affairs Committee, where he had worked for Senator Johnny Isakson. After the *Post* ran the story about Tom's imminent departure, a reporter contacted Senator Isakson's communication director, Amanda Maddox, for a comment from the senator. Amanda emailed Tom to tell him that the sources for the original story about him had been Darin Selnick and Brooks Tucker. Tom called Amanda and said, "Are you sure you want to put that the information came from Darin and Brooks in an *email?*"

She confirmed, "Yes, Tom, I am fine with putting this in writing."

Tom asked me to call the *Washington Post* reporter to set the record straight and contact the White House to have them issue a retraction. I called the White House and left a message for press secretary Sarah Huckabee Sanders, and I also spoke to Raj Shah in Communications, who assured me that they would clear this up. Nobody ever did.

43

Fighting an Uphill Battle

I DIDN'T WANT THE IG REPORT TO CATCH GENERAL KELLY OR THE president by surprise, and luckily I already had a meeting scheduled where I could tell them myself. A few days before the report was to be released, the three of us met for lunch in the small, elegant dining room next to the Oval Office.

Facing a large flat-screen TV tuned to Fox News, with the remote control positioned adjacent to his plate, the president sat at the head of the table, with General Kelly and me on both sides. While the president focused on his lamb chops, assorted vegetables, and Diet Coke, I made my case.

"Mr. President, we're making good progress at the VA, and I am certain this will continue, with your support. But I have to tell you I'm very concerned about this IG report about to be released."

I had his attention now. The president understood media scandals and how much damage they can cause. "Okay, go on."

I described every allegation, countering each one with a factual description of what had really occurred. Throughout, the president and his chief of staff interrupted with questions.

"Who does the IG work for?" the president asked. General Kelly explained to him that inspectors general were independent of the agencies they were assigned to and reported to Congress.

"So you got approval from your ethics official for your wife to go?"

"Yes, that's right."

"So what's the problem? Seems like you should get through this. But you know what? Go talk to Stefan Passantino, our ethics attorney here at the White House. He's a great guy and will know what to do."

Before I left, as he usually did, the president asked me how Ike was doing and whether he was happy with the progress we were making.

Kelly added that he wanted me to meet with the White House communications team so that they would be prepared for the upcoming inquiries and could help with the messaging.

By the time I reached the Eisenhower Office Building, a short walk across Executive Avenue, Stefan Passantino was waiting for me. He told me that he had called his boss, Don McGahn, to let him know I was coming over. I went through the report in detail, and Stefan listened intently before offering an assessment.

"It doesn't really seem all that bad. Seems like there's a reasonable explanation for everything. Most important is for your department to push back *hard* on the IG and get your agency legal counsel involved. The response can't come from the White House, but if the VA's legal counsel needs some advice, please have them call me."

Encouraged, I then went to see Kellyanne Conway, Hope Hicks, and Sarah Huckabee Sanders—three of Trump's key communication officials. Hope's advice was to pay the government for the cost of Merle's ticket. "They won't stop hounding you until you do," she said. "So you might as well do it now."

Most of the other communications professionals I asked told me not to pay the money, because it would look like an admission of wrongdoing, but I took Hope's advice and mailed a check for $4,312 to the VA Finance Department for the coach ticket that the VA had bought Merle.

The VA attorney who was provided a copy of the IG report told me that something seemed seriously off, especially because I had only been given two days to review the document. He had never seen a review time shorter than thirty days. Why was there such a rush to release this report? Why didn't they want the secretary of the VA to have sufficient time to respond to such a high-stakes matter?

Then, incredibly, the IG issued a revised draft report with new materials. This new version contained an interview with Vicky Gosling—something that the first draft did not. Apparently the IG's office had been in a hurry to publicly issue the report, despite not having had the opportunity to interview such a key person. Since the first version of the report had already found our relationship with Vicky to be improper and not based on genuine friendship (despite not having interviewed her before making these findings), it seemed like the IG's office made conclusions first and only gathered evidence later as an afterthought. Here again, I was given two days to review this new version. Justin called the IG again and requested an extension to review the new information that had been added to the report. The IG granted an extension from the due date on Friday until Sunday at 5:00 p.m.

Working through the night, Merle and I went through the report in excruciating detail. Where the investigators got it wrong, we documented it. Where they left out the documentation and detail we'd provided in our earlier submission to the IG, we reiterated them. Where their logic was not supported by the facts, we offered a reasonable interpretation. Our submission to the IG, after a thorough review and edit by Justin and his team of attorneys, was a fifteen-page report. In addition, Justin obtained an independent review by an ethics official, who discussed in detail our attendance at Wimbledon and found no ethical violation. Finally, we included a signed statement of fact from Vicky Gosling, who agreed to an interview with Justin and his team.

Vicky's interview, as reported by the IG, struck us as so unusual and one-sided that we wanted to have her talk to our lawyers and record her statement of the facts ourselves. Merle called Vicky and found out how horrific her experience with the IG had been. She said the investigators ambushed her—calling her without any notice while she was driving on a highway and demanding to speak with her despite her communicating that she didn't feel comfortable taking calls while driving. She said what followed was one of the most upsetting and disrespectful conversations of her life. She said she was so rattled that she almost wrecked her car.

"They twisted all of my words around, Merle! They kept saying that you weren't my friend and accused me of wanting something from David. My face turned red, and I started to have a panic attack. I was so flustered that when they asked me what your name was, my mind went blank! I just couldn't think because I so desperately wanted to get off the phone with these horrid people."

This turned out to be a huge issue in the mind of the IG and something picked up on by the press—that the "friend" who had given us Wimbledon tickets couldn't even recall my wife's name.

In Vicky's signed statement of fact, she described the time she and Merle had spent together and all the personal issues they had discussed. Vicky also described the circumstances of inviting us to Wimbledon, including her sister's cancellation. She also made clear that she had no business connection to the VA, that she did not seek or solicit any business from the VA, and that no company she worked for at the time had any such interest. She ended by saying that she considered us friends, and the tickets would have been offered to us regardless of whether I was a cabinet secretary.

All this was submitted to the IG by the 5:00 p.m. Sunday deadline. Justin and I requested a meeting with the IG the following day to ensure that they understood the substance of what we had submitted. These documents were attached as an addendum to the IG's report when it was finally released, but as is usually the case with retractions of stories or corrections of smears, I assume few people took the time to read them.

Ironically, one of the VA's most senior attorneys—one who personally advised me on a number of critical issues during my tenure at the VA—experienced his own downfall at the hands of the IG. Speaking out against the manner in which the IG conducted its investigation into his own behavior, the VA attorney filed a lawsuit in 2018 claiming that the investigation was reckless and malicious and that the results were inaccurate and predetermined. Specifically, the complaint stated that the investigator from the IG's office shared statements of wrongdoing with witnesses and asked them to change their opinions to conform with his own.

44

Reporting the News

USA Today's DONOVAN SLACK ASKED TO INTERVIEW ME, AND judging from her questions, I could only assume that she had inside sources tell her what the not-yet-released IG report was going to say. I asked her if she wanted an exclusive interview with me where she could ask me anything she wanted. My only condition was that she publish her interview before Wednesday, when I thought the report was going to be released. With the VA Press Office unwilling to defend or support me (they were completely silent, in fact), I thought this was the best way to tell my side of the story.

On Monday, February 12, a staff member on the tenth floor of the central office came to my chief of staff, Vivieca, and said, "I can't hold my tongue any longer." She said she'd heard the politicals admit to planting the story about Tom Bowman's imminent firing and their intention of taking down the secretary and privatizing the VA. But then, within twenty-four hours, this same staffer denied that she'd ever said anything to Vivieca. I found out later that she had received threats of physical harm, which obviously had the desired effect.

Other voices were saying they "smelled a rat" and that this whole thing was "not about Shulkin" or travel but rather about a political agenda. The theories circulating were that the politicals were using these reports as a decoy to plan the real agenda of privatizing the VA.

That afternoon, I met with the IG himself, Michael Missal, and I pointedly shared my displeasure with the leaking of the IG report to the press. He insisted that his office had nothing to do with it.

Justin went on to say, "I was a DOJ prosecutor, and at DOJ, anybody who acted the way your people did in those interviews would have been fired immediately." Justin was referring not just to the hostility and aggression displayed but also to the transcript of the VA ethics chief's report in which the IG investigator said something about pushing the interviewee "to get to where this needs to go." Why had they predetermined where this *needed to go*? The investigator persisted in trying to reverse the VA ethics official's original opinion that the acceptance of the Wimbledon tickets on the basis of friendship was appropriate.

As our meeting with the IG continued, I went through my rebuttal of their draft point by point to address inaccuracies that we had identified, while Missal sat stone-faced. Eventually, when Missal spoke, he acknowledged that it could be appropriate for a spouse to travel to Europe at VA expense and that my wife had been preapproved with travel orders as an official invitee of the delegation. He clarified that the real issue was his belief that my staff had altered an email in order to ensure approval. Yet he acknowledged that there was no evidence of my awareness of an altered email. So why wasn't that much more nuanced, limited, and moderate assessment reflected in the report?

Donovan Slack's story was published in *USA Today* online Tuesday evening, just before the IG report's public release. It was not as kind to me as I had hoped for, but at least she included my responses and my overall opinion of the report along with the IG's allegations.

The *Washington Post* and others were not as balanced. The IG report was released on the IG website at about 11:45 a.m. on February 14, 2018—the one-year anniversary of the happy day when my family and friends traveled to DC to witness my swearing in as the United States' ninth secretary of the VA. Several of the major media players published articles covering the IG report within minutes of its release. Considering the length of the IG report, this wouldn't have been possible without advance copies or inside information. Interestingly, several of the reports included information only from the first-draft report, dated February 5—information that was no longer present by the time the final report was published on February 14. These reporters never bothered to read the finalized version that acknowledged that I had no knowledge of the altered email. As soon as the story broke in the *Washington Post,* Congressman Mike Coffman called for my resignation, and CNN's Jake Tapper retweeted the congressman's statement. I had worked with Coffman for years and generally felt that he acted before he thought. The voters of Colorado eventually realized this, and he was not reelected in 2018.

I immediately went to Capitol Hill and met with Senator Tester, Senator Isakson, and Congressman Walz. When I spoke to them about the IG report, Senator Isakson said he had heard all about it the week before. Once again, why was I the last to know about *my* IG report? Isakson continued, "Don't do anything rash, and call me later tonight." But then he added swiftly, "Here's what you do: you confess, you apologize, and you promise never to do it again."

Clearly, he had given this speech to others who found themselves in politically hairy situations. But this world wasn't the world I was used to, and I wasn't interested in accepting blame for sins I hadn't committed. I had come to Washington idealistic and well intentioned, and I wasn't prepared to compromise my values as part of this ugly game.

Senator Tester confided to me, "Look, I'm gonna have to beat you up about this in public, but you're a good guy. Know that I support you."

Ranking Member Walz said, "I know this gets ugly. At least once a year, my political enemies try to get me to resign by coming out with something about me. Just try to hang tough."

With the political appointees leaking stories to the press and the press eager to find a way to embarrass the Trump administration, no one in DC was willing to call for a stop to the madness. Once there was blood in the water, the feeding frenzy only intensified.

I had always suspected who was behind the leaks, but I only had shreds of evidence. Then, in mid-February, I was sitting with a reporter when something extraordinary happened. She had her phone placed upright in front of me to record the interview. The phone rang, and the caller ID said "Darin Selnick." She glanced at the phone and said, "Sorry, I have to get this." She listened for a few seconds before saying, "Okay, thank you," hanging up, and then turning back to me. "Sorry to change topics so suddenly, but I have to ask: Do you disagree with the White House about coverage for Agent Orange? Are you pushing for new presumptive conditions against the objections of the Office of Management and Budget?"

I was stunned. This was highly sensitive information, the details were still being worked out between the VA and the OMB, and any public disclosure of this would further alienate me from the administration. But now I saw firsthand what Darin Selnick was doing.

Eventually, I spoke to Andrew Bremberg. On a number of occasions, I confronted Andrew with my concern that Darin was the source of the White House leaks. Andrew always appeared to take these concerns seriously, but then invariably, after he had "looked into them further," he would declare that he didn't believe this to be true. And so even after I confronted Andrew and stated that I had witnessed Darin's call to the reporter with my own eyes, he chose inaction once again.

The VSOs arranged a meeting with John Kelly to let him know that the political appointees in VA were wreaking havoc and not representing what veterans wanted. They also wanted to let Kelly know that their ability to provide feedback to the White House was being cut off by Darin Selnick and Jennifer Korn, deputy director for the Office of Public Liaison. Privately, many of the VSO leaders said they had been in DC for years and had never been treated with so much disdain and disregard as they were by this White House. They also wanted to tell Kelly directly that they supported me and recognized that I was being sabotaged. But apparently the meeting did not go well; Darin and Jennifer had invited representatives from Concerned Veterans of America, who sat front and center and intimidated everyone else.

Apparently Kelly asked, "Why doesn't David just fire them?" Verna Jones from the American Legion responded that she believed I was not allowed to do so, which was certainly my understanding. The White House staff had told me in no uncertain terms that I couldn't touch the politicals.

45

The Plot Becomes Clearer

I DID ANOTHER IN-PERSON INTERVIEW WITH *USA TODAY*'S DONOVAN Slack, and she brought with her a leaked internal VA travel schedule showing an upcoming trip to Colorado for the VA adaptive sports winter event. I had not yet confirmed that I was attending, but this leaked itinerary had been prepared by the VA travel department just in case. Somehow, this important part of my job in supporting disabled veterans was being characterized as an attempt to score a ski vacation on the taxpayers' dime.

When I got back to the department, I asked Jackie how this travel schedule could have been leaked to the press. She said, "I have no idea. This never happened to any of the other secretaries." This made me wonder just how deeply the VA had been infiltrated by those attempting to take me down.

Scott Blackburn, the VA's interim chief information officer, informed me he was going to quit soon because the political appointees had completely poisoned the culture. I liked and trusted Scott, and I was feeling more and more alone.

On the same day of the IG report release, Tom Bowman came into my office holding three pieces of paper. "Sir, you have to see this," he said. "A member of my staff just gave this to me." He said someone slipped it under his door that morning. The pages contained an email from Jake Leinenkugel, the senior White House adviser assigned to the VA, addressed to Camilo Sandoval, another White House political appointee.

Jake, who viewed himself as the senior White House adviser as well as the lead political appointee, was the one who assembled the politicals in his office each day to meet behind closed doors. When one of these appointees wanted to speak with me, Jake usually accompanied him.

In the email Tom showed me, dated December 4, 2017, Jake outlined a plan to Camilo recommending that Vivieca, Tom, and I all be replaced by individuals of their choice. Vivieca, Jake wrote, was under investigation by the IG in connection with the Europe trip. This reference to the IG investigation, however, was made almost three months before the report was released, making me and Tom wonder how he was aware of details of an ongoing confidential investigation. In making a number of other allegations about Vivieca, Jake also noted her status as a Democrat.

As for Tom, Jake said that he was disloyal to the president's agenda with respect to Choice and should be replaced by Jake himself. Finally, he suggested that I be replaced after I had achieved one last political victory for the president. He further recommended that the current acting under secretary be returned to her old job and replaced with Mike Kussman, a former VA under secretary. Dr. Kussman was one of the leaders of the VA reform report sponsored by the Koch brothers–backed organization, Concerned Veterans of America. Jake went on to recommend that Camilo be appointed as a White House adviser to oversee the electronic health record projects. And to run the VHA, Jake recommended the career physician who wanted the position when President Trump was first elected: Dr. Richard Stone. I felt the heat rising to my head when I realized how specific and well thought out this conspiracy was.

Shortly after the IG report was released, Jake and John Ullyot barged into my office. Red-faced, seething, and shoving hands in my face aggressively, John shouted, "You lied about me in this report! You said that you never reviewed the press statement that we released to the *Washington Post*!" Here I was thinking that my career was completely destroyed, and John was traumatized about this one essentially insignificant part of the report.

Jake jumped in. "This is just outrageous that you would do this. I mean, we have always supported you in everything we do."

Now, *that* was outrageous. Having just read Jake's email, I could have laughed if this hadn't been far too serious of a situation. I lowered my voice to avoid yelling and said as calmly as possible, "Now, Jake, we both know that's a lie."

I didn't want Jake to know that I had a copy of his email. Instead, I offered, "Jake, if I'm mistaken, then I owe you an apology." They stormed out of my office.

Because the VA's Media Relations Office refused to offer any response to the IG report on my behalf, I had no choice but to prepare my own statement. My statement was factual, and it directed interested parties to the documents I submitted to the IG. I then called Tom Bowman and Jim Byrne into my office and asked them if I had the authority to post a statement on the department website. Byrne checked into it and within the hour reported, "Yes, you absolutely have the right and authority to do so."

The statement was up on the website for about ten minutes before I received a call from Cabinet Affairs at the White House. "Mr. Secretary, this is Bill McGinley. You are instructed to take down the statement on the VA's website immediately."

"Why shouldn't there be a response from the department?" I asked. "And, Bill, it's been cleared by Jim Byrne, our general counsel."

"I've been told by White House Communications to take it down, so take it down."

I called Scott Blackburn and asked him to remove the statement. Shortly thereafter, a different statement was posted by Media Relations stating that the report was being reviewed and that further accountability actions were being considered. Clearly, the Office of Public Relations was not just failing to do their job;

they were throwing me—and the department's reputation—under the bus.

Because reporters who called the Office of Media Relations for statements or to request an interview with me received no response, they began to email and call me directly. Out of frustration, they asked me, "How can there be no response to this report?" The White House was silent as well.

Since becoming secretary, I made sure to be accessible to the press when issues arose and did not shy away from the hard questions. When there was a problem at the VA, I told them, and when we made progress, I told them that as well. I wasn't about to change my policy by hiding behind a "no comment"—especially when I thought I had nothing to hide. So I started to take calls, respond to emails, and grant on-camera interviews. I heard that the VA Office of Media Relations and the White House communications team were furious.

On February 15, I had a one-and-a-half-hour meeting with Bill McGinley at the White House Cabinet Affairs Office, where McGinley made it clear once again that I was prohibited from removing or demoting the politicals. The politicals appeared to view this meeting as a green light to no longer respect any of my wishes in any way.

Encounters like this reinforced my understanding that there were two parts to the White House: First, there was the president, John Kelly, and those surrounding them in the West Wing. Second, there were the politicals who had given up their previous jobs to support the Trump campaign. These opportunists had their own agenda and were working behind the scenes to accomplish it, and then they were going to the media and attributing their own viewpoint to the White House.

46

A Breaking Point

THE DAY AFTER THE IG REPORT WAS RELEASED, I WAS SCHEDULED for a Senate hearing. That morning, before leaving for the hearing, Vivieca opened the door of her office adjoining mine and whispered, "You have to see this." She was holding a printout of an email, supposedly from her, which authorized VA to wire a sum of money to an external address. The finance department flagged this as a strange request and called Vivieca to confirm its authenticity. Vivieca did not write the message. After showing it to me, Vivieca gave the falsified email to Scott Blackburn, our acting chief information officer, who soon confirmed that it had been sent on the VA server. So maybe there was truth to the IG's finding that an email from Vivieca had been altered; it just hadn't been altered by her.

For Vivieca, this was the last straw, and she told me she was going to resign. I was devastated, but I knew her well enough to know that she wasn't going to change her mind. Her logic made sense; if things had gotten so out of control that she was being targeted for something she didn't do, why risk further humiliation? Moreover, after thirty-one years of service, she didn't want to jeopardize her government pension.

I lost a key teammate when Vivieca resigned, and I was left feeling even more alone. But I had no intention of leaving the mission. I was going to keep serving the veterans, as I had sworn to do, for as long as I was allowed. The remainder of my tenure would prove to be the longest and hardest month and a half of my life.

The press was now relentlessly pursuing me with questions about the IG report, including questions about the hacked email. I responded, "Yes, this morning we found that our chief of staff's email was hacked, and we're looking into it. I am not an expert in these areas."

After further investigation, I discovered that the correct term for what had happened to Vivieca's email was not *hacking* but *spoofing,* meaning the creation of a fraudulent message that purports to be from someone else's email. But the server had not been compromised. Consequently, there were now allegations that I deliberately concocted the spoofing to try to deflect the attention away from me and create an untrue conspiracy theory. The IG quickly stated that they were launching another investigation, and shortly after, his staff came to remove Vivieca's computer for evidence. Sadly, none of this was surprising. This was just another day at the office at this point.

The coverage on the IG report went from bad to worse. Most accounts described the trip as an extravagant sightseeing tour or a luxury European vacation. But now several stories suggested that Merle had taken a per diem of thousands of dollars, when in fact she had received no reimbursement for any expenses other than the coach airfare, which we subsequently repaid. Unfortunately, another victim of collateral damage from this episode was the Five Eyes conference. Would any future VA secretary ever be willing or able to meet with our allies overseas again?

Soon there were daily leaks coming from "anonymous sources" at the White House, spreading rumors that I had underreported the seriousness of the IG findings. There were other rumors that the president was going to fire me very soon.

On the other hand, Ronny Jackson, the president's personal physician and a friend of mine dating back to the Obama administration, called me to say that he had just been with the president, who said, "Your friend David is doing a good job and is going to be okay." The conflicting reports about what the president was thinking made it increasingly difficult to know what to do.

With Vivieca gone and Tom and me weakened, the politicals knew the balance of power had shifted in their favor, and they began to flaunt it. Within hours of Vivieca's announcement, John Ullyot and Jake Leinenkugel were in my office. "Mr. Secretary, we will let you know who your new chief of staff will be." I was flabbergasted. Can you imagine any other organization in which the underlings tell the boss who he must hire as his closest associate?

Not long afterward, I received a call from Bill McGinley. "We want Peter O'Rourke as your new chief of staff. I assume you are going to be okay with this?" As if I really had a choice.

47

Presidents' Day Weekend

ICONTINUED TO HEAR FROM IKE, BUT LESS FREQUENTLY. IT WAS CLEAR that he was still having active discussions with the White House, but he was distancing himself from me. I can only assume that the misinformation fed to him by the politicals played a large role in this.

By this time, picking up the phone felt like receiving the next set of instructions from a kidnapper. I jumped every time my phone beeped or lit up, which, unfortunately for my blood pressure, was constantly. That weekend, Ike let me know that he was having breakfast with the president and said, "I'll let you know where you stand." I was waiting for my death sentence. Whether I was going to be fired started to feel less like a question of *if* and more like a question of *when*. I heard back from Ike a few hours later. "I will tell you your fate at 3:00 p.m., and if it's not at 3:00 p.m., then at 5:00 p.m.," he said eerily. I was alive for a few more hours.

Ike didn't call back before my evening train from Philadelphia back to Washington. It had been a very disconcerting and long Presidents' Day weekend for me and my family. Danny, Merle, and I were together in Philadelphia, and we had Jennie on family conference calls for hours of both Saturday and Sunday. We were losing hope but still trying to hold on and strategize. My family was now my PR team and essentially the only ones I felt I could trust. As I said before, serving in this type of position involves the entire family, and my time in government did and continues to affect all of us.

While I was on the train, John Kelly called to say, "You're still on the team." I breathed a sigh of relief but knew my troubles weren't over.

Back at the VA, I began excluding some of the politicals from my morning report. It was now just me, Tom Bowman, the under secretaries of health, benefits, and memorial affairs, the general counsel, and my new chief of staff, Peter O'Rourke. O'Rourke unfortunately was closely associated with the politicals, which was the reason they handpicked him for the position, and he was undoubtedly reporting back to them.

Tom Bowman informed me that he received a call from the staff at the House Veterans Affairs Committee telling him that John Ullyot and Curt Cashour went to Chairman Roe's staff on Thursday and demanded him "to call for the secretary's resignation by the end of this weekend." These were my own PR people—the same ones who took down my statement responding to the IG report and replaced it with an incriminating statement that the White House would continue to investigate the allegations. They also refused me access to my official Twitter account and did their best to prevent me from having any access to the media. For months now, they had failed to pass along requests from reporters, saying instead, "No comment."

On February 22, I suspected that the politicals leaked to the *Washington Post* that I was scheduled to travel to the Vatican, where I had been asked to speak with other federal officials on our approach to personalized medicine. Apparently they were not satisfied with the traps they had already set and were now creating as many as they could. The trip to the Vatican conference was approved months beforehand, but I had already decided that it wouldn't be prudent for me to attend. Someone leaked a copy of my tentative schedule for the trip anyway to rile things up. It was clear that the politicals weren't thinking about helping veterans but only about their narrow ideological obsession with removing me from my position so that they could control the agenda at the VA.

I continued to hear one set of directions from Kelly and the opposite from White House staff. If I could have managed even twenty minutes to talk to Kelly alone, I think we might have been able to halt the damage, but the politicals were blocking my access to him, too. Bill McGinley was now saying he spoke for the West Wing and was the only person I could reach.

Three Sundays in a row, I was contacted by Jonathan Swan, the political reporter for *Axios*. On each occasion, Swan sent me defamatory statements from unnamed "White House staff" and provided me with a four-hour window to respond before sending the article to print. But I was on my own, without the support of my own press office, and I had no way to get the White House to put together a proper response. One story reported that the White House had lost confidence in me and that I was becoming "unhinged." Other outlets were reporting that I was paranoid and, as evidence, cited the armed guard outside my office. Of course, there had always been armed security posted outside my office, which is a precaution taken for most cabinet secretaries. But readers didn't know that. It seemed that certain parts of the Washington press corps had descended to the level of the supermarket tabloids.

I had long since given up hope that the VA's media office would respond appropriately. All I heard now from the White House, the new VA chief of staff, or the VA press office was a lengthy and intricate runaround.

On Sunday, I spoke briefly with John Kelly by phone and told him about the political appointees' continued efforts to undermine me. Kelly said matter-of-factly, "You are the secretary, and the president has confidence in you. We'll figure out the rest tomorrow."

Each time Kelly communicated something like this, I felt a tiny bit of hope. I knew there wasn't much Kelly could do, but it felt good for him to hear me and acknowledge my struggles. He then asked about the rumors spreading of a new IG report on my use of security. I explained that the allegation was that security accompanied me whenever I went on errands or out for dinner. Kelly interjected, "As they should."

I also told Kelly about the reporter who was going to publish the piece saying that I had become unhinged and that the story needed a comment from the White House by 4:00 p.m. Kelly said he would talk to Sarah Huckabee Sanders and take care of it. The White House never offered a comment or correction.

Before I got off the phone, Kelly arranged for me and Tom Bowman to meet him the next day. To prepare for the meeting with Kelly, I spent time with Tom Bowman lining up the things we needed to discuss. Here is a sample:

1. Jake Leinenkugel's email to Camilo, discussing their plan to replace the deputy secretary, the chief of staff, and the secretary.
2. The telephone call to Amanda Maddox in Senator Isakson's office from a reporter, informing her that the story on firing Tom Bowman had been planted by Darin Selnick and Brooks Tucker.
3. John Ullyot and Curt Cashour lobbying Chairman Roe to call for my resignation.

Under normal circumstances, any of these allegations on its own would have been enough for an employee to be fired. But nothing about these circumstances was normal.

Tom Bowman and I met with General Kelly as well as Andrew Bremberg, Bill McGinley, Peter O'Rourke, and Sean Doocey. Tom showed Kelly the email evidence of the politicals' efforts to have us removed and reviewed the other information we had uncovered. Kelly reacted in disbelief. He told me, "You're the secretary, and it's going to stay that way. If they're being like this, you have to fire them. Actually, I can't see why you haven't already."

I said, "Because McGinley told me I wasn't allowed to."

Kelly said, "Well, you have to."

McGinley sat silently staring into space. Sean Doocey squirmed in his seat. O'Rourke tapped his foot nervously.

I left the meeting and went home, where I breathed another small sigh of relief. Finally, a small victory.

Someone at the meeting must have told John Ullyot that Kelly had given me the green light to fire him and others. John took a vacation immediately so that he could avoid me.

Yet reports continued. The politicals . . . politicals were leaking stories to backstab me, including assertions that I was not staying in office long; Kelly was not happy with me; I was paranoid and unhinged, hiding behind an armed guard. Increasingly I was being referred to as the "Obama holdover," as though that indicated an inherent disloyalty to Trump that would be reason enough to remove me from office.

I received an email from Senators Tester, Blumenthal, and Casey requesting that I submit all my receipts from the European trip so they could assess if we needed to pay back any additional costs. I guess this is what Senator Tester meant when he said he'd have to "beat me up about this in public." While it was very stressful and time-consuming to find receipts from a trip that had taken place more than seven months earlier, I was glad to supply documentation and put on record that everything not only was in order but had been approved in advance. The receipts would also show that Merle's only expense paid by the VA was a single coach airfare. There had been no per diems or any other reimbursements. I had also written a check to the government for the full face value of the Wimbledon tickets, even though Vicky had gotten them for buy one, get one free, and no government funds were used to purchase them.

Then Fox's Pete Hegseth opened up a new front while on air, trying to paint me as a bureaucrat maintaining the status quo and averse to the president's agenda. But Hegseth called me to say, "We're being unfairly accused of trying to overthrow you." Grasping his word choice, I asked, "Who's *we?*" Hegseth, with his ties to Concerned Veterans of America, had always been the mouthpiece for the political appointees; now he seemed to be implicating himself in their scheme.

I tried to have a rational discussion with him. "Pete, I want Choice for veterans too, but it needs to be done in a phased-in approach that is thoughtful and does not hurt the veterans who need help the most. And your version of Choice would cost billions more per year, bankrupting the system. How can we responsibly pursue this?" Unfortunately, he didn't want to engage at the level of budget and other aspects of day-to-day reality. He seemed to prefer his sound bites on television.

48

Words of Encouragement

O N MARCH 1, I DECIDED TO WATCH THE NATIONAL NEWS FOR THE first time since the story broke, thinking that enough time had passed that I wouldn't be risking my sanity by watching. But only twelve minutes into *ABC News with David Muir*, they launched into a story about six cabinet secretaries: Ben Carson, Scott Pruitt, Jeff Sessions, Steven Mnuchin, Ryan Zinke, and me. The segment began with Ben Carson's $31,000 dining room table. Then they cut to the "scathing report" on the secretary of the VA. The next two to three minutes were focused solely on me, although it felt like hours to me. They flashed shots of Merle's emails with Gabe as well as multiple pictures of Merle and me, including one of us taken by paparazzi on the red carpet at the Kennedy Center, which we had never seen. This was crazy! Three years ago, I was running a hospital in New Jersey and was only known within my industry. Now, Merle and I were staring at our pictures on the *national news*.

ABC did zero fact-checking. They simply took the original *Washington Post* story from September 27 and the original IG draft (not even the final version) and reignited the story. When they described our Saturday morning at Wimbledon, the reporters spoke with such disdain, as though Merle and I were working on behalf of an international spy ring. They acted like no regular person could possibly watch a tennis match at Wimbledon; one could only score tickets to such a coveted event by being part of the queen's entourage. Since when was attending a sporting event with friends on a weekend worthy of coverage on the national news?

Having my character maligned on a public stage every day was pure torture. I wish I could say that my skin was thick enough to not let it bother me. But as I've mentioned, it deeply affected not just me but the rest of my family. Ever since I became secretary, Merle had received letters, emails, Facebook messages, tweets, and phone calls from veterans who needed assistance. Now she was getting emails and calls from reporters and random strangers with nasty messages about how unethical we were to steal from taxpayers. Merle had never been appointed as a public official. She had never sworn an oath. She had never asked for any of this.

Merle's patients, my son's coworkers, and Jennie's law school classmates either ignored them—not knowing what to say—or offered condolences as though there was a death in the family. My front-office staff was battered. Each time I was scheduled to attend an event, even a cabinet meeting, they would check with me to confirm that I was still planning to go. Meanwhile, my schedule lightened as people who otherwise might have sought appointments wanted to avoid the awkwardness of my situation. I started to feel like I was carrying a contagious disease that nobody wanted to catch.

In March, Peter O'Rourke passed along the White House's request that he and I pay a visit to Ike at Mar-a-Lago. It was even clearer to me from this meeting that Peter was now calling the shots and coordinating messages from the White House and the team of politicals. While we were at the beach club, Marc Sherman followed me into the men's room at one point. Then, looking around to make sure nobody else was within earshot, he whispered, "David, don't touch the politicals. You're playing with fire. They're more powerful than you realize." That would be my last visit with the three Mar-a-Lago gentlemen.

Upon my return to Washington, I asked Tom to remove Curt Cashour from his position as press secretary, and I asked Peter O'Rourke to be there as a witness. Curt, in my opinion, was not able to represent the VA with the media because he had lost my trust, and judging from regular and ongoing feedback from the press, he had lost their confidence as well.

Curt never left the agency. Instead, he took paid leave, probably assured by other politicals that the situation would soon resolve itself in such a way that he could return to his position. Peter O'Rourke kept the politicals aware of current White House thinking as well as his ongoing conversations with Ike and the team. I often wondered what Peter did during the day, other than meet for hours behind closed doors with the VA politicals. Certainly, he was not overly engaged in performing the duties of my chief of staff, which included the daily operational issues facing the VA.

Most of the career staff at the VA simply carried on while giving me occasional words of encouragement along the lines of "Hang in there, it's going to get better." It was hard to tell whether they actually believed this. The veterans service groups were largely supportive, too. They shared information with me about what they were hearing and tried to correct inaccuracies when they could.

Surprisingly, members of Congress were the most supportive. One afternoon, I was at the Capitol meeting with Senator Bernie Sanders when he kicked everybody out of his office and asked me, "What's going on?" I tried to explain this intricate web of scheming. Shaking his head, Sanders said, "These are bad people. We're proud of you for standing up to them." As an afterthought, he added, "But when are you going to get your name off the front page of every newspaper?"

Chairman Isakson and Chairman Roe provided me with consistent encouragement. Senator Carper sent me a handwritten note of support and made public comments about my positive impact on veterans. Senator Tester reminded me of a conversation we'd had during my confirmation process. He said, "David, you told me that when you took this job, you were prepared to leave if you were forced to violate your principles. You might have to." Congressman Wasserman-Schultz showed a great deal of empathy, saying that she had been through her own difficult times. On March 7, 2018, Bill McGinley phoned me and instructed, "Just to be clear, you are not to fire anyone." I protested. Both the president and Kelly had said that it was acceptable for me to move people out if that was what I needed to do to get the VA back on track. McGinley denied this. I wondered: Who was really calling the shots? And did Kelly have any idea what McGinley was saying? If I couldn't exercise authority over my staff, there was no way I could continue running the VA. When I tried to contact Kelly for clarification, he was unavailable and didn't return my call.

There was a cabinet meeting the next day, and Rex Tillerson, then secretary of state, did not attend. He normally sat to the right of the president, and because Kelly didn't want an empty seat next to the president, he told me to move down, and then Zinke moved over to the seat next to mine. I also think Kelly wanted me to be seen sitting next to the president in order to send the message to everyone that I still had the president's support. It was a gift. My family was shocked to see me on television, smiling next to the president as if nothing had changed. It was moments like these that made us think we could actually get through this and that I would get to stay in government.

On March 9, NBC News broadcast a picture of Merle and me at Wimbledon. Then in an interview with reporter Lisa Rein, Chuck Todd said that people were getting tired of VA war stories. Lisa gave a good account of what I was facing with the political operatives. But Chuck's bottom line was, "At some point, you can't recover." This was exactly my fear.

On Sunday, another early-afternoon preview arrived from *Axios*'s Jonathan Swan, again with a 4:00 p.m. deadline for comments. I sent a copy to Sarah Huckabee Sanders at the White House. Swan had details of a private meeting between Kelly, the president, and me. More tellingly, despite the fact that it had been a good meeting, Swan's account was clearly biased against me. The

White House chose not to respond. So *Axios* ran with a story head-lined, "Trump Finally Losing Patience with VA Sec. Shulkin."

On Monday, I called Bill McGinley and said, "You're not let-ting me defend myself. You have people in the White House like Darin and others leaking things to the press, and the White House won't say a word." As usual, Bill listened, said that he would get back to me, and never did.

The next day, Rex Tillerson was fired by a Trump tweet, and the president nominated Mike Pompeo to replace him as secretary of state. Danny said to Merle, "I sure hope we don't wake up to a tweet firing Dad one day."

Dave Philipps of the *New York Times* called to ask for my com-ment on a rumor that the president had been talking to Rick Perry about taking over the VA. This was exhausting.

The situation was getting out of control, and I found it hard to believe that the White House actually wanted a cabinet where everyone felt threatened at all times and unsure when the next round of firings would take place. Then again, this was a president who had risen to prominence on reality television, where he had turned firing people into a kind of sport. Maybe this was just the next series: *White House Apprentice,* or better yet, *Survivor: White House Edition.*

At an Ides of March breakfast with Senators Sanders, Isakson, Test er, and Cassidy, we discussed Choice, still trying to get language into the omnibus by Thursday to get the budget passed. Nancy Pelosi said that it was leaning too much toward privatization, so she couldn't support it.

The next day, acting FBI director Andrew McCabe was fired just twenty-six hours before he would have been eligible for retirement.

Picked up by CNN, Jonathan Swan's *Axios* article was now trend-ing, which exemplified the sad truth of political reporting in such a highly partisan time: a leak becomes a story, which gets picked up and repeated without corroboration and then reprinted and recycled until it becomes the accepted truth, and finally, a self-ful-filling prophecy.

That same evening, my son, Danny, sent me an article from *Politics USA*: "The Koch brothers are about to make their move to privatize the VA." The forces for privatization of the VA were closing in on me. Concerned Veterans of America, the Koch brothers' veterans service organization, hadn't just gained a seat at the table; they had stolen the head of the table. CVA was at the White House on a regular basis and showing up at meetings when I hadn't invited them. At every turn, White House staff made sure CVA was given a strong voice.

The Koch brothers were well known to have paved their way to influence by making financial contributions to several of the most pro-privatization members of Congress. Significantly, Koch Industries was the number-one contributor to Senator Jerry Moran's campaign in 2014, number four in 2016, and number six in 2018. They were also regular contributors to Mike Coffman, the representative from Colorado who had called for my resignation. As reported by *Public Citizen*, others with a known connection to the Kochs included forty-four senior Trump officials and White House staff, including Andrew Bremberg, head of the DPC; Don McGahn, chief White House counsel; Marc Short, chief of legislative affairs; Darin Selnick, White House adviser on veterans affairs; and Kellyanne Conway, assistant to the president. While it is not clear if any of these people intervened on the Kochs' behalf, there was unquestionably a great deal of support for CVA within the Trump White House.

A few days later, I got a call from John Kelly asking, "Did you talk to the *New York Times*?"

I acknowledged I had.

"Did you say you'd been authorized to purge people within the VA?"

That I denied. "I said I was given the authority to get the VA back on track, and people needed to focus on issues of importance to the VA or they would need to leave the organization."

"Okay," he said, "that sounds right. But you have to come over right now to see the president." Then he hung up.

I rushed to the White House and waited outside the Oval Office for forty-five minutes. Staff and visitors going in and out passed by without making eye contact. I began to feel like a nonperson.

Kelly and the president were already seated when I came in. President Trump said, "How's that travel stuff going? Is it still going on?"

To my relief, his question implied that he wasn't seeing the plethora of bad media coverage about me. Then he switched gears and asked, "How's the Choice Program?"

I told the president that I had just been with Senator Isakson discussing it. "We're putting the final touches on the Senate legislation, and Senator Isakson is preparing to introduce it. He's hoping for unanimous consent."

Then the president asked me, "What does Pete Hegseth think of this Choice thing?" But before I could answer his question, he yelled to Madeleine Westerhout, his assistant who sits outside the Oval Office, "Get Pete Hegseth on the phone!"

We were actually bringing a Fox News commentator and former director of Concerned Veterans of America into our conversation. Within a minute, Hegseth was on speakerphone.

"Pete, what do you think about this Choice stuff?"

"Mr. President, I don't think Isakson's bill gets you what you want. We want to have full choice where veterans can go wherever they want for care."

"Pete, I have the secretary here with me, and he says we can't do this all now, because it would cost us over $50 billion. So, Pete, we have to take our time."

"Mr. President, I agree, but we can find the money from within the VA."

Hegseth never worked in the VA and, as far as I could tell, knew nothing about managing a health care system and had little understanding of the clinical and financial impact of the policies he was advocating. To me, his suggestion was the worst-case scenario, reflecting the ugly truth behind the benign-sounding push for greater "choice" from the Koch brand of conservatism. It was a stalking horse for dismantling the VA entirely.

After the president hung up, he said to me, "I needed to do that." It was times like these when I realized how politically astute the president actually can be. In a one-minute phone call, the president disarmed a key voice of opposition to a policy that both he and I wanted to go forward.

John Kelly then switched gears. "Mr. President, we have to talk about the situation with the political appointees and David at the VA."

I explained the situation to the president.

The president listened and then asked, "Did I appoint them?"

"Yes, they're your political appointees, Mr. President."

"Well, that makes it tough, but you got to do what you gotta do with these people. But they'll cause trouble from the outside if they go, because they won't be happy."

To my amazement, a few days later, the media reported a fairly accurate account of this private meeting in the Oval Office. The president, General Kelly, Hegseth, and I were the only people involved in the conversation. Who leaked the information?

Listening to the radio on my way home, I heard MSNBC claim that everyone who agreed to work for this administration now had a ruined reputation. The story gave me an uneasy feeling, but it was too late to turn back now.

I didn't know it then, but I had just had my last meeting with the president.

49

My Final Days

I N LATE MARCH, THE WHITE HOUSE HOSTED A PREVIEW OF A FILM about veterans without bothering to invite the secretary of veterans affairs. There was also a Medal of Honor ceremony, where I had been front and center the year before, but from which I was excluded this year. Clearly, the political appointees were happy to give veterans the impression that I had lost interest in them. One of the sad ironies was my failure to realize just how much General Kelly, the person I would otherwise turn to for help in this politically charged situation, had been marginalized himself. In retrospect, I think Kelly was unaware of all the people providing the president with counsel and misinformation. When I was with him and the president in meetings about the VA, Kelly was always openly supportive, and he continually reinforced that I had the veterans' best interests at heart and that I had the confidence of the congressional leadership and the VSOs. He may have been offering his endorsement because he was more aware of the threats to my position than I was. But I wondered how Kelly could not have been aware that, despite his open support for me and endorsement of my authority, his staff and the other politicals contradicted his instructions without consequence.

With the political appointees in attack mode, the accusations of wrongdoing were flying fast and loose. Anyone can make an anonymous allegation to the IG, and once the IG opens an investigation, it can take on a life of its own. As soon as the interviews with staff begin, the rumor mill starts to churn. In Washington, allegations become reality, particularly when people on the inside are fanning the flames.

With the IG's new allegations that my security agents were claiming more hours than they had worked as well as allegedly receiving unjustified overtime payments, my security detail's overall mood was melancholy. There was no longer any small talk or joking. My agents just stared straight ahead and tried to get through their shifts. A few lamented that in all of their years in federal service, their integrity had never been questioned the way it had been in recent weeks. We all started to feel like a pack of wounded dogs licking our wounds.

The media continued to contact me on a regular basis, saying they were told that a second IG report was imminent and would show my misuse of security. Journalists were assured that this report would be much more damning than the first IG report. In addition to inquiries from the press, Congress and White House staffers continued to ask me what the controversy was. I responded to everyone with the same simple summary: I had been given a written security protocol. I complied with those instructions. I was unaware of anything improper.

Most government officials understood that every cabinet member has a security detail. Many have 24-7 protection—whereas I was on my own at home until it was time to venture out again. Protection was provided anytime I was in public, though, whether for official or for personal reasons, for the obvious reasons that harassment and physical harm were just as likely at the supermarket as at a VA function.

This new round of allegations made it all the way up to the president's office. John Kelly asked me about this second IG report on two occasions. When the president said, "David, I hear there's a very bad report coming out soon about you and your security detail," I wondered how he had heard about a report that hadn't been released. Apparently someone had been feeding this rumor directly to the West Wing.

All I could say was, "Mr. President, from what I know, the allegations are unsubstantiated."

On March 22, there was a White House celebration for Greek Independence Day. As Merle and I entered the State Room, we saw General Kelly, who came over and gave Merle a hug. Kelly looked her in the eyes, put his hand on her shoulder, and said, "Don't worry, it's all going to be okay. The president has confidence in David, and he just needs to keep doing what he is doing. It's going to blow over." Then he walked her over to the bar, handed her some wine, and clinked her glass. Merle smiled, but it was an uneasy smile.

Shortly thereafter, a new story broke under the headline: "McMaster firing upends plan to oust other top Trump officials." National Security Adviser H. R. McMaster had been fired by tweet the day after John Dowd, the president's personal lawyer, resigned. According to the story, I was first on the list of expendables who might now be given a reprieve, followed by Ben Carson. The story, of course, said I was going to be fired for my "extravagant travel."

That evening, Merle and I went to the Kennedy Center to see Lin-Manuel Miranda's *In the Heights*. During the show, I started getting texts and phone calls from reporters, so at intermission, I went outside to respond. Apparently, the Washington press corps was buzzing with rumors "from the White House" that I was going to be the next one in the Trump administration booted. So I spent the remainder of the intermission and most of the second half of the show conducting interviews from my cell phone.

I got messages from people all over the country telling me to hold on and stay strong. Others characterized being fired by this president as a badge of honor.

50

The Fateful Last Call

SIX DAYS LATER, ON MARCH 28, I WAS IN MY VA OFFICE WHEN I first heard from a reliable source that I was going to be fired that day.

I called General Kelly's office and communicated that I needed to speak with him immediately. Kelly returned my call pretty quickly, and when I told him what I had heard, he sounded surprised. He said he knew nothing about it but would get back to me. Within thirty minutes, he called back and told me he did not believe this information to be true and that nothing had changed. According to the chief of staff, I still had the president's confidence.

Tom Bowman came into my office to tell me that the politicals stripped him of his autopen privileges, meaning he could not sign off on anything. This was when I realized I no longer had my autopen privileges either.

At about the same time, Merle received a call at her office from a woman using a blocked number. Merle recognized her voice as the same person who had called her office two weeks earlier. The woman spoke with urgency, communicating that they needed to talk, but would not leave her name or number because she was too afraid. Merle gave her our home number, went home, and sat by the phone. When the woman called again, she informed Merle that there were five ex-marines in the administration plotting my demise. She said she worried for our safety and warned us to watch our backs. Merle, upset and shaken, pleaded with her to go public or at least tell her more. Over the phone, this woman read Merle snippets from texts that Peter Shelby, the political appointee who headed human resources, had supposedly sent to other politicals. In these, Shelby said, "Shulkin messed with the wrong group of people. He's going down. He's working against Trump." Merle asked her to send screenshots of these texts to her, but the woman hesitated. She said she might be willing to meet Merle somewhere in Washington to show her the texts, but she was too afraid to send them electronically. Before hanging up, the woman repeated that she feared for Merle's safety and for mine.

It was around this time that Jackie told me the president was on the phone.

"David, you're killing me with all the bad press coming out of the VA," the president bemoaned. He hadn't bothered to say hello.

"Mr. President," I said, "as I told you the last time we met, there are a number of people in my organization continuing to leak inaccurate information. But we are making progress within the VA still, and in the next ninety days, I'll have three major policy wins for you."

I told him about our work to finish the modernization of the electronic record, complete the legislation that would permanently reform Choice for veterans, and finalize our restructuring plan to streamline the management of the organization. It was a productive conversation, but I could tell that he was losing patience.

The president also asked about the Cerner contract for electronic health records. "Can't you find a cheaper alternative?"

I tried to explain that I hadn't seen the final contract and that we were still in the process of confirming that it contained all of the requirements needed to ensure real interoperability and a successful outcome.

Then he said, "Okay, I have to go. But come over tomorrow at eleven, and we'll talk some more."

I told Merle and the kids that I was meeting the president the following day, which we assumed meant I was going to survive another day as secretary.

Later that same afternoon, I sat in my office, signing letters to the family members of soldiers who had been killed recently in a helicopter crash. As solemn and painful as this duty was, I was honored to have these letters come from me.

Around five o'clock, the phone rang, and it was John Kelly. "David, I'm sorry to tell you this, but I think the president is likely making a change and picking a new VA secretary. I think it's a terrible idea, and I didn't know anything about it until just now, but there's nothing I can do. I just wanted to give you a heads-up."

"But when I spoke to the president today, he didn't say anything about this. He asked me to meet with him tomorrow," I stammered.

"You spoke to the president today?" Kelly asked, surprised.

"A little before noon. He called, and we talked about a number of issues, but he never mentioned anything about letting me go."

"I had no idea. He did the same thing with Rex. I just don't know what to say." Kelly seemed embarrassed.

"Do you think he still wants to meet tomorrow?"

"Not likely. I think he's going to make an announcement any minute now."

With that, Kelly hung up. I would never hear his voice again.

I put my hands over my bewildered and exhausted face. I wished desperately that this was all a nightmare and I could wake myself up.

I gathered my briefcase and coat and left the building to go home for the night. As soon as I got to the apartment, I called Merle, and as I was telling her about my conversation with Kelly, she gasped. A new tweet from the president posted just after five o'clock: "I am pleased to announce that I intend to nominate highly respected Admiral Ronny L. Jackson, MD, as the new Secretary of Veterans Affairs. . . . I am thankful for Dr. David Shulkin's service to our country and to our GREAT veterans!"

Merle and I held our phones to our ears in silence, each listening to the other breathe, not knowing if we should yell, cry, console, or argue. We were speechless.

Apparently, the politicals at the department had known this was coming, because almost instantaneously, my access to my work email and phone were shut off. Three years of events and memories vanished in a second. All my contacts, all my documents, all my photos . . . gone.

I then received a call on my personal cell phone from the office, saying that they planned to box up my personal possessions and ship everything to me. Treated like a leper, I wasn't allowed back in VA headquarters, not even to say goodbye to my staff or to clean out my own desk. I wasn't even given the opportunity to send the VA workforce a note expressing my gratitude and admiration for what they had accomplished during the three years I had the honor of working with them.

I heard nothing further from the White House, but that same evening, I received an urgent call from a VA colleague, saying that the politicals were planning to make new allegations that I had walked off with government property, some of it containing sensitive information. I asked for a government driver to come to my apartment that evening so I could return any and all government electronics and possibly sidestep new accusations. At 10:00 p.m., I went down to the street and turned over everything ever assigned to me by the government. I turned away empty-handed and heartbroken.

51

Vindication . . . but Not Quite

D URING THE THREE YEARS I SERVED AT THE VA, I GAVE UP A GREAT
deal financially, professionally, and personally. I worked basically fourteen-hour days, 365 days a year. I poured my heart into
fighting for the veterans I represented. And *this* is how it ended.

Immediately after Trump's tweet broke the news, I was
swamped with texts and calls (on my personal cell phone) from
reporters interested in my reaction. How did they *think* I was
reacting? I didn't respond initially to any media requests, knowing
that I needed to cool down first. I knew I wanted to say something, but I wanted to say it perfectly.

The evening I got the news, I was alone in our Washington
apartment when I sat down at my computer and began to write
an op-ed about the privilege of serving, what we at the VA had
accomplished, and the real reason I was fired. The politics of Washington are harsh, and the forces striving to dismantle government
are real. That story needed to be told, and I wanted to be the one
to tell it. Besides, I was tired of my enemies and the press telling
my story and of being unable to defend myself. Contacting the
editors of the *New York Times* editorial pages at night isn't easy,
but I managed to reach them, and they published my editorial
online just before midnight. Its title was simple: "Privatizing the
VA Will Hurt Veterans."

There seems to be an unwritten rule in Washington: when your time comes, go quietly. That wasn't going to work for me, mostly because this fight was not just about me but also about the veterans I served. Shortly after my op-ed was published, many other media outlets realized there might be more to this story than a travel issue. Also in response to my op-ed, I received calls and emails from hundreds of people around the country who expressed solidarity. It seemed that many people were finally beginning to see the political scheming at work. But realistically, most of the country didn't, and that's deeply disturbing to me.

The next morning, I received a call from my apartment building's front desk, informing me of the news crews and reporters assembled outside the building since 6:30 a.m. Invitations from Anderson Cooper, Jake Tapper on *State of the Union*, Chuck Todd on *Meet the Press, Morning Joe*, NPR, Brett Baier, *PBS Newshour, Good Morning America, CNN Good Day*, and *USA Today* flooded my inbox and call logs. I went on the air and told my story to several different news outlets. I defended myself on a big stage, perhaps for the first time. And I advocated for veterans on a big stage, perhaps for the last time. After a three-day media blitz, I had said what I needed to say and refused further interviews.

That evening, Rachel Maddow, who once viciously attacked Merle and me about our European travel, acknowledged the political forces at work against me and advised her viewers not to believe all the stories they heard about me. Some reporters like her were starting to see that there was more to the story than what was first alleged. Maddow reported that she no longer believed I was fired for travel-related issues. I appreciated her diligence and willingness to acknowledge a mistake.

Walking the streets of Washington and without security for the first time in quite a while, I was touched that so many people stopped me to express support and thank me for speaking out.

After a few days, Kelly sent me an email. It read: "I honestly do not know why you were treated in this way. Honestly I do not.

I apologize and will find out why this happened. I am angry over the way you were treated. It should NOT have happened."

It was reported in the papers that Kelly was so disturbed by the way I was ousted that on March 28 he told people in the White House that *he* was going to resign. It was reported that Secretaries Mattis and Nielsen talked him off the ledge that day and convinced him to stay for the greater good. Kelly would survive for another ten months before officially quitting.

On Sunday, April 1, the headlines were asking, "Was Shulkin fired or did he resign?" If you're wondering who cares, I don't blame you. But the White House claimed that I resigned, which according to the Vacancy Act of 1998, would give them far more latitude to replace me. Because I was fired, Tom Bowman as the deputy secretary should have become the acting secretary. But the politicals managed to circumvent the rules, and Robert Wilke became the acting secretary.

Over the next few days, my voicemail and email were packed with people weighing in on the issue. Several of them who seemed to be in the know believed that my firing was all related to my intention to complete a contract with Cerner. I had been planning to sign a contract only if it adequately addressed the issues of interoperability and fully met the other requirements specified by the VA's IT team. Camilo Sandoval was incorrectly telling people that I was going to sign it the next day. In my view, the contract was close to completion but was not there yet.

A number of other people were catching on to the real reasons for my firing. They were starting to understand that the IG investigations had been a red herring to distract from the bigger picture of the Koch brothers' and the politicals' game plan, Choice and the overarching desire to eventually privatize the VA. With me out of the way, not only could progress toward strengthening the existing VA stop, but it would be much easier to reverse direction and work toward breaking down the entire system.

A week after I was fired, there was a reception in my honor at the Disabled American Veterans (DAV) headquarters, hosted by the DAV, the Veterans of Foreign Wars, and the American Legion.

When I got there, the hosts brought me up on stage, and Congressman Roe made some formal remarks. He was followed by Senator Isakson and Senator Tester, and everything they said was warm, personal, and very meaningful to me. The comment that stuck with me most was made by Senator Tester. He told the crowd and reminded me of what he had once said to me: "Shulkin and I had a lot of conversations in my office, and I used to say to him, 'You know, David, there may come a time when you have to fight against privatization, even if it costs you your job.' And it did." The whole event felt like I was attending my own funeral, and Merle was in tears at several points.

Many people from the veteran community came up to me at the party to thank me for speaking out after I was fired. Sherman Gillums, a leader at AMVETS, told Merle, "David was the martyr who awakened the country and let them know what was going on." Others said that my willingness to speak out for what was right gave them hope and that people knew I had stood up for my principles. Vivieca and her husband, Jim, were there, and I was so pleased when Vivieca was asked to come on stage and be recognized for her hard work and incredible contributions to the VA. Tom Bowman had called at the last minute to say that he couldn't attend. Unspoken but very clear to me was Tom's fear of retribution from the new VA regime with whom he still worked. While I understood, it stung that he and other VA leaders weren't there to show their support for me.

The press continued to hound me for months. Most wanted me to comment on how the politicals worked against me and what their strategy might be going forward, but I had no interest in prolonging this ugly fight. My goal all along had been to work toward positive change for veterans, and that remains my only real concern.

The entire episode was unfortunate for many reasons that radiated well beyond me. One was the sad irony that journalists, even those who considered themselves antagonistic to the Trump administration, allowed themselves to be played as if they were the administration's own hatchet men and women. Another was the absurd cost of all the time spent investigating a supposed transgression that, even if it had constituted a violation, involved modest sums at best—all of which I paid to the VA anyway. Yet the most troubling aspect of all was the nature of the single-minded bullies who simply didn't believe in the ideas of compromise, respect, or playing by the rules.

A few weeks later, the VA sent Vivieca, Poonam, and me letters requesting that we repay more money for our European trip. The logic was distorted and nonsensical, and it was clearly just one more political hit job.

Vivieca, Poonam, and I each responded, and while I never saw their letters, mine laid out the facts of the trip clearly and factually. Tom Bowman communicated by phone that the information I had submitted would be considered by an internal group at the VA and then referred to him as deputy secretary. He assured me that my letter would be given fair consideration.

I was not surprised when, a few weeks later, Tom called again to say that Peter O'Rourke, the new acting secretary, would not allow Tom to be part of the review process. Several days later, Tom announced his retirement.

My letter was scheduled for consideration by a committee at the VA that was part of the regional office in Saint Paul, Minnesota. In August, I received the committee's response, which said unequivocally, "*There was no indication of fraud, misrepresentation or bad faith.*"

Finding none of these, they were waiving any request for any further compensation. They explained that since the travel authorization had been reviewed and approved prior to the trip, VA staff members were at fault. They concluded that I had followed all federal travel regulations, stating specifically, "*No fault is found on the part of Dr. Shulkin as he could reasonably expect his travel plan and authorization to be vetted prior to execution. Unjust enrichment has not been found as Dr. Shulkin received funds that were approved related to his travel. There is no indication that he sought unfair gain at the expense of VA.*"

Unsurprisingly, this report clearing my name was never leaked or picked up by the press. It wasn't a sexy story, I guess. I've heard it's almost impossible to erase a smear, which is why the tactic is so effective for those willing to stoop low enough to utilize it. I wish the media would consider its complicity in perpetuating false rumors and ruining lives—both in publishing inaccurate stories based on partisan leaks and then allowing misperceptions to persist by not correcting the record.

I am not just troubled about the impact on me and my family. I'm also troubled by how such negligence affects the reputation and stability of an entire agency, particularly when it was making good progress. In this case, millions of veterans were left with real concerns over the future direction of the VA.

In the weeks following my departure, there was significant management chaos at the VA. Scott Blackburn, the acting chief information officer, left. The official leading the Choice Program left. The head of innovation left. The new principal deputy under secretary for health left. Many other talented career professionals also left. All of these were gifted people who had left the private sector but had had enough.

Moreover, I have no idea what motivates angry, bare-knuckled partisans like the political appointees who came to the VA, but I felt that they never took the time to learn the basic issues facing the organization that they were trying to turn upside down. Maybe they just didn't want to see a government-run health care system succeed. They had nothing to offer but their narrow and aggressive antigovernment ideology. I also felt that without any relevant experience, they never understood the implications of making decisions in a complex environment, especially one with such a profound impact on the lives of extraordinary Americans who served their country honorably. I fear their aim was winning a power game, not serving veterans.

52

Becoming Law

WITHIN A FEW MONTHS OF MY FIRING, ALL THREE OF MY MAJOR policy objectives were implemented. The restructuring plan for the VA was moving forward; the Cerner contract was signed, and the Choice bill (renamed the Mission Act) was penned into law—largely as I had proposed and supported it, including the provision for caregivers. And as I had advocated, the administration even eventually dropped its opposition to providing Blue Water navy veterans with the support they deserved. I received none of the credit, but I was happy about a win for veterans.

The final phase of the Cerner negotiations grew even more complicated when Camilo Sandoval started to attend the meetings on electronic health records. Supposedly, he was also speaking regularly with the Mar-a-Lago team about how the VA IT team was managing the process and sharing his concerns about the contract. All of this interference and the toxic environment it created became too much for Scott Blackburn, my acting chief information officer, and as mentioned earlier, he resigned within weeks of my departure from the VA. Advancing past a great number of competent career people in the VA's IT department, Camilo was made acting CIO. Who decided this and what background Camilo had to do the job was unclear.

Nearly seven weeks after my firing, the political appointees apparently determined what I had known all along: the options for IT modernization were limited, and the Cerner contract was the best option for VA and for taxpayers. In the end, the right decision was made, and the VA was on its way to gaining a cutting-edge system to propel it into the future. The Cerner contract was ultimately signed on May 17, 2018.

On June 6, at an event in the Rose Garden, the president also signed the Mission Act. President Trump talked about what a great day it was and that he had delivered on his commitment to giving veterans choice over their health care. He also talked about other progress he had made since taking office: the accountability bill, the new electronic health record, and now Choice. With him were Republican members of the Senate and House and representatives from several of the VSOs. No Democrats were included, and few (if any) career VA professionals were present. By this time, of course, I was at home in Philadelphia and never mentioned. But the irony was not lost that these same politicals who had fought me bitterly were now celebrating and taking credit for each of the policy objectives that I had worked tirelessly to achieve.

The Mission Act, which I had worked on for almost three years, represented a major reform to help the VA become a contemporary health system. I brought this bill close to the finish line despite two strong objections from individuals at the White House. First, they did not want to expand caregiver support. I am sure the only objection here was the cost, despite the fact that supporting caregivers for the older veteran population would actually reduce government costs in the long run. Second, they wanted open access without clinical criteria. I knew this would be prohibitively expensive and lead to cannibalizing the VA itself. The bill gave the secretary the necessary latitude to create regulations that would allow the program to succeed. I was confident that as long as I was there, I would find the appropriate balance between access to the private sector and strengthening the VA system. But, of course, I was no longer there.

Despite my outspoken support for the expansion of caregiver support and the almost unanimous support of the Senate and House committee members, the Trump administration would not support this provision. Andrew Bremberg fought me bitterly on it. Yet Bremberg never took the time to understand the data on the tsunami of costs rising to care for aging veterans, who without this support would require institutional care at taxpayer expense. Not only was supporting veterans in their homes the right thing to do for the veterans' sake, it was also the most economical in the long run. In the end, in its push to get the Choice bill done, the administration dropped its objections to caregiver support.

Nevertheless, following the president's signature on the Mission Act, the handshakes, and the slaps on the back, there remains uncertainty about what happens next. The most concerning provision included in the Mission Act relates to the eligibility for care in the private sector of the community. While the definition of this eligibility is rather complicated, the provision may ultimately determine the long-term sustainability of the entire VA system. It is left to the discretion of the secretary to determine who can receive private care and under what circumstances. This could result in a narrow definition of eligibility (meaning most veterans would continue receiving care at the VA) or a broad definition (allowing veterans to seek private care on the VA's dime whenever they please) that would pave the way for privatization. Privatization would not come in a single step—from a quick vote in Congress or an executive order—but rather as a result of gradually widening the conduit to the private sector while simultaneously draining the resources from the VA.

The secretary released the new access standards for the Mission Act on January 30, 2019. These represented a stark contrast from what I had worked toward during my time at the VA. In fact, the only aspect of these access standards I agreed to was the idea of giving veterans greater involvement and choice in their health care decisions by eliminating the 40/30 rule (forty miles from a VA provider and thirty-day wait times). But these new proposed access standards called for the VA to bypass the clinical capabilities of the system. Incredibly, what they proposed was administrative standards of thirty-minute and sixty-minute drive times for primary care and specialty care, respectively, as well as new wait times of twenty and twenty-eight days for primary care and specialty care, respectively. This meant that even veterans who lived in the same town as the VA but faced a thirty-minute drive—as would many residents in any major city with traffic—would now have the ability to access private care with no copays, deductibles, or other means of care coordination.

The blood drained from my face when I read these details. My first thought was that the politicals at VA simply had no idea what they were doing. But as I thought more about it, I realized that they knew exactly what they were doing. Access standards like this would provide millions of veterans with the ability to get care in the private sector and lead to the rapid dismantling of the current VA system. If you were designing a path toward privatization, this would surely be it.

In proposing these new standards, it was as if the VA ignored everything that had happened in health care over the past twenty-five years. Industry professionals know that without controls on utilization and greater cost shares from patients, overutilization and spiraling costs are almost inevitable. The rest of the health care industry has been moving toward value-based care and the ability to develop systems of care that select for quality and outcomes. The system the VA was proposing was exactly the opposite—a simple, administrative criterion for eligibility and no ability to control or coordinate the care that would be delivered outside of the VA system.

In the Mission Act, the potential to expand community care through broadening access standards means that more expenditures for care outside the VA will come from funds that were previously utilized within the VA. It is difficult to understand how the VA has projected that no patients who currently receive care in the VA will move to community care. This flawed assumption shows the deep lack of understanding of the impact of this policy. Regardless of whether this was simply a mistaken assumption or a deliberate spin minimizing the impact of these standards, the results will be the same. A VA system starved of capital and operating funds with an open aperture to the private sector will, by definition, lead to privatization of the system, which will paradoxically result in less choice for the veterans in the end.

I believe that a patient with an urgent clinical need, even if he or she lives next door to a VA medical center, should be seen immediately by *someone*—either at the VA or elsewhere. As I've mentioned previously, I also believe that the VA should focus more resources on services that are needed most by the veteran population—namely, foundational services such as rehabilitation and specialized care for traumatic brain injury and posttraumatic stress. My vision for the system also allows for veterans to access services in the private sector that the VA may not be doing as well or where it doesn't have the expertise or experience. The VA now appears to be moving away from this approach and choosing instead to open the floodgates.

These new access standards, as proposed, will likely have the unintended consequence of leading to more fragmented care for veterans. Recent research has shown that veterans who received care from both within and outside of the VA system had three times as many medication errors than those who received care solely from within VA. In my opinion, these new findings provide more evidence that we should be building a VA system that utilizes a clinical assessment and coordinates the care for those who receive care in the private sector.

Still, the most pragmatic criticism of the VA's proposed approach is the cost of the new access standards. The cost of paying for veterans to get care in the community needs to come either from the current VA medical centers or from Congress (who would have to authorize new funds). The VA has estimated this additional cost to be more than $17 billion, a projection that I believe is grossly underestimated. This money, whatever the true amount, will need to come from somewhere. My suspicion is that it will come at the expense of the current VA system and will consequently cannibalize its capabilities. Again, if VA insiders were scheming toward privatization, this was the way to do it.

There is a big difference between providing veterans greater access to care in the private sector (which I support) and privatization. Greater choice can be achieved through appropriate access standards based on clinical criteria, which would allow veterans to utilize the private sector where it makes sense medically. At the same time, appropriate clinical standards allow for a strong and sustainable VA that could provide essential services to veterans. In contrast, unfettered access to private care based on drive and wait times paves the pathway for the dismantling of the government-run system set up to serve veterans. For some, this distinction is hard to see, but for those who understand the political brinksmanship at work, this marks the major difference for the future vision of caring for our veterans.

I am convinced that the path now chosen, if allowed to continue, will leave veterans with fewer options, a severely weakened VA, and a private health care system not designed to meet the complex requirements of high-need veterans. The result, I believe, will be a fundamental inability to fulfill our sacred responsibility of caring for the men and women we send into harm's way.

Darin Selnick and his fellow political appointees were undoubtedly behind this policy shift. And Concerned Veterans of America was directing from the sidelines. While largely unaware of his political appointees' scheming, President Trump was most likely pleased with the result, because it fit well into a political sound bite and was consistent with his campaign platform. Most likely he does not realize the long-term implications of the wrong access standards. But years from now, if these policies are implemented, I fear that the country will lose a truly invaluable national asset, and the damage will take decades to undo. I believe that empowering political appointees, with no experience in health care, no interest in involving industry experts, and no accountability to voters, will prove to be one of the larger mistakes of the Trump administration.

On June 5, 2019, the VA released the final community care regulations for the Mission Act. Even with these, there remains much unknown about how the program will be implemented. The VA received 23,557 comments on these regulations, many of which expressed support and many others identifying concerns. Let me be clear: I want the Mission Act to be successful and to improve care for veterans, and I favor greater choice for veterans. Although many of the concerns expressed in these comments are real and deserve careful attention, I wish that the VA would be more transparent with its plans and define and implement the new access standards more clearly, if only to allow for appropriate policy debates and oversight by Congress. To date, there has not been enough transparency, and this causes me great concern. Time will tell.

I do appreciate some of the advances that have been made since I left office. One of the groups of veterans I fought for during my service was the Blue Water navy veterans, and when I began writing this book, I planned to make their case. There have been significant developments since then. The VA's appeal of a court decision granting Blue Water navy veterans benefits had kept the issue stalled and veterans waiting. To get the issue unstuck, it looked like a legislative solution would be required. In June 2018, the House voted 382 to 0 to pass the Blue Water Navy Veterans Act, which granted presumptive benefits to these Vietnam War sailors. The next step was to have the Senate debate and vote on the bill, but this didn't happen. At the time, Secretary Wilkie came out against granting benefits to the Blue Water navy veterans, most likely because of financial considerations. Four prior secretaries— Nicholson, Peake, Principi, and McDonald—authored a letter to the Senate leadership that also recommended against moving forward with the bill until the issue could be studied further.

The problem, of course, is that fifty years had already passed since these exposures, and there is no new data on which to base further studies. Political forces successfully delayed a decision for these veterans once again. It's become far too easy for the VA to call for further study and consequently delay a resolution of an issue.

Aware that I was in favor of granting these benefits, veterans around the country contacted me by email, phone, and Twitter and requested that I make my voice heard. While I was hesitant to once again put myself in the crosshairs of the administration, I decided to send a letter to Chairman Isakson, Ranking Member Tester, Chairman Roe, and Ranking Member Walz to urge them to move forward with granting the benefits. My letter was picked up by the press and reported as a debate between me and prior VA secretaries. Much to my delight, in June 2019, the Department of Justice decided to drop its appeal of a federal court decision that would provide compensation to disabled Blue Water navy veterans. After almost fifty years for some of these veterans, the wait seemed like it was finally over.

53

More Trouble

IN AUGUST 2018, A *PROPUBLICA* REPORT EXTENSIVELY DETAILED THE involvement of Ike Perlmutter, Bruce Moskowitz, and Marc Sherman as influencers of VA policy. I declined to comment when dozens of media outlets reached out to me. Anything I could've said would have been pure speculation because, despite being painfully aware of their involvement, I never had a clear understanding of the exact duties that the president delegated to them or their relationships with the president and other members of the administration. Moreover, I wasn't aware that any of the three did anything wrong other than occasionally giving some bad advice and speaking to me harshly. I saw them as well-intentioned, politically connected private citizens who wanted to be involved because they cared about helping the president improve life for veterans. More than occasionally during my time working with a disorganized and unconventional White House, I saw them as instrumental in getting the attention of people who I myself (as a cabinet secretary) often had trouble accessing.

Perhaps what surprised me most was that few members of the press reported on the published email where Jake Leinenkugel laid out the plan to get rid of me, my deputy secretary, and my chief of staff—a plan to be coordinated through *Ike*. Specifically, the email read: "SECVA (Secretary of VA)—put on notice to exit after major legislation and key POTUS VA initiatives in place. Utilize outside VA team (Ike) and strong political candidates." Jake spoke about me like a racehorse, with the politicals waiting for one more trophy before putting me to sleep.

After a close reading of the *ProPublica* report on the Mar-a-Lago trio's involvement in the VA, it became clear to me that the source of the story must have been someone who worked in the IT department at the VA. The issues discussed in the report involving Ike, Bruce, and Marc were largely IT related, and I was aware that they pushed back so hard on the Cerner contract that they made some enemies within the VA to the point that they might inspire a malicious leak like this. I also recalled Camilo Sandoval, who dropped Ike's name on a regular basis around the VA's IT department where he worked. Camilo knew what he was doing. As suggested in Laurence Leamer's recent book on Mar-a-Lago, when a call comes "from an individual who has the president's ear, it's not a suggestion but an order." Staff by and large despised Camilo, and everyone knew he was there for only one reason: the politicals at the VA and the White House wanted him there.

I later heard that Camilo was telling anyone who would listen that I had been hurrying through a flawed Cerner contract, that the signing was imminent, and that I needed to be stopped. The same source told me that Camilo and several others from the VA, possibly with some outsiders' help as well, had told the White House that I needed to be removed before a bad contract was signed. Neither Camilo nor others from the White House confronted me with any such concerns so that I could address any objections head on. Moreover, as mentioned, Camilo's allegation was unwarranted because I wasn't planning to sign any contract until I was fully satisfied that we ensured the presence of appropriate safeguards.

Also in August 2018, I became aware that some of the politicals at the VA were still trying to publicize my trip to Europe as a strategy to deflect attention from their exposure in *ProPublica*. Almost a year later, the VA's press secretary, Curt Cashour, released an official statement saying, "In his brief stint at VA, Secretary David Shulkin made misleading statements to the press, directed the misuse of a subordinate's official time, and improperly accepted Wimbledon tickets in conjunction with a questionable taxpayer-funded trip to Europe." Why were they still so focused on me? My attorney, Justin, told me that he had never seen a government spokesperson be this outwardly hostile and malicious, and no other administration would have tolerated it.

Long after I left government, some of the press continued to report that I was fired because of a travel scandal. It's frustrating for me that reporters chose to repeat rumor as fact, even after the allegations against me had been largely discredited. To add to my frustration, and to put the whole affair into context, current Trump secretaries (and certainly past cabinet secretaries) frequently travel with their spouses on trips at government expense without criticism. Secretary Rick Perry's wife, Anita, took three overseas trips. Rick Perry upgraded his travel to business class on both international and domestic flights at an additional cost of over $50,000 to the government. Similarly, Secretary of State Mike Pompeo took his wife, Susan, on a multicountry tour during his service. As mentioned above, Karen Kelly, Chief of Staff John Kelly's spouse, traveled at government expense to the Invictus Games in Toronto. Karen was part of the official delegation, which should have been treated no differently than Merle joining the official delegation in Europe. And while Merle and I were villainized for some sightseeing in London, multiple members of the president's family visited many of these same sites in June 2019—a trip that reportedly cost taxpayers over $5 million.

In September 2018, FEMA director Brock Long allegedly used government vehicles for personal travel. FEMA's IG simply required him to pay back the money and promise to put safeguards in place for the future. Even the VA's prior deputy secretary was investigated by the VA's IG and found to have inadvertently missed paying for a number of personal flights. The IG required him to reimburse the department, and staff was retrained on proper authorization procedures.

My point is neither to criticize my former colleagues (or their spouses or families) nor to point fingers and say, "Well, they did it, too." Rather, my point is that there was no clear line that I crossed or could've been aware that I crossed when I was following standard practice. I certainly had never traveled on charter or military flights (with the exception of travel on the planes that carried the president, the first lady, or the vice president). My point is really that comparable actions were not treated comparably. I was essentially forced out of office, while those more philosophically in sync with the administration stretched the bounds of propriety without penalty. To me, it was clear: I was pushed out of the VA because of a partisan desire to get rid of me and any other obstacles standing in the way of privatizing the VA.

54

Getting It Right for Veterans

Throughout my career, the VA has been a leader in clinical outcomes and patient safety, which may seem counterintuitive. In contrast, despite greater access to capital to put toward facilities, equipment, and salaries to attract the best and the brightest, improvements in quality and safety rarely happen in the private sector unless they align with financial incentives. Often, the wrong financial incentives lead to worse outcomes. For example, shorter hospital stays reduce the chance of patient infections, yet hospitals and doctors are sometimes reimbursed for each day the patient spends in the hospital.

One of the benefits of working in the VA is not having to worry about how things will be paid for, which allows professionals to simply focus on doing what's best for the patient. Moreover, the VA offers many additional services, some not considered "health care" per se but that have a huge impact on health and well-being. For example, the VA provides income supplementation when a person is disabled or unable to work, transportation services, caregiver support, peer counseling, housing subsidies, medication subsidies, long-term care, and medical equipment and supplies. The VA's ability to sidestep the economic disincentives existing in the private sector is one of its greatest superpowers.

Some people within the Trump administration told me privately that they believed the VA system was unfixable and that the real estate was too valuable. They suggested restricting the eligibility of new veterans into the system so that after the wave of current veterans died off, the VA would finally be able to display an "out of business" sign on its front door. These beliefs are not based on any evidence but rather an adherence to ideological bias. When you bring a chief financial officer's or a real estate mogul's mind-set into human services, you immediately face a contradiction.

There have been many attempts to "privatize" public schools, for instance, based on the hypothesis that if we could just get rid of all the children who are disruptive, slow learners, and unpromising, then we could really make some money. But the whole point of public education is not to push the kids who are easiest to educate through the system and then collect a financial reward! The point is to create a social fabric that strengthens society by educating everyone. Similarly, privatizing the VA would lead to some veterans' health care needs being met while others' needs totally slip through the cracks. The private sector is entirely capable of arranging mundane things for veterans like eyeglasses fittings and lab tests, but when it comes to the more complicated and chronic issues that disproportionately affect veterans (e.g., posttraumatic stress, traumatic brain injury, complex surgeries following war-related trauma, severe service related behavioral health issues, etc.), the private sector is sorely underprepared. In contrast, the VA has the capability and the desire to cater to these difficult issues. If the United States intends to honor its promise to take care of all its veterans, then we need the VA. It's that simple. Taking care of the men and women who served and sacrificed for our country is a moral obligation undertaken by society at large.

I have always favored a middle-of-the-road strategy for the VA, meaning that I want to strengthen the institution while simultaneously moving toward greater coordination with the private sector. I was never pro-privatization nor anti-privatization. I was simply pro-veteran. When I became under secretary, roughly 19 percent of veterans received care in the community. When I left the VA as secretary at the end of March 2018, the figure was nearly 36 percent. We were working with the private sector more than ever before, and at the same time, we were strengthening the core foundation of VA services.

My stance was confusing to those with a "you're either with us or against us" approach. Governing in a democracy is always a matter of compromise and coalition-building, but unfortunately, the Trump administration brought in zealots who cared less about governing (or serving veterans) than they did about driving an ideological agenda. Making matters worse, they engaged in subversive behavior and defamation instead of the open and free debate that makes our democracy so strong.

In June 2018, I published another article in the *New England Journal of Medicine,* arguing that government-run health care doesn't mean there shouldn't be competition and implementation of industry best practices. My thinking evolved during my time as secretary, and I came to see that driving change in a system as large and bureaucratic as the VA requires extra incentives. Nothing motivates like competition, and with competition comes accountability. If a VA facility is performing poorly, it needs to develop a plan for improvement with clear goals, metrics, and timelines. If the plan doesn't materialize, then the local management should be supplemented or replaced. If there is still no improvement, veterans shouldn't be held hostage to an inferior system of care and instead should have the ability to opt out of the VA system and seek care in the private sector. This is what happens in the private sector when higher-quality hospitals grow their market share at the expense of lower-quality facilities.

The VA is currently locked in an outdated reimbursement model, which requires the agency to pay fee-for-service to its providers and, with a few exceptions for rural locations, a Medicare fee schedule. It isn't participating in the more contemporary value-based models of care, such as bundles of care or differential payments based on quality or efficiency measures. Yet for the VA to be competitive, it must have this kind of flexibility.

On another note, I also strongly believe that the VA has become too top-heavy and bloated with administrators. The result is decisions that take too long to make and a diffusion of accountability that leads to less-than-favorable outcomes. The VA's central headquarters has more than 150 different program offices, each with its own culture and bureaucracy, and the inefficiency bleeds into the field. The accountability for operational decisions and outcomes needs to shift more to local executives and clinical leaders that care for veterans and away from administrators in Washington.

Restructuring efforts are very time-consuming and emotionally draining for a large agency. As under secretary, I felt we needed to fix the wait-time issues before trying to reorganize. Once becoming secretary, and having confidence that we had already significantly improved access, I launched a major effort to revise the management structure. The first objective was to trim at the central office, and I charged our Office of Enterprise Integration with the responsibility of overseeing this. We asked the VHA to revisit the role of the Veterans Integrated Service Networks (VISN), the layer of management between the field and the central office. Every large, geographically spread-out organization has some regional management structure, yet many decisions and actions were being held up at the VISN level. I felt it was time to remove or redesign the VISN, but we were still in the design phase when I left office.

I also believe, as first recommended in the 2016 Commission on Care Report, that the VA needs a new model of governance, complete with its own board composed of health care experts, veterans, and business leaders. It should remain a government entity but with a structure that allows it to develop strategies free of political influence. The Obama administration was unsupportive of this idea. I feel strongly, however, that this is the level of dramatic structural change necessary to fix some of the systemic

problems that are nearly impossible to address in a highly politicized environment.

This new governance structure would mean the end of political appointees. People who serve our veterans should be chosen
not on the basis of political ideology or their commitment to a
particular elected individual but rather because of relevant experience, competence, and commitment to the mission. The VA also
needs to ensure continuity of leadership, which is why I think the
secretary should have a term of at least four years, with the possibility of renewal. This is similar to the model used by most medical
schools for appointing deans as well as by the Federal Reserve for
maintaining the independence of its director.

In order to survive and flourish, the VA needs to evolve. The
big picture is that the VA needs to change from being a pure provider of care to being a network coordinator of care. This would
require a huge change in mind-set, but it is one I believe the VA is
fully capable of. Time and time again, I have seen personally how
when VA professionals and staff are given the right mission and
clear direction, they deliver.

Something else to consider is how critical it is for VA officials
to not become too distanced from the veterans themselves. That's
the reason I kept practicing medicine during my time as secretary.
When I stepped into an exam room with my white coat, I wasn't
the secretary of the VA anymore; I was simply a doctor caring for
a patient. This helped me stay in touch with veterans' day-to-day
issues.

One day during my time in office, we gathered six hundred of
our top leaders from around the country at the National Conference Center in Leesburg, Virginia. After a two-day session filled
with presentations, we had a panel of veterans speak about their
experiences at the VA. One of the panelists was Lauren Augustine,
who shared her thoughts on a new app we developed to allow
veterans to schedule appointments online. We had been working
internally on this software for more than two years. Over budget

and well past the original timeline, we had finally launched the app and then sat back and waited for our well-deserved accolades.

To our surprise, Lauren gave us an account of trying unsuccessfully to schedule an appointment using our technology. First she went to Google for instructions but found nothing. Next, she struggled with the login process. Eventually, when she got in, she was unable to find the appointment she wanted, so she gave up. The room of six hundred VA leaders fell silent. Lauren made everyone realize that despite millions of dollars spent on developers and technology contractors, we neglected to ask for feedback from the users themselves.

If I had to simplify my approach to reform and improvement for other leaders, I would say this: The formula I use is "set, do, and report." By "set" I mean setting the big-picture strategic objectives for the organization. I don't believe that setting goals is about achieving consensus or listening to what the organization wants. It's about listening to the customer or end user and then figuring out the right steps to take as a result. "Do" means focusing on implementation to get the job done. I am a believer in the iterative approach to achieving goals. Start somewhere, try something, and keep track of what works. Then try again. Don't wait until all of the unknowns are known. I have never met a great leader who was afraid of taking risks or was paralyzed by a fear of failure. Finally, "report" means transparently sharing your progress with others. Reporting results is essential to being able to ask others for help.

55

Reflections: It Shouldn't Be This Hard to Serve Your Country

When I reflect on my time at the VA, I feel both pride in what we got accomplished and regret for what we left on the table. I feel great satisfaction in knowing that we saw more than a dozen pieces of legislation signed into law, improved access to services for veterans, directed the modernization of VA infrastructure, and oversaw the implementation of a veteran-focused culture. None of this could have happened without a dedicated workforce and Congress's cooperation and willingness to set aside partisan politics to focus on shared goals. To this day, I am forever grateful to the many veterans I met who made my experience so worthwhile. It was a privilege to serve them for three years.

Yet I strongly believe that we as a society have allowed public service to become far too unpleasant. When we were recruiting for the VA, many wonderfully qualified people expressed a sincere desire to learn more about joining the team. Some came to visit and seriously considered signing on, but ultimately, few did. Once they learned about the limitations on outside activities, the number of regulations and restrictions, the reputational risks, the toxic political culture, and the low salary, they refused to take the leap.

In the nineteenth century, high levels of patronage, graft, and corruption within government led to the creation of bureaucratic controls intended to guarantee fairness and transparency. The unintended consequence, however, is the very omnipresent sense of mistrust toward those serving. This sense of mistrust, combined with inflamed partisanship and a news media that thrives on sensationalism, makes it possible for a mere allegation, even if ultimately refuted, to destroy a career. And along the way, the battle of trying to publicly defend against accusations of impropriety is so painful that it's understandable why so few people decide to take the risk of joining government.

I strongly believe that Washington needs to transform into a more welcoming environment for talented individuals who can bring significant real-world experience to government. For one, we need to create a system of true professional oversight rather than rampant allegations and internal investigations. This is the way professional societies work, with self-regulation and professional competence driving their standards. The system of inspectors general is far from ideal and, in my opinion, instills fear in leaders and causes an unwillingness to take risks and make changes. Our current whistleblower culture flourishes in government, largely because of this system of distrust. Of course it's necessary to uphold laws and maintain ethical standards, and we should hope that people do report true wrongdoing. But government could approach this the way the private sector does—with better management practices and more accountability rather than "secret police" who come in after the fact. At the VA, the IG's office employs nearly one thousand people and has become a highly feared part of the agency. Having borne the brunt of what I thought was an unfair and unjust investigation, I believe we can do better.

After I left and the politicals were given free rein, it became clear that these appointees had few innovative ideas of their own. While they excoriated my approach and policies, they continued to follow my precise policy playbook after my exile. They supported the Mission Act—a legislative objective I pushed for throughout my entire tenure as secretary. They signed off on the Cerner contract—the path I had paved and was moving toward completion. They dropped their objections to granting benefits to Blue Water navy veterans—a position for which I had advocated. They continued working toward suicide prevention—my main clinical priority as secretary. But the politicals soon crumbled under their own weight.

In May 2018, a number of Democratic lawmakers signed a letter asking the president to remove Camilo Sandoval. They reasoned that he didn't have the necessary experience to serve as acting CIO and cited several allegations of inappropriate use of data from his past. Unsurprisingly, the VA responded with a statement of support for him. Eventually, however, he was moved to a less powerful and more poorly defined role within the department.

Having worn out his welcome at the White House, Darin Selnick also reported in May that he was leaving the Domestic Policy Council to return to consulting for the Koch brothers–backed organization Concerned Veterans of America. A few months later, Darin came back to the VA as Secretary Wilkie's policy adviser on Choice and was influential in developing the flawed access standards I already mentioned. Jake Leinenkugel also announced in July 2018 that he was leaving his role as senior White House liaison and instead was appointed to run VA's commission on mental health. Also in July, Peter Shelby, the political appointee who served as the assistant secretary for human resources, was reportedly escorted out of the building. Another political appointee, Don Loren, the assistant secretary for security and preparedness, was supposedly fired or resigned. Peter O'Rourke, the chief of staff forced upon me after Vivieca resigned and who was later named as acting secretary, left the department in a hurry. John Ullyot quickly announced his departure in March 2019 as well. The politicals could carry out political sabotage, but when their scheme was finished and they were forced to confront the substance of the VA issues themselves, they were clueless. I worry most about this when it comes to the implementation of the Cerner system. Getting a contract signed is one thing, but carrying out the real work involved is quite another. My years of experience with EHR implementations taught me that doing this well will require participants with real experience and knowledge that is unfortunately in short supply within the VA's political leadership today.

Some people say I should've had thicker skin. I resented the tactics that were used, and are still being used, in this administration. The environment we see in Washington today, modeled by the administration, is consistently one of personal attacks. I believe that people who launch personal attacks rather than focusing on the issues often do so because they lack intelligence. This is why the political appointees focused their efforts on attacking my character rather than debating ideas on which we disagreed. They used the media to their advantage to leak stories on allegations of ethical and moral issues—none of which were true.

While serving as secretary, I knew standing up for veterans and fighting the political battles against privatization would put a large target on my back, yet what truly amazed me was that the attacks continued for more than a year after I left office. At the end of 2018, when the VA was criticized by the Government Accountability Office for their suicide-prevention outreach efforts, the official VA response issued by Curt Cashour was to blame *me*. Then in December 2018, when I acknowledged Secretary Mattis on Twitter for standing up for his principles in his resignation letter to the president, the response from Dan Caldwell at Concerned Veterans of America was again a personal attack against me.

In my view, there is no place in civil society for this kind of behavior, and certainly no institution with a mission as important as the VA's should tolerate it. If the United States wants to set an example for other nations to follow, this is surely not the way to do it. And if the United States wants to attract rather than repel qualified public servants, then it needs to make government a less toxic place to work. It shouldn't be this hard to serve your country.

I remind myself and my family that this was never meant to be an easy job but that our struggles could never compare to those of the veterans who fought and sacrificed so much for their country. To be clear, the title of this book—*It Shouldn't Be This Hard to Serve Your Country*—is a play on words. It primarily refers to our men and women in uniform who deserve the best care from the VA but are being held hostage to political infighting, Washington red tape, and biased agendas. It only secondarily refers to the backlash and harassment I faced once I entered the spotlight, despite playing everything by the book as best I could and doing all I could to make a real difference in veterans' lives.

To this day, people ask me how I could have worked in the Trump administration, and my answer is simple: I didn't serve because I particularly wanted to work for Donald Trump. I served to give back to our veterans and continue the work I was already invested in. I hope many others would and will continue to make the same choice—even though more than a dozen cabinet members in this administration have already passed through the revolving door. Because if people let their political differences stop them from entering public service, we are all going to be much worse off.

Politics is meant to be a rough sport. Some say I should've known what I was getting myself into, since almost nobody leaves Trump's administration with his or her head still above water. They may be right. I was overly optimistic and perhaps naïve when I assumed that political scandals and turbulent firings only happened to people who engaged in actual wrongdoing. I also still don't see how I could've said no when I was asked to serve my country—first under President Obama and then under President Trump. If my skill, experience, and leadership could help our veterans, then it was my duty to say yes. I'm not sure I would make a different choice if I could go back and do it all over again.

One of the greatest honors of serving as under secretary and secretary of the VA was getting to know the veterans and their families. Serving others, especially those who have sacrificed for the nation, is one of the most gratifying experiences one can have.

And sharing such a meaningful common purpose with so many hardworking VA employees who were there for the right reasons was invigorating.

This past winter, Merle, Danny, Jennie, and I attended the 2018 Army-Navy Game in Philadelphia. No longer a member of the cabinet, I had no security or entourage. We proudly watched America's game as the young cadets and midshipmen competed and their classmates cheered them on. President Trump spoke from the field at halftime. The whole afternoon was bittersweet. Merle and I couldn't help but think of the past couple of years at the Army-Navy Games, when I was still serving and we felt much more included in the day's festivities. As we were walking out of the stadium at the end of the game, though, about a half-dozen middle-aged veterans approached us, and one said, "Hey, aren't you the former VA secretary?"

I nodded.

"We just want to thank you for all that you did. It really made a difference," another said.

A third chimed in, "We always knew you had our backs."

I thanked them, and as we walked away, one of them turned to me and said, "You know, for us veterans, Trump may have fired you, but you will always be our secretary."

Author's Note

IT WAS SOMETIMES DIFFICULT, BOTH FACTUALLY AND EMOTIONALLY, to put this story down on paper. As mentioned above, my access to my VA calendars, emails, and documents was shut off moments after my firing. As a result, I did my best to accurately recall the events as they happened and referenced outside materials as much as I could. However, my memory of the events—some of which occurred years earlier—is by no means perfect. I often quote people to the best of my recollection and admit that it may not always be verbatim. If I have made any mistakes, I can assure you they were not intentional. Similarly, my reference to Trump's political appointees assigned to the VA is not meant to generalize all appointees. There are many political appointees serving for the right reasons and who are talented, dedicated, and competent. In my reference to the "politicals," I am referring to just a select group of appointees who were at the VA for what I felt were the wrong reasons and, even if they were well intentioned, had a lasting and harmful impact on the agency.

I realize that there are strong political divisions within our nation today. I understand that some who read this book will feel differently than I do, and I respect that. But the purpose of this book is to share my experience, present the facts as I see them, and let the readers evaluate the direction that the VA should head in the years to come. Ultimately, this book is written to persuade others to do better for veterans, shed light on the toxic and dysfunctional political environment in Washington, and work toward creating a world where it is not this hard to serve your country. It is only then that I believe that good people will want to raise their hands, go to Washington, and fight to make the system better for all.

This book is also meant to recognize the incredible work that is done in the VA system every day and, most importantly, the contributions that our veterans and their families have made and continue to make to our country.

Finally, I want to acknowledge and thank my family. I could not have written this book without them, but more importantly I could not have served without them. My wife, Merle, fully embraced the job and the Washington experience as much as I did. She lived the ups and downs of going from private life to public scrutiny, and she was with me every step of the way. Merle dutifully kept a diary of our time in Washington, which helped me immensely in recalling the details of the narrative written here. Merle also reviewed version after version of this book with me to ascertain that I accurately told the story that, in many ways, is as much hers as mine. I also want to acknowledge William Patrick, who helped organize my writing and translate my ideas into a publishable manuscript. I especially want to thank my daughter, Jennie, for taking on this project as her own (despite working a full-time job), reworking my writing, and painstakingly editing the entire book to make sure it communicated my story accurately and through an authentic voice. Danny, too, was instrumental in diligently keeping track of the many relevant video clips, articles, reports, and tweets so that I could reference them throughout the book. Both Jennie and Danny lived this experience with us and embrace the meaning of service. I will be forever grateful for my family's love and support.

References

Note: In preparing this manuscript, I have relied on my recollection of events, my wife's journal, and some personal notes. In addition, I referred to a number of documents I have noted below.

Chapter 2

Veterans Health Administration. "Review of Alleged Patient Deaths, Patient Wait Times, and Scheduling Practices at the Phoenix VA Health Care System." August 26, 2014. https://www.va.gov/oig/pubs/vaoig-14-02603-267.pdf.

Chapter 3

Shear, Michael D. "Trump Weighs Letting Veterans Opt Out of V.A. Medical Care." *New York Times*, December 28, 2016. https://www.nytimes.com/2016/12/28/us/politics/trump-weighs-letting-veterans-opt-out-of-va-medical-care.html.

Chapter 6

Shulkin, David. "How the VA's 'Stand-Down' Resolved 56,000 Plus Urgent-Care Consults." *NEJM Catalyst*, April 14, 2016. https://catalyst.nejm.org/va-stand-down-resolved-56000-plus-urgent-care-consults/.

Chapter 8

Slack, Donovan. "VA Officials Didn't Mislead Congress on Wait Times, Investigation Finds." *USA Today*, August 6, 2016. https://www.usatoday.com/story/news/politics/2016/08/05/skye-mcdougall-va-official-wait-times/88304490/.

Chapter 10

Shulkin, David. "Preventing Veteran Suicide: A Call to Action—Vantage Point." Veterans Administration, February 3, 2016. https://www.blogs.va.gov/VAntage/25625/answering-the-call-the-veterans-suicide-summit/.

Jordan, Bryant. "VA Concedes It Had No Role in Developing Hepatitis 'Miracle Drug.'" Military.com, March 11, 2016. https://www.military.com/daily-news /2016/03/11/va-concedes-it-had-no-role-in-developing-hepatitis-miracle -drug.html.

Chapter 11
Orlando.va.gov. "Working-Class Heroes: VA Responds to Mass Shooting— Orlando VA Medical Center." July 25, 2016. https://www.orlando.va.gov /features/orlando_shooting_va_response.asp.

Chapter 15
Ortiz, Erik. "Members of the Designated Survivor Club Describe How the Perceived Power Came—And Went." NBC News, February 28, 2017. https://www .nbcnews.com/storyline/trumps-address-to-congress/designated-survivors -recount-nights-doomsday-presidents-n720691.

Chapter 16
Selnick, Darin, and Stewart Hickey. "Transforming VA Care: A Way Forward." *The Hill*, July 25, 2016. https://thehill.com/blogs/pundits-blog/healthcare /288850-transforming-va-care-a-way-forward.

Crampton, Liz. "Sam Clovis Is Leaving USDA." *Politico*, May 3, 2018. https:// www.politico.com/story/2018/05/03/sam-clovis-leaving-usda-518109.

Keefe, Josh. "Is the VA Being Privatized? Critics Say This Koch-Backed Group Is Fighting to Do Just That." *Newsweek*, April 5, 2018. https://www.newsweek .com/koch-brothers-backed-group-could-determine-future-va-870693.

Kesling, Ben. "Koch Groups to Mount Hard Press to Expand Private-Sector VA Services." *Wall Street Journal*, November 3, 2017. https://www.wsj .com/articles/koch-groups-to-mount-hard-press-to-expand-private-sector-va -services-1509734707.

Drum, Kevin. "The Koch-Fueled Plot to Destroy the VA." *Mother Jones*, March 13, 2016. https://www.motherjones.com/kevin-drum/2016/03/koch-fueled -plot-destroy-va/.

Chapter 19
"Donald Trump Joins Queen for 75th D-Day Anniversary." *BBC News*, June 5, 2019. https://www.bbc.com/news/uk-48522401.

Chapter 21

Pittman, David. "HHS Responds to Global Cyberattack." *Politico*, May 15, 2017. https://www.politico.com/tipsheets/morning-ehealth/2017/05/hhs -responds-to-global-cyberattack-220308.

Chapter 22

The White House. "Press Briefing by Secretary of Veterans Affairs David Shulkin | The White House." May 31, 2017. https://www.whitehouse.gov/briefings -statements/press-briefing-secretary-veterans-affairs-david-shulkin-053117/.

Chapter 23

Veterans Administration. "News Releases—Office of Public and Intergovernmental Affairs." November 29, 2016. https://www.va.gov/opa/pressrel /pressrelease.cfm?id=2837.

Veterans Administration. "News Releases—Office of Public and Intergovernmental Affairs." March 12, 2019. https://www.va.gov/opa/pressrel/pressrelease .cfm?id=5216.

Allen, Arthur. "A 40-Year 'Conspiracy' at the VA." *Politico*, March 19, 2017. https://www.politico.com/agenda/story/2017/03/vista-computer-history-va -conspiracy-000367.

Allen, Arthur. "Shulkin's Move to Dump Vista Seen as Bold, Risky." *Politico*, June 6, 2017. https://www.politico.com/story/2017/06/06/shulkins-move -to-dump-vista-seen-as-bold-risky-239189.

Weinstock, Matthew. "Shulkin: VA Poised to Break Interoperability Logjam." Modern Healthcare, March 9, 2019. https://www.modernhealthcare .com/article/20180309/NEWS/180309895/shulkin-va-poised-to-break -interoperability-logjam.

Chapter 25

Jordan, Bryant. "Lawmaker Questions Why VA Reinstated Employee Linked to Armed Robbery." Military.com, March 23, 2016. https://www.military.com /daily-news/2016/03/23/lawmaker-questions-va-reinstated-employee-linked -armed-robbery.html.

Druzin, Health. "Appeals Board Reverses Another VA Executive's Punishment." *Stars and Stripes*, February 8, 2016. https://www.stripes.com/news/appeals -board-reverses-another-va-executive-s-punishment-1.392980.

Wentling, Nikki. "Employee Watching Porn on the Job Is the Reason VA Needs More Firing Authority." *Task & Purpose*, April 4, 2017. https://taskandpurpose .com/employee-watching-porn-job-reason-va-needs-firing-authority.

Veterans Administration. "News Releases—Office of Public and Intergovernmental Affairs." March 31, 2017. https://www.va.gov/opa/pressrel/pressrelease .cfm?id=2876.

Fandos, Nicholas. "V.A. Plans to Fire Its D.C. Medical Director—Again." *New York Times*, August 9, 2017. https://www.nytimes.com/2017/08/09/us /politics/veterans-affairs-brian-hawkins.html.

Arnsdorf, Isaac. "Trump's VA Firing Spree Falters in Court." *ProPublica*, May 15, 2019. https://www.propublica.org/article/trump-va-firing-spree-falters-in -court.

Chapter 26

GOV.UK. "Joint Communique on International Ministerial (5-Eyes) Conference on Veterans' Issues." July 21, 2017. https://www.gov.uk/government /news/joint-communique-on-international-ministerial-5-eyes-conference-on -veterans-issues.

Watson, Kathryn. "Report: Office Responsible for Vetting Trump Appointees Plagued by Personnel Problems." CBS News, March 30, 2018. https://www .cbsnews.com/news/report-office-responsible-for-vetting-trump-appointees -plagued-by-personnel-problems-report/.

"Manchester VA Medical Center Officials Removed over Care Allegations." *Military Times*, July 17, 2017. https://www.militarytimes.com/2017/07/17 /manchester-va-medical-center-officials-removed-over-care-allegations/.

Chapter 28

Bennett, Jonah. "VA Secretary: Dishonor to Vets to Let Nazis Go Unchallenged." *Daily Caller*, August 16, 2017. https://dailycaller.com/2017/08/16 /va-secretary-dishonor-to-vets-to-let-nazis-go-unchallenged/.

Chapter 31

Slack, Donovan. "Exclusive: VA Chief Dismisses European Travel 'Distraction,' Buzz over HHS Post." *USA Today*, October 27, 2017. https://www .usatoday.com/story/news/politics/2017/10/27/exclusive-va-chief-dismisses -european-travel-distraction-buzz-over-hhs-post/804661001/.

Chapter 34

Shulkin, David, and Kyle Sheetz. "Reforming Veterans Benefits Will Be Controversial, but Necessary." *The Hill*, January 6, 2019. https://thehill.com/opinion/white-house/424037-reforming-veterans-benefits-will-be-controversial-but-necessary.

Veterans Administration. "News Releases—Office of Public and Intergovernmental Affairs." November 1, 2017. https://www.va.gov/opa/pressrel/pressrelease.cfm?id=3967.

Shane, Leo. "Former VA Secretaries Spar over 'Blue Water' Navy Benefits." *Military Times*, September 20, 2018. https://www.militarytimes.com/veterans/2018/09/20/former-va-secretaries-spar-over-blue-water-navy-benefits/.

Wentling, Nikki. "Gulf War Veterans with Brain Cancer Denied Fast Track to Compensation." *Stars and Stripes*, November 18, 2016. https://www.stripes.com/gulf-war-veterans-with-brain-cancer-denied-fast-track-to-compensation-1.440142.

Veterans Administration. "VA Announces New Work Group to Study Brain Cancer in Gulf War Veterans—Public Health." Spring 2015. https://www.publichealth.va.gov/exposures/publications/gulf-war/gulf-war-spring-2015/khamisiyah.asp.

Chapter 35

"Veterans in America: A Conversation with VA Secretary David Shulkin." *Washington Post*, November 9, 2017. https://www.washingtonpost.com/post-live-2017-veterans-in-america/?utm_term=.8223027da7eb.

Bur, Jessie. "VA and Union Clash in Negotiations for a New Contract." *Federal Times*, May 6, 2019. https://www.federaltimes.com/management/2019/05/06/va-and-union-clash-in-negotiations-for-a-new-contract/.

Chapter 37

Lee, Michelle Ye Hee, Lisa Rein, and David Weigel. "How a Koch-Backed Veterans Group Gained Influence in Trump's Washington." *Washington Post*, April 7, 2018. https://www.washingtonpost.com/politics/how-a-koch-backed-veterans-group-gained-influence-in-trumps-washington/2018/04/07/398b67c4-3784-11e8-9c0a-85d477d9a226_story.html?utm_term=.359b004e29aa.

Editorial Board. "A Coup at Veterans Affairs." *New York Times*, March 29, 2018. https://mobile.nytimes.com/2018/03/29/opinion/shulkin-out-veterans-affairs-koch.amp.html.

Cassidy, John. "The Conservative Plot to Oust an Able Secretary of Veterans Affairs." *New Yorker*, March 29, 2018. https://www.newyorker.com/news/our -columnists/the-conservative-plot-to-oust-an-able-secretary-of-veterans-affairs.

Easley, Jason. "The Koch Brothers Are About to Make Their Move to Privatize the VA." *Politics USA*, March 25, 2018. https://www.politicususa.com/2018 /03/25/koch-brothers-privatize-va.html.

Barkan, Ross. "If the Department of Veterans Affairs Head Is Sacked, the Koch Brothers Will Rejoice." *The Guardian*, March 20, 2018. https://amp .theguardian.com/commentisfree/2018/mar/20/david-shulkin-department -veterans-affairs.

Chapter 38
Isakson, Johnny. "Veterans' Affairs Committee Approves Isakson's Bipartisan Legislation to Improve Veterans' Community Care, VA Services." November 29, 2017. https://www.isakson.senate.gov/public/index.cfm/2017/11/veterans -affairs-committee-approves-isakson-s-bipartisan-legislation-to-improve-veterans -community-care-va-services.

Shane, Leo. "Trump's Go-To Guy at VA Faces First Major Opposition from Republicans on Capitol Hill." *Army Times*, January 19, 2018. https://www .armytimes.com/news/2018/01/19/trumps-go-to-guy-at-va-faces-first-major -opposition-from-republicans-on-capitol-hill/.

Chapter 40
Shulkin, David. "Beyond the VA Crisis—Becoming a High-Performance Network." *New England Journal of Medicine*, March 17, 2016. https://www.nejm .org/doi/full/10.1056/NEJMp1600307.

Chapter 41
Veterans Administration. "Administrative Investigation. VA Secretary and Delegation Travel to Europe." February 14, 2018. https://www.va.gov/oig/pubs /VAOIG-17-05909-106.pdf.

Krause, Benjamin. "You're Fired: Thomas Bowman Termination 'To Knock Shulkin Down a Peg or Two.'" *Disabled Veterans*, February 9, 2018. https://www.dis abledveterans.org/2018/02/09/fired-thomas-bowman-termination-shulkin/.

Rein, Lisa. "Ugly Power Struggle Paralyzes Trump's Plan to Fix Veterans' Care." *Stars and Stripes*, March 9, 2018. https://www.stripes.com/news/veterans /ugly-power-struggle-paralyzes-trump-s-plan-to-fix-veterans-care-1.515825.

Slack, Donovan. "VA Secretary David Shulkin's Top PR Aide Lobbied Congress to Get Him Fired, Sources Say." *USA Today*, February 28, 2018. https://www .usatoday.com/story/news/politics/2018/02/28/va-secretary-david-shulkins -top-pr-aide-lobbied-congress-get-him-fired-sources-say/380726002/.

Robert Fleck v. Department of Veterans Affairs, Office of the Inspector General, United States District Court for the District of Columbia, Civil Action No 1:18-cv-1452, filed June 20, 2018.

Chapter 44
Sisk, Richard. "Kelly Meets at White House with Vets Groups on VA Chaos." Military.com, February 26, 2018. https://www.military.com/daily-news/2018 /02/26/kelly-meets-white-house-vets-groups-va-chaos.html.

Chapter 45
Slack, Donovan. "VA Secretary David Shulkin Says He Learned Lots of Lessons from Handling of Travel Report." *USA Today*, February 27, 2018. https://www .usatoday.com/story/news/politics/2018/02/27/va-secretary-david-shulkin -says-he-learned-lots-lessons-handling-travel-report/374247002/.

Philipps, Dave, and Nicholas Fandos. "Intrigue at V.A. as Secretary Says He Is Being Forced Out." *New York Times*, February 15, 2018. https://www.nytimes .com/2018/02/15/us/veterans-affairs-david-shulkin.html.

Allen, Arthur. "Shulkin's Move to Dump VistA Seen as Bold, Risky." *Politico*, June 6, 2017. https://www.politico.com/story/2017/06/06/shulkins-move -to-dump-vista-seen-as-bold-risky-239189.

Cassidy, John. "The Conservative Plot to Oust an Able Secretary of Veterans Affairs." *New Yorker*, March 29, 2018. https://www.newyorker.com/news/our -columnists/the-conservative-plot-to-oust-an-able-secretary-of-veterans-affairs.

Arnsdorf, Isaac. "The Trump Administration Goes to War—with Itself—over the VA." *ProPublica*, February 16, 2018. https://www.propublica.org/article/the -trump-administration-goes-to-war-over-the-va.

Chapter 46
Rosiak, Luke, and Julia Nista. "Shulkin Says Impersonation of Top Staffer Occurred Hours before Facing Congress about Altered Email." *Daily Caller*, February 17, 2018. https://dailycaller.com/2018/02/17/david-shulkin-email-hack/.

Shane, Leo. 2019. "VA Inspector General Finds No Evidence of Computer Hacking in Travel Scandal." *Military Times*, February 28, 2018. https://www

.militarytimes.com/veterans/2018/02/28/va-inspector-general-finds-no
-evidence-of-computer-hacking-in-travel-scandal/.

Mangan, Dan. "Top Aide to VA Chief David Shulkin Announces Departure Two
Days after Travel Scandal Explodes." CNBC, February 16, 2018. https://www
.cnbc.com/2018/02/16/wright-simpson-aide-to-va-chief-shulkin-retires-amid
-travel-scandal.html.

Chapter 47

Estepa, Jessica. "VA Secretary Shulkin Discloses Official Travel Details." *USA
Today*, September 29, 2017. https://www.usatoday.com/story/news/politics
/onpolitics/2017/09/29/va-secretary-david-shulkin-discloses-official-travel
-details/717598001/.

Rosiak, Luke. "Exclusive: The Second 10-Day European Vacation Shulkin
Wanted Kept Secret." *Daily Caller*, April 9, 2018. https://dailycaller.com/2018
/04/09/shulkin-veteran-affairs-vatican-vacation/.

Yglesias, Matthew. "How Veterans Affairs Secretary David Shulkin Became the
Trump Cabinet's Most Endangered Member." *Vox*, March 4, 2018. https://www
.vox.com/policy-and-politics/2018/3/14/17109230/david-shulkin-veterans
-affairs.

Chapter 48

"David Shulkin's Firing at the VA Is Latest Step in Trump-Koch Push to Privatize Veterans' Healthcare." *Democracy Now*, March 30, 2018. https://www
.democracynow.org/2018/3/30/david_shulkins_firing_at_the_va.

Editorial Board. "A Coup at Veterans Affairs." *New York Times*, March 29, 2018.
https://www.nytimes.com/2018/03/29/opinion/shulkin-out-veterans-affairs
-koch.html.

Zibel, Alan. "The Koch Government: These 44 Trump Officials Have Close
Ties to Right-Wing Billionaire Brothers." *Corporate Presidency*, 2018. https://
corporatepresidency.org/koch/.

Samuels, Brett. "Shulkin Says He Has White House Approval to Root Out
'Subversion' at VA." *The Hill*, February 20, 2018. https://thehill.com/policy
/healthcare/374790-shulkin-says-he-has-white-house-approval-to-root-out-sub
version-at-va.

Fandos, Nicholas, and Dave Philipps. "In Battle over Future of Veterans' Care,
Moderation Wins, for Now." *New York Times*, March 6, 2018. https://www

.nytimes.com/2018/03/06/us/politics/veterans-affairs-shulkin-koch-brothers .amp.html.

Thomsen, Jacqueline "Trump Called 'Fox & Friends' Host for Opinion on Veteran Care during Meeting with VA Chief: Report." *The Hill*, March 11, 2018. https://thehill.com/homenews/administration/377874-trump-called-fox -friends-host-for-opinion-on-vets-healthcare-during.

Chapter 50

Shane, Leo. "What We've Learned from David Shulkin's Post-Firing Media Blitz." *Military Times*, March 30, 2018. https://www.militarytimes.com/veterans /2018/03/30/what-weve-learned-from-david-shulkins-post-firing-media-blitz/.

Restuccia, Andrew, and Louis Nelson. "No Longer Muzzled, Shulkin Takes on Trump's White House." *Politico*, March 29, 2018. https://www.politico.com /story/2018/03/29/david-shulkin-responds-firing-491272.

"Sen. Jerry Moran—Kansas." Open Secrets, accessed 2019. https://www.open secrets.org/members-of-congress/contributors?cid=N00005282&cycle=2014 &type=I.

Chapter 51

Shulkin, David. "David J. Shulkin: Privatizing the V.A. Will Hurt Veterans." *New York Times*, March 28, 2018. https://www.nytimes.com/2018/03/28 /opinion/shulkin-veterans-affairs-privatization.html.

Restuccia, Andrew. "Did Shulkin Get Fired or Resign? This Is Why It Matters." *Politico*, March 31, 2018. https://www.politico.com/story/2018/03/31/did -shulkin-get-fired-or-resign-veterans-492877.

Stewart, Emily. "David Shulkin Says He Was Fired. The White House Says He Quit." *Vox*, April 2, 2018. https://www.vox.com/policy-and-politics/2018 /4/2/17188096/david-shulkin-va-veterans-affairs-fired-quit.

Chapter 52

Sweeney, Evan. "VA Signs $10B Deal with Cerner, but Implementation Challenges Still Loom Large." *Fierce Healthcare*, May 21, 2018. https://www.fiercehealthcare .com/tech/va-cerner-ehr-contract-10b-dod-shulkin-wilkie-mhs-genesis.

Tahir, Darius. "Shulkin Out before Signing Cerner Contract." *Politico*, March 29, 2018. https://www.politico.com/newsletters/morning-ehealth/2018/03 /29/shulkin-out-before-signing-cerner-contract-153768.

Steinhower, Jennifer, and Dave Philipps. "V.A. Seeks to Redirect Billions of Dollars into Private Care." *New York Times*, January 12, 2019. https://www .nytimes.com/2019/01/12/us/politics/veterans-administration-health-care -privatization.html.

Wentling, Nikki. "VA Moving Forward with Shulkin's Nationwide Restructuring Plan." *Stars and Stripes*, May 22, 2018. https://www.stripes.com/news/va -moving-forward-with-shulkin-s-nationwide-restructuring-plan-1.528556.

Wentling, Nikki. "Former VA Secretaries Join Fight over Agent Orange Benefits for Blue Water Navy Vets." *Stars and Stripes*, September 20, 2018. https://www .stripes.com/news/veterans/former-va-secretaries-join-fight-over-agent-orange -benefits-for-blue-water-navy-vets-1.548519.

Shulkin, David. "Implications for Veterans Healthcare: The Danger Becomes Clearer." *JAMA Internal Medicine*, forthcoming, July 22, 2019.

"News Releases—Office of Public and Intergovernmental Affairs." Va.gov, June 5, 2019. https://www.va.gov/opa/pressrel/pressrelease.cfm?id=5263.

Kime, Patricia. "Justice Department Won't Appeal Agent Orange Ruling Benefiting Blue Water Navy Vets." Military.com, June 6, 2019. https://www.military .com/daily-news/2019/06/06/justice-department-wont-appeal-agent-orange -ruling-benefiting-blue-water-navy-vets.html.

Chapter 53

Arnsdorf, Isaac. "The Shadow Rulers of the VA." *ProPublica*, August 7, 2018. https://www.propublica.org/article/ike-perlmutter-bruce-moskowitz-marc -sherman-shadow-rulers-of-the-va.

Levin, Bess. "Three of Trump's Mar-a-Lago Buddies Are Secretly Running the V.A." *Vanity Fair*, August 8, 2018. https://www.vanityfair.com/news/2018 /08/three-of-trumps-mar-a-lago-buddies-are-secretly-running-the-va.

Spitzer, Julie. "Trump's 'Mar-a-Lago Crowd' Reviewed VA's $10B Cerner Contract Before Signing, Pushed for Apple App." *Becker's Hospital Review*, December 4, 2018. https://www.beckershospitalreview.com/ehrs/trump-s-mar-a-lago-crowd -reviewed-va-s-10b-cerner-contract-before-signing-pushed-for-apple-app.html.

"At Least 5 Investigations Opened on Trump Cabinet's Luxury Travel." *Axios*, October 9, 2017. https://www.axios.com/at-least-5-investigations-opened-on -trump-cabinets-luxury-travel-1513306054-07f49a73-a99a-44eb-a583-1e9b75 eed2e5.html.

Weiss, Brennan. "$1 Million in Private Flights and a $31,000 Table—Here Are the 6 Trump Cabinet Members under Scrutiny for Their Lavish Spending of

Taxpayer Money." *Business Insider*, March 17, 2018. https://www.businessinsider
.com/trump-cabinet-officials-spending-taxpayer-money-under-fire-2018-3.

Abadi, Mark. "Trump Cabinet Members Have Racked Up Millions of Dollars of
Taxpayer-Funded Travel—Here's Who's under Scrutiny." *Business Insider*, October 10, 2017. https://www.businessinsider.com/trump-private-jet-cost-cabinet
-security-2017-10.

Leamer, Laurence. *Mar-a-Lago: Inside the Gates of Power at Donald Trump's
Presidential Palace*. New York: Flatiron Books, 2019, 242.

"Memorandum," Department of Veterans Affairs, Va.gov, March 29, 2017.
https://www.va.gov/oig/pubs/admin-reports/VAOIG-17-00730-174.pdf.

"Energy Department Spent $63,500 on Upgraded Flights for Rick Perry in First 6
Months." May 13, 2018. ABC News. https://abcnews.go.com/Politics/energy
-department-spent-63500-upgraded-flights-rick-perry/story?id=55538173.

"DOE: Anita Perry in Paris on 3rd Trip Abroad for Agency." November 7, 2017.
E&E News. https://www.eenews.net/stories/1060065887.

Chapter 54

Sheetz, Kyle, and David Shulkin. "Why the VA Needs More Competition." *New
England Journal of Medicine*, June 21, 2018. https://www.nejm.org/doi/full
/10.1056/NEJMp1803642.

Chapter 55

Mazmanian, Adam. "Hill Dems Want VA's Acting CIO Out." *FCW*, May
16, 2018. https://fcw.com/articles/2018/05/16/blumenthal-walz-va-cio-ehr
.aspx.

Jones, Christopher. "Farewell to the Trump Political Appointee Who Brought
IT Chaos to the Department of Veterans Affairs." *Pacific Standard*, February
19, 2019. https://psmag.com/social-justice/farewell-to-the-trump-political
-appointee-who-brought-it-chaos-to-the-dept-of-veterans-affairs.

Shane, Leo. "Outgoing White House Adviser Disputes Shulkin's Accusations
of VA Infighting, Conspiracies." *Military Times*, March 30, 2018. https://
www.militarytimes.com/veterans/2018/03/30/outgoing-white-house-adviser
-disputes-shulkins-accusations-of-va-infighting-conspiracies/.

Neefus, Chris. "Darin Selnick Rejoins Concerned Veterans for America as Senior Advisor." *Concerned Veterans for America*, May 8, 2018. https://cv4a.org
/press-release/darin-selnick-rejoins-concerned-veterans-for-america-as-senior
-advisor/.

Rodack, Jeffrey. "Shulkin Critic Darin Selnick Returning to Work at VA." *Newsmax*, March 27, 2018. https://www.newsmax.com/politics/darin-selnick-veterans-affairs-david-shulkin-white-house/2018/03/27/id/850936/.

Rein, Lisa, and Josh Dawsey. "Trump Loyalist Peter O'Rourke Forced out of VA after Collecting His $160,000 Salary while Doing Little Work." *Chicago Tribune*, December 11, 2018. https://www.chicagotribune.com/news/nationworld/ct-trump-peter-o-rourke-veterans-affairs-20181211-story.html.

Ogrysko, Nicole. "Another Top Executive Leaves VA, Where Leadership Vacancies Are Already Widespread." *Federal News Network*, July 11, 2018. https://federalnewsnetwork.com/veterans-affairs/2018/07/another-top-executive-leaves-va-where-leadership-vacancies-are-already-widespread/.

Cohen, Zachary. 2019. "Embattled Trump Appointee Resigns from Post at VA." CNN, March 14, 2019. https://www.cnn.com/2019/03/14/politics/department-of-veterans-affairs-official-jon-ullyot-resigns/index.html.

Dyer, Andrew. "Amid Shake-Up, Trump Taps Beer Magnate to Lead Veterans Affairs Mental Health Commission." *Hartford Courant*, July 24, 2018. https://www.courant.com/sd-me-va-leinenkugel-20180724-story.html.

The **Honorable David Shulkin, MD**, joined the Department of Veterans Affairs in 2015, first as under secretary for health and then as the ninth secretary of veterans affairs. He was the only Obama holdover who served in President Donald Trump's cabinet and the only member of the cabinet unanimously confirmed by the Senate. Prior to his government service, Shulkin worked in a number of health care administration roles, including as president and CEO of New York's Beth Israel Medical Center and president of Morristown Medical Center in New Jersey. He is the Distinguished Health Policy Fellow at the Leonard Davis Institute of Health Economics at the University of Pennsylvania, professor at Jefferson University's College of Population Health, and chief innovation officer at Sanford Health. A board certified internist, he practices and teaches medicine in New York City and still advocates on behalf of veterans. More information can be found at www.DavidShulkin.com.